Please Don't Call Me Dumb!

Please Don't Call Me Dumb!

Memoirs of Unique Cognitive Processing:

Dyslexia, Sequencing, or What?

Regular and Special Education Teacher

Argie Ella Hoskins

Cover design © 2018 Daniel Joseph Reneer

Please Don't Call Me Dumb! Memoirs of Unique Cognitive Processing: Dyslexia, Sequencing, or What?

This book was written for educational purposes. It shares helpful insights experienced by students, parents, seasoned elementary and high school teachers, and significant others with many years of observing and researching the human condition.

Dedicated gratefully to the memory of Dr. Betty Harrison and Dr. Robin Steed: my professors, my esteemed mentors, and my friends. Their light of hope led my mind out of confusion. They made a seminal contribution to my understanding and involvement.

Appreciative of Dr. Gene Shumway for hours spent with me, conversing over the text, and making suggestions that made the content more understandable. He has been a fellow traveler in the pursuit of making life better. Gene is one of the special lights who believes that we have the power to choose to be happy and have a reason to have hope.

Know you and me,
More alike than unalike,
Intriguing gifts are we,
Search and you will find,
A bit of everything in me and thee.

—Argie Ella

Intelligence along with natural curiosity compensates for deficits. Curiosity is powerful. For me there is an Intelligence—Natural Curiosity Intelligence. A bit of everything in me and thee.

—Argie Ella

Content

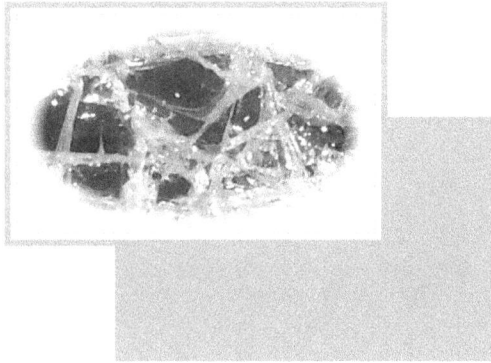

How do our brain cells look? Here we have a piece of broken glass.
Might this be somewhat analogous to the complexity of the human
brain? I don't know but desire to understand the story within the
confines of the structure. Patterns are fascinating. There is a oneness in
patterns because they are patterns. They hold the mysteries of the
universe. I have experienced the beauty of my ever-changing brain.
Patterns can be changed to create an evolving uniqueness.
Beauty!

Acknowledgments

Heartfelt thanks to many friends and family who have shared their advice, support, and patience during the process of making my experiences into a book. The list would read as a book within this book. I am grateful for assistance received while bringing this writing to finish. Together, we painted a picture of hope for many who have wandered and wondered about the complexity of the brain while knowing little about this astonishing creation. Thanks to the nature of our brains for pulling together a mixture of bits of intelligence to create a spectrum of beauty with knowledge and creativity. Beautiful!

Contained herein are stories, research, and insights from contributors who have allowed me to share the unfolding of the cognitive processing *Why* and *how* to survive the *Why*. I appreciate the opening of doors for us to continue to journey and find answers to the mysteries of the brain that are treasures for us to enjoy. With a grateful heart and a sharing spirit, I say, "Thank you. Together, we learn!" It is with gratitude that I appreciate the brilliant researchers and scientists who continue to search.

Gratitude for sons who have no bounds for what they have taught me. Everything I have experienced from being a mother has given me a peek into creation. Trying to walk the road back home, I am grateful.

Thanks from my heart for the complexity of my parents' example for being at the crossroads with love to understand *me*.

Kathy Senior, Effie Gertson, Marne` Reneer, Jeneal Webber, Lynn Walker, Noel Reneer, Kathy Caballero, and Harmony Legge have been valuable sets of eyes, along with Julia Blair's interest. Generous hours of encouraging me, sharing hearts, and inquisitive minds shared! Caring!

Thanks to grandsons Daniel and Benjamin, and husband Gene for understanding my stress. I have made a choice to show my weaknesses and strengths so that I can bring hope to others. **I am grateful for awareness.** In the end, I take responsibility for the content of this book.

Preface

To be a member of this intense and gifted tribe:
Awareness of cognitive uniqueness,
Admit your uniqueness,
Celebrate your uniqueness,
Share your uniqueness,
Include the gifts of others' uniqueness.

The unfolding of understanding cognitive processing has come from my involvement as a special education teacher. The purpose of this book is to share what I have come to know. I feel that we are working ourselves out of the "dark ages" of education. Let us continue the positive direction and change the picture! The jargon in this book comes from the specialized language of the educational and medical professions, which is unavoidable but understandable. Jargon can be helpful because it consists of unique words either borrowed or created to help one understand and apply concepts to a particular field of study.

I am not an expert in any field; however, this book is an expression of my experiences. I have been influenced by those who know much more about brain processing than I. Becoming aware of learning challenges has taught me a lot about me. And others!

I know some of our brightest, most creative, and gifted people are often misdiagnosed and misclassified with terms that revolve around behavioral and emotional challenges. Labels are generously used, such as Bipolar, Oppositional Defiant Disorder, Obsessive Compulsive Disorder, Attention Deficit Hyperactivity Disorder, and the list can go on and on. The uniqueness of each person finds ways to explain differences. Cognitive processing differences!

The labels don't stop. The *experts* point fingers and define a person: Learning Disabled! Dyslexia! Asperger's! Gifted! Retarded! Autistic! And again the list can go on and on. Labels can be overwhelming and sometimes ridiculous! The essential question I ask, "Why do we need to label?" Labeling can be positive, but it is more often negative. It may even create an overwhelming false sense of identity. Are the many associated behaviors defined as symptoms, syndromes, disorders, or what? Where on the continuum of severity do the behaviors fall? Dig deeply to find the causes and the effects! Explore the subjects that grab your interest: study, ponder, and continue to read. Connect the dots.

Can one identify the problem, design the intervention, and move on with or without a label? Can a label be carried like an unwanted *wart* on the face or a *blister* on the heart? For me, learning about and understanding an identifier called dyslexia brought massive relief that redirected my thinking to know why I had labeled my cognitive processing as a *monster*. I can now call it dyslexia. I am relieved. I found it is also a gift. As you find your gifts, you will be inspired and relieved.

Do we process information differently? Processing information in a different way can be an admirable thing. I have a son who picked up this book and said, "If this book had only one sentence on each page, I would read it!" I missed my chance! That would result in reading about three hundred sentences. That's commendable and comfortable! I should have taught my son that reading one sentence on each page was acceptable and even could be outstanding. He would have then begun on the path of learning to learn! When do we start to teach an individual how to learn, and whose responsibility is it?

How do we learn to learn? I was born with what some would label dyslexia including a deficit of not being able to sequence. I didn't know what my brain was doing until I became a mature adult. As I academically stumbled through kindergarten to high school, I concluded that the struggle was firmly in place because I felt both *dumb* and smart. My 3rd grade teacher voiced that I would never graduate from high school. Ouch! On the other hand, I have had experiences in my adult life, which when pieced together, seemed to make it clear that I am not dumb; I might even be smart. Yes, smart! What a confusing and burdensome dilemma! Can you have it both ways: *dumb* and intelligent?

This book will open a door through which others who think they are *dumb* can pass. Such an unanticipated passage can give them an understanding of their unique talents. These can be a platform from which they can craft an ultimately successful approach to a challenging life. They will master the essential skills of *learning to learn* by understanding the way their brains are wired to receive information.

Understanding the nature of cognitive processing is critical. Knowing how we think and what we can do with that thinking is the beginning of the story. I heard *words* at an International Dyslexia Association meeting that described the process: acquisition, interpretation, organization, application, and recall of sensory input. Wow! Is there more?

Cognitive processing is a collection of mental skills that are essential to our functioning. Intelligence forms the foundation.

The reason I wrote this book will be understood as we journey, day after day. Are there questions about cognitive processing? Yes, perhaps someday, someone will say, "I understand now! Aha! I knew there was an answer!" Keep looking! It will matter.

I have contemplated what I know, what to do with what I know, and what I am not sure I know. I shout, "Heaven forgive me as I stumble."

It would be well to write a book for the student audience, a different version for parents, another for teachers, and one for everybody else. Therefore, my goal is to roll the essence of what is appropriate into one book. As I look through my lenses, I desire that we will emerge with an understanding of how we process information. I will share how accepting differences in processing is an essential key. I am passionate about this subject. As we deepen our understanding, our empathy will increase, and we can bring the message of Hope.

I know of cases where not understanding how the brain is processing information has led some, step-by-step, to prison, to suicide, and others to murder. Hopelessness! My tears care, and I am grateful for you!

Introduction

In a nutshell, this book is an informal presentation from a caring and concerned heart; it attends to the feelings of my heart. I make no pretext about being a professional writer. It is about cognitive processing with its impact upon feelings, thoughts, and the range of human behavior. It peeks through a window to have a look at learning differences, and the effect of differences can be overwhelming on education and upon social interaction. I am not saying I have all the answers; I don't. I continue to search! However, I know that you may learn something about your cognitive processing as you journey seeking further light and knowledge, you will be inspired. This information will be useful. It will be a benefit to students, parents, teachers, and others. Yes, explore monsters with knowledge and application. *You are smart!*

We need to understand brain processing and how it can bring order out of chaos. For those seeking such understanding, this book will be broadly and deeply helpful. Those who have concerns about cognitive processing, its genesis, and its applications will find a compass.

What is brain or cognitive processing? Knowing *What* is to understand *Why.* **Cognitive processing** is the *Why.* I want to know *Why.* Help!

The memories that brought this writing about have an ever-changing trail of emotions. Memories in long-term storage are triggered by unpleasant emotional associations or by joyful snapshots. Day by day, memories will lose focus of the real picture. I figured out that to solve my brain mystery, I needed my memories to fit somewhere in the complicated brain puzzle. Blurred but helpful!

I remember at a very early age, with some awareness of the world around me, I started creating a picture of what success meant to me. A child who could read!

I dug into my brain to discover how memories fit in the puzzle of reality. I cried! With awareness, I paint a picture of a frustrated child asking, "Am I failing or succeeding?" I was failing with my verbal language skills. Communication complicated, and I knew it! I knew that I was out of concert with who I thought I was: a bright child. I was a child who couldn't read or communicate—delayed verbal language associated with learning to read, a nightmare! However, reading can come much more easily than verbal language—spoken communication. Language intervention should start sooner than later.

However, when the picture of a child reading, the one that I had made up in my head to be me, didn't happen, where could I turn to make my picture come true? From that mind-creation came a sense of confusion. Life seemed hopeless. Did you ever feel like that as a child? Some would call it dyslexia, minimal brain dysfunction, specific reading disability, or a perceptual deficit. I express it this way; my young brain learned differently then I was being taught. It seemed like a secret.

When mind-creations—expectations fail, we cope in various ways. People sometimes become ill. I have seen students become ill, so they wouldn't have to go to school. Look for the real *why*. We can have real or unreal reasons why mind-creations or dreams fail. Some disguise or blame the following: finances, education, opportunity, freedom, support, knowledge, or a dysfunctional attitude, such as "I couldn't care less." "Yes, I fail because it is someone else's fault!"

Pulling together elements as to *why* reading has been challenging for me has been a rocky road. Looking the causes straight in the eye has been a giant and essential step. No more denial and self-pity! "I am going to figure this thing out and create an accurate picture." And I have! Farewell, unreal *monsters!*

I am sharing; I have lived it. I have survived by understanding and learning to compensate. Hate or make monsters your friends. The *riptides* that tear at the soul along with the beauty of the sun shining through the turquoise waves are part of our tangled and colorful tapestry. To save us from negative entanglements, identification is critical. Early! Look for unique gifts to strengthen weaknesses. Hope!

Welcome and enjoy!

Argie Ella

1

Dyslexia:
Plea to Teachers and Parents
Jeneal Webber, Parent

Dyslexia
By Jeneal Webber

I had never heard the word dyslexia, let alone know what it meant and how it would affect my life as a young mother. My first child was Rebecca. She was a beautiful daughter with lots of energy and a love for learning. She walked early, talked early, and had great excitement for just about everything that came into her life. I know I have described almost every child. Amazing!

Our days were full of activities. Rebecca loved reading. I had a stack of around ten books. She would not be satisfied until we finished all of them, every day. Her favorite one was *In a People House* by Dr. Seuss. Rebecca would read the books back to me. I knew she wasn't reading. It was more like she had memorized them.

At the age of one, Rebecca could stand and faithfully repeat the *Pledge of Allegiance* with her little hand over her heart. She was not only adorable but very smart.

As Rebecca grew, I noticed some little things. She would get the left and right confused. She would talk backward: *runny babbit* or *flutterby*. She would often write her letters and numbers upside down and backward. Those dreaded 2's, 3's, 6's, 7's, 9's, p's, q's, b's, d's, etc. I had the same trouble while I was growing up. Rebecca's uniqueness didn't concern me.

Fast forward a few years, I had two more children. Together we would read books, count numbers, and learn colors. I always had lots of crayons, coloring books, and play-doh. We played outside in the dirt and on the swings and went for walks together.

Life was great. Then, it was time for Rebecca to start kindergarten. I was excited. She was excited. She loved school and her teachers. The teachers would tell me Rebecca was an excellent student. The only thing they noted was she would write her letters and numbers backward. They told me she would outgrow this. About the age of ten, Rebecca started taking piano lessons. She loved music and learning to play the piano. She had a talent for being able to play music by ear and transposed music to any key. Her teacher was frustrated. I overheard the teacher telling Rebecca, in a very stern, somewhat angry voice, "You need to learn the notes, and you can't transpose music. I haven't taught you that yet." I found another piano teacher that would be a better fit, one that would require Rebecca to learn notes while encouraging her creative talents.

Year after year, the teachers told me the same thing, "Rebecca is very smart, but she struggles with reading, writing, and math. She doesn't understand directions. Rebecca is failing most of her tests and has a hard time reading. She refuses to read out loud. Rebecca just needs to try harder." That was it, TRY HARDER! So, in kindergarten, first, second, third, fourth, we all tried harder. I helped Rebecca at home along with my other children. We read more, we wrote more, and we counted more. We tried harder until we were all sick of trying harder. With every school year, Rebecca would fall further behind. My bright, happy girl wasn't feeling very bright and wasn't very happy. She hated school. Rebecca was passed from grade to grade with no real plan to help her improve.

It was time for Rebecca to start the 5th grade. She was sad. Rebecca was sick. She had stomach aches at the thought of going to school. Rebecca even started throwing up. My heart broke for her. I felt helpless.

My daughter, Jamie, was starting the 1st grade. She had some of the same problems as Rebecca but not as severe. I could see Jesse, my three-year-old, would follow Rebecca's path. I quickly got him into pre-school, hoping that would help.

2

By this time, I hated school as much as Rebecca. It was a struggle to take her to school every day. Tears, sickness, and feeling defeated were a daily battle. I promised to help her any way I could, knowing very well I didn't know what to do anymore. Every day in school was so hard for Rebecca. She was failing test after test. She was not learning or progressing. No matter how much I told her how smart she was, she believed she was *dumb* and stupid. She was upset over feeling *dumb*. Her self-esteem was crushed, and I was making her face another failing year. My thoughts were *trying harder!* She has been trying harder! Why don't the teachers try harder? Tell me something different! Tell me how to help her. I was in over my head so were the teachers. I prayed for a miracle.

Soon it came time for the dreaded parent-teacher conference. With Rebecca failing one test after another, my hopes weren't very high for a good report.

I sat down in the little desk chair across from the teacher waiting to hear more of the same. He said, "I think Rebecca is a very smart girl. She is always willing to help when she can. She is friendly and kind to everyone. She doesn't cause any trouble." He also said, "When I listen to Rebecca read, she will read something different yet come up with the same meaning." Text: The long road went through the forest. Rebecca read: The long road went through the trees. She couldn't read the word *forest,* but she knew it had to do with trees. No, the irony wasn't lost on me. It was like Rebecca was screaming, "I can't learn because this big thing is blocking my way."

The teacher went on to tell me he had never had a student struggle with reading, writing, and math, yet be so smart. She has a lot of horse sense or common sense; this you can't teach. He suggested testing and a resource class. Rebecca might have a learning disability of some kind. He would talk to the principal and the resource department.

This information was something different! Finally! A teacher was willing to see Rebecca and her struggles. He knew that working harder wasn't the answer. He thought the resource program would help. I was happy and scared to death at the same time. Any children sent to resource classes were ridiculed. The classroom teacher assured me that it was different at this school. Mr. Garrett, one of the resource teachers, had made it such an inviting class. Other children wanted to go there as well. I'm sure it took a lot of effort on all the teaching staff to make this happen. I signed the permission papers to start the testing.

After a few weeks, I wondered about test results. I met with the principal, the counselor, and the resource teacher. They went over all the testing results and scores. I didn't understand the testing and was confused by the scores. It was very overwhelming and new to me. Rebecca was smart, behind in grade levels, and had an unnamed learning disability. She did, though, qualify for the resource program.

I signed more paperwork to start Rebecca in the resource program, but I knew I couldn't stop there. What was this disability that could take a smart, happy, and well-adjusted child that loved to learn and turn her into a crying mess with low self-esteem, hate for school, and now affect her physically? I needed to know more; I needed to teach myself how to teach my daughter to learn. Also, as I had more children facing the same disability, I went to school with Rebecca. I went to the resource teachers and asked if I could volunteer in the resource class. I planned to watch and learn. I love children, so this came naturally to me. Thankfully, the resource teacher said yes. Soon, I was spending at least an hour, or so, a day at school. I helped with cutting, gluing, taping, and anything they wanted. I met a teacher named Argie Hoskins Shumway. She was a kind and gentle teacher. I would soon learn the children loved her. The other teacher, Mr. Garrett, was a remarkable teacher. The kids would say that he made the class fun while teaching.

Argie worked with Rebecca, getting to know her and her learning disability. After a short time, Argie handed me a book saying, "I think you need to read this." The name of the book was *Dyslexia in the Classroom*. Through the years, I have loaned the book to so many parents that I have lost track of it. As I said, I had never heard the word dyslexia, knew what it meant, or how it would change my life and Rebecca's life.

I took the book home and started reading. Before I finished the first chapter, I learned the definition of dyslexia and how it affects the learning process. Dyslexia is a general term for disorders that involve difficulty in learning to read or interpret words, letters, and other symbols. But for Becky, her general intelligence was high! Difficulties come on a spectrum from mild to severe. Each child is different because each child has a unique brain. There it was in black and white. The more I read, the more all the missing pieces came into place. I was learning about my children's disability *and* my own. Finally! Someone had given it a name. Not a label, a name. I was determined to understand dyslexia and how to teach my children *how* they could learn.

The next few months, Rebecca and I were like sponges soaking up all the new information. I would read anything Argie gave me and watched her put that knowledge into teaching. Teaching with all modalities to provide the student the best chance for learning: visual, auditory, kinesthetic, and tactile.

I learned that learning to spell using the motor movements was essential. Students learn to use fine motor movements, by tracing the letters with two fingers and enforcing that with using large motor movement by writing the letters in the air. Repeating this process over and over, the students learned their spelling words.

I learned about cognitive processing, spatial relations, and sequencing. These are all very critical when it comes to an understanding of the brain of a person with dyslexia. I learned to teach using the student's strengths while addressing their weaknesses. It is a given that you always praise the child for their efforts and accomplishments. They become more willing to do this hard work when they see the progress they are making.

I remember back to my grade school years; it was during a period when educators felt it was better to learn to read using sight words, not phonics. Just the rote method of saying a sight word like *chair* over and over, I found that some words did stick in my brain. The way I mastered reading was by singing hymns at church. There I could see the word, point to it with my finger, while singing slowly in syllables. This method worked for me. I loved reading. Math was a different story. I transposed numbers, always making it difficult to understand math. Forget algebra, with all its numbers and letters all mixed up in one equation. I just begged my math teacher not to fail me. I, too, was quickly passed on from one grade to the next hoping the next teacher could help me. Now, there was a chance for me to help my children.

It came time for Rebecca to take her first spelling test in her regular classroom. She had worked on this list for a week using all her new skills. I went to her class that day to pick her up. She had her spelling test in her hand and a big smile, one I had not seen in a long time. She held the paper out for me to see. "Mom, Mom, I'm not *dumb*! Look! I'm not *dumb*!" She had scored a 100 percent on her test. She cried, I cried.

Rebecca caught on very quickly what worked for her. From then on things would be different for her. She was learning how her brain worked and how she needed to learn.

Argie helped me in so many ways. She was willing to teach me, help me learn, and further my education on dyslexia. I attended classes at the Slingerland Institute for Reading. I went to the seminars given by the Orton-Gillingham Institute. I worked with Argie in a successful summer school program for children with learning disabilities. I eventually started doing private tutoring.

Everything I learned, I could use to help my children, from making letters and numbers out of sandpaper for the rough texture to be traced with tiny fingers to clapping out syllables. Also, helping them understand more about how their brain learns brought relief.

I wish I could say that the middle and high school resource programs were as successful as my experience with Highland Elementary. Sadly, even with my grandchildren, there are some resource classrooms where the student is just told to read a book, do homework, or ask for help if needed. The most significant requirement is not to cause trouble.

In a perfect world, a team is made up of educators and joined by parents who understand that parental involvement is crucial. It is essential that students know they have a caring support group, those who are willing to teach them, no matter what it takes. In turn, the students need to be part of the team. Having all the members of this team on the same page can significantly reduce the stress and pressure children with dyslexia feel. At least, we can keep trying to make a difference for our children, especially the ones who are getting left behind and feeling *dumb*! *It is so much easier to teach a young, happy child to read and write the correct way than to reteach a sad, angry, older child.* Again, I would like to express my gratitude and love to Argie Hoskins Shumway. Her willingness to pass on her knowledge and help me understand our incredible, brilliant dyslexic brains has meant the world to my children and me.

Thank you, Jeneal Webber!

Given my experience, I have a belief that good teaching for the person with dyslexia is good teaching for all. Teachers of teachers need to be trained to understand the issues about language-related skills and the learning process. As my children and I have encountered university teachers, few are aware of how the brain functions around how language is processed, and they do not perceive it to be core to everything they say. I want my grandchildren to have teachers who know how necessary it is to have access to language through language education. I have found myself bewildered by what language means.

Dr. Orton observed reading challenges. He stressed the relationship between reading efficiency and oral language skills. My mission is to bring awareness that language is a means of understanding ourselves.

I **see** a broken leg; I know there are challenges. Empathy! I don't **see** cognitive processing challenges—invisible. The challenge is like being blind. Empathy?

The purpose of this book is to bring understanding to the blindness.

Jeneal is consistently committed to her stewardship. Dedication to her responsibility is an example of caring. She has been at the "cross-roads" for her children. She found her personal power and used it.

Jeneal, I am grateful for the privilege of being your children's teacher. Students hold my serious intent. My desire is for all of us to have the power to create success; success builds success. We can't do everything, but we can do something. It is like this . . . the sun keeps coming up, and Heaven willing, I will also. Each day, Daddy said as he turned on the stove, "Sis, get up and amount to something!" Something!

2

Private Summer School:
Making a Difference

J eneal and I continued to educate ourselves and others. Sometimes the road was rocky, dim, and without direction. Then it would happen! We could see where the next step should be taking us and excitedly, we were on our way. The reward was to have students learn. This teaching and learning was energizing and gave hope to others to do the same. Don't give up! Don't give in! We had a successful private summer school. Our lessons fit individual learning styles and intellectual gifts. *Success builds success!* We appreciated using our acquired skills for academic changes.

We sent this information to parents:
Argie's Summer School
Teachers: Argie and Jeneal (Slingerland trained)

Diagnosis and Remediation of Learning Development
TESTING: Intelligence, Academic, Personality, Cognitive processing
BASIC SKILLS: Reading, Writing, Spelling, Math
REMEDIATION: Dyslexia
MULTISENSORY TRAINING: Auditory, Visual, and Motor
STUDY SKILLS   COMPUTER TUTORIAL   GROSS MOTOR

July 9 through August 18 (6 weeks)   Monday through Thursday
9:00 to 12:00   Small groups
1:00 to 5:00   Individual instruction

TEACHERS
Argie Shumway – Regular Ed. and Special Ed. Certificates in Behavioral Disorders and Resource. Presently teaching in the Alpine School District as a Resource teacher. Argie is an experienced regular classroom teacher. Jeneal Webber – Parent and teacher.

SCHOOL PSYCHOLOGICAL SERVICES (optional)
W. Richard Ellison has served as Director of Special Education in Woodland, Kansas and Guidance Specialist in the Jordan School District. Presently a psychologist for the Alpine School District.

SCHOOL SOCIAL WORK SERVICES (optional)
Dr. Gene Shumway served as a school social worker in the S.L.C. District. He taught full-time at the University of Utah for twelve years. He is currently teaching at Brigham Young University. He has a private practice in marital and individual therapy.

For more information:
Days—Jeneal Webber   Evenings—Argie Shumway
(End of flyer)

The years of 1986 and 1987 found Argie's Summer School along with the years 1988 through 2005 for private tutoring extremely busy. During this time I was also teaching in the public school system.

Brigham Young University, School of Education, and Department of Counseling Psychology and Special Education would send me tearful referrals. Parents would call the university asking for a teacher who could help their child learn skills they needed to survive in the classroom. It was not unusual to receive a call from BYU asking if I were available. Summertime was a very busy time for me.

I met committed parents who were concerned about their children's frustration with school. They would drive for hours to have a visit. One family moved from southern Utah to Orem to have their child tutored for the summer. One year parents bought tickets for all of us to go to the conference of the Orton Dyslexia Society that later changed the name to International Dyslexia Association. Parents were caring. It brought joy to me to help in a way that would change a child's life from discouragement to hope. Along with the student, parents were relieved to be aware that their child was not *dumb*. *Please Don't Call Me Dumb!* With understanding came the realization that they, the parent or parents, were not *dumb* either. A story that ends well.

A lump in my throat comes from thinking about seeing grateful faces, not different from my relief when I became aware that I had a special gift. Brains are unusual and beautiful!

I found myself doing workshops for our school district. Another teacher and I taught workshops at a university. We had a story to tell to children and adults. We desired to bring another lens to look beyond discouragement and change it to *hope*. **Bring hope! Hope is the reward.**

By artist Daniel Joseph Reneer

11

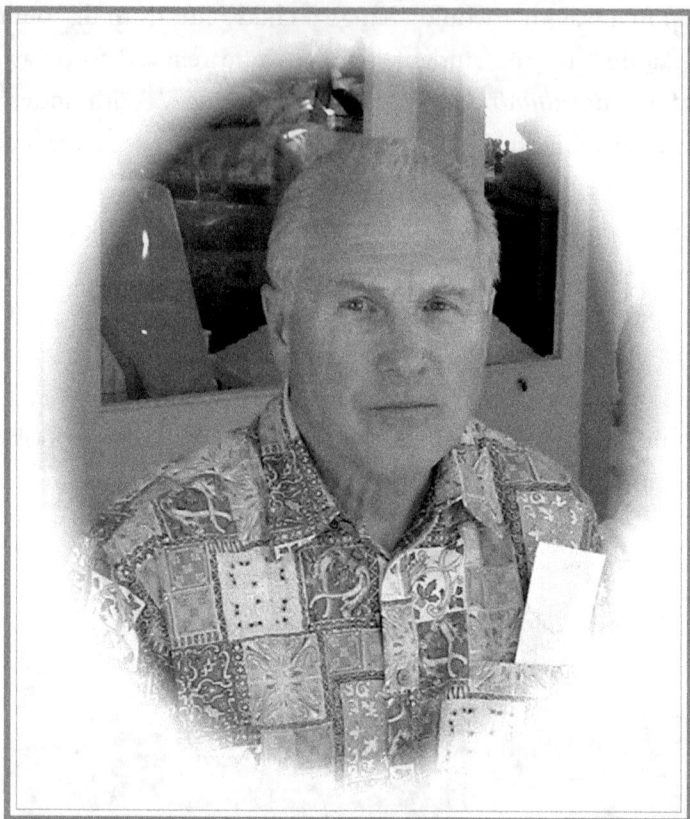

James Young

Dr. Young reached into the hearts of many individuals to help them find
solutions to difficult challenges. Those who have known him and his
wisdom have enjoyed a reward.

3

Not Dyslexia:
Lack of Opportunity
Dr. James Young, University Professor,
Marriage and Family Therapist

I am privileged to know **Dr. James Young. He was one of the professors who watched me teach Dr. Robin Steed's reading program. I had not previously known him. Years later one of his daughters married one of my sons. Lucky me. I remember him well. He has been an influence on many students and others who know him as he continues to spread his sharing and caring heart. Dr. Young received his doctorate from Peabody College, Vanderbilt University in Nashville, Tennessee. It is a research university offering a full-range of undergraduate, graduate and professional degrees. He points out that not all reading disabilities are dyslexia. For some, it is the lack of learning opportunities and for others the lack of focused intent on the reading process.**

Why Jimmy Couldn't Read
By James Young

Introduction

I'm Jimmy. Fortunately, I do not have any specific identifiable language disabilities. January of 1955, at 17 years of age, in the last month of my senior year in high school, I left public education and entered the Air Force. I guess you could say I was technically a "high school drop-out." My mother went to the principal and obtained my graduation certificate

13

while I was in Basic Training. I was not overly anxious about my lack of academic preparation. I had no planned career counseling, no real understanding of education and its relationship to future work. I had no academic pursuits. I didn't know nor cared what my grade point average was. I was bored with schoolwork and was looking forward to a new adventure. I had learned how to relate well to people and was not afraid to leave my home on my own. I had done so the last summer, taking a farming job up in Canada. I did not at the time realize that I simply did not have proper preparation in the basic language skills of reading for understanding or writing a coherent paper with correct spelling and punctuation. I could read well enough to get a decent score on the Air Force entrance exam and accepted into that armed service. I went on to be a successful airman in my four years of military service. I earned the rank of Airman first class.

Experiencing Public Schools

My language skills were not developed, mostly because of the lack of teaching. In grade school, I learned to "word call." I would say the name of a written word, but I was very slow at this "word calling." "Breaking the code" was mostly taught by memory or "sight reading" of the good old *Dick and Jane* basal series and using picture clues to get the meaning of the narrative. The phonetic decoding I picked up was incidental and not from consistent, organized teaching. Because of this lack of phonetic instruction, I was also a poor speller. Spelling for me was mostly from sight memory.

Because of my poor decoding skills, my reading comprehension was also slow and tedious. After slowly reading a paragraph, I had difficulty in recalling the meaning of that paragraph and would have to go back several times to get the meaning. As I got into the higher grades and had to read in the different content areas, I remember many times I would "read" a paragraph and then think, "Now, what was that I just read?"

My dear mother was working full-time to feed and clothe our family of four young children. She and my father were divorced when I was eight years of age. She also went to night school at a junior college in the evenings. She was my best "language arts" teacher. She would correct me in my language usage as all good parents do. I learned to speak correctly through the everyday speaking in our home. I learned the proper conjugation of verbs not by understanding the tenses and person but by experiencing spoken language in my home. Again, this is the way most children learn to speak their native tongue.

Mom had little time to monitor what we did at school. She left it up to us to do our schoolwork. Most of the time, I would bring schoolwork home and put it on the dining room table so that she would notice it. Much of the time I never looked at my schoolwork until I picked it up and headed out to school.

By the time I went into the Air Force, my math skills were as poor as my language arts skills. Early on, I learned to dislike math mostly because of how it was presented to me. Math was taught by rote memory. I remember trying to memorize the multiplication facts. The teacher would have an oral drill at the end of the week. The person who could recite that week's facts received a sucker. My best friend who lived across the street from me was good at memorizing math. He would always win the sucker. I never won one. When I got into algebra and geometry, I could do the problems but in my own way. I would always try to visualize in my mind the problem using diagrams and visual timelines, etc. I remember taking a standardized achievement test at the end of junior high. When I got to high school, the geometry teacher said I had a really interesting test results profile. I did poorly on simple tasks like computing percentages, yet could do problems that required spatial reasoning.

My Real Underground Curriculum

So, what did I learn during those public school years? In those elementary years, I did learn how to play the violin thanks to my mother arranging the lessons for me. I became First Chair in the 6th grade. As I attended high school, I perfected my motor skills and became a good competitive gymnast. I did learn how to type on a manual typewriter while attending junior high school. My girlfriend suggested I take this class with her, but what I was most interested in learning had very little to do with the formal school curriculum. I was a very friendly yet somewhat timid younger boy. I could make friends easily. I was a peaceful boy, shying away from conflict.

As I have looked back over that time in my life, I always had a mild sense of anxiety when I was young. I think this had the most to do with my family milieu. There was always an undercurrent of emotional strife caused by my father and mother's relationship accompanied by sibling quarreling. I was a "bed-wetter" until about 12 years of age. Part of that was due to the nondiagnosed congenital kidney defects. The other part was probably emotional. I was afraid of my father more than I loved him. As a young boy, I was fearful of bullies. I would avoid them if possible.

On a more positive side, in those younger years, I was most interested in making things, doing art, and crafty things. I was very mechanically inclined. I liked to take things apart and put them back together. This included old bicycles, appliances, a motorbike, and an old 1930 Chevrolet. I also had a talent for visual arts. I loved to draw and do watercolor painting at home and in school. I would receive congrats and encouragement from my teachers about my artwork. I became quite good at making leather wallets and belts. I had my own marble piece on my bedroom table where I would work my leather crafts. I had all the various carving tools. I remember building my own crystal radio set. I put up an antenna from my garage to a telephone pole. I built my own sleeping place in the corner of my backyard out of an abandoned chicken coop. I set up an army cot with blankets and my railroad lantern. My dog Smokey would sleep back there with me as I listened to my crystal radio.

I loved the outdoors. When I first lived in the San Fernando Valley, it was still quite rural. There was a large dairy farm two blocks west of our house. I spent many an afternoon exploring this dairy. It eventually closed down, and then my friends and I spent hours exploring inside the barns and buildings. Further to the west, there was this dry, sandy wash bed that ran from the north of the valley to the south end. Now and then, with heavy rainfall, this wash bed would be full of water rushing down to the Los Angeles River. I would go wading in the water and swimming in the deeper pools. I would spend many hours exploring this dry wash bed from Hansen Dam on one end to Sepulveda Dam on the other. I would sometimes get up early, while the others in my family were still asleep, and pack some bacon, eggs, and bread, with a frying pan and matches to start a fire. With these items in my army pack, I would head out to the wash. A few miles to the north, a set of railroad rails crossed over this wash. I would set up my camp and cook my breakfast under this overpass. Snakes, lizards, horned toads, frogs, tadpoles, skunks, possums, guinea pigs, rabbits, turtles, and chickens were all a part of my backyard menagerie. The reptiles and jackrabbits were prolific in the brush on the sides of this wash bed.

Developing My Social Skills

My social skills came slowly. I was a loner in the crowd. I liked to observe from the edges and ease into the social interactions. Like most young boys, I was shy around girls. I liked girls, but I was timid in asking them out. That continued during all my school years. In junior high, I had a particular girlfriend who was very calm and quiet. We became good friends. When I entered our large high school, I felt somewhat socially overwhelmed. At that time, our high school had about 4,000 students attending. We had to have two lunch periods. To maintain control of the campus, it was technically a closed campus during school hours. We had an eight-foot chain-link fence around the main campus. This ineffective, inasmuch as you could find big gaps in the fence way out in the back of the school where the agricultural classes were taught.

I was nervous as to where to eat my lunch, where to *hang out*. That first semester at lunchtime, I would go out to the back of the school where they had a large sandbox full of metal gymnastic equipment, such as high bars, swinging rings, and parallel bars. There was a small group of us who had played around the gymnastic sandbox near my home. We would eat our lunches and then work on different gymnastic tricks. I was perfectly comfortable staying out of the large quad in the center of the school where all the different social groups would gather at their specific park lunch table and "check out" each other. This was scary to me.

My dear sister who was a year older than I was, very pretty and popular, had made many friends. She was in the middle of the popular social circles. At home, I met a few of her boyfriends who took a liking to me and invited me to "rush" for one of the two most popular men's social groups. At first, I said I was not interested. It sounded too uncomfortable for me. I eventually took my sister's nudging and rushed for the Esquires' social group. I passed the initiation hazing and was now an official member. At noon I had to meet in the center of the quad and sit on the large park table that this group had marked as their own. Looking back, this was a great blessing to me. I learned to love and appreciate these young men like they were my family. We had a party every month where we would dance and have refreshments. Some in the group were beer drinkers. Some smoked. Like myself, there were others who did not drink or smoke. There was a group of us who all participated in one or two of the school athletic programs. I was somewhat uncomfortable having to find a date for those Esquire parties. I managed, and by my senior year was elected by my buddies to be the president of this group. I have fond memories of the good times. A couple of the guys from this group went into the Air Force with me.

My Athletic Life

I continued with my gymnastics and lettered all three years in high school. Participating in a sport where I had to perform all by myself out in the middle of the gym floor as everyone was quietly watching your every move was terrifying for me. It was an oxymoron for me as the shy self-conscious person to do this type of athletics. I would dread when the season would come time to perform. I learned to psych myself up and completely ignore the spectators. I learned to get in my own head and concentrate on my routines. I learned to conquer my fears and work through them. I performed well and had a good reputation as a competent gymnast. I took first place all Valley in Floor Exercise my senior year. I also long jumped in track and played football "on the side."

My sports and social club experiences kept me interested in going to school every day. The formal curriculum was something I had to do. I never was much interested in the end product of my time in school. I went because I was an obedient son and that was what young people did. I never got "hooked on learning" nor could I see how it would bless me my whole life. And, that is the mindset I was in when I left high school and joined the Air Force.

How I Learned to Learn

I did well in the service. Basic Training was like a big glorified Boy Scout camp. I learned to "play the game" of keeping your space neat and clean, answering "yes sir" and "no sir" at the appropriate times. Others would kick against the rules and always be getting reprimanded. I didn't. I liked the routine, order, and predictability of Basic Training. Tech school in Mississippi went smoothly. I learned how to operate radar equipment.

After I had gone to tech school, I was assigned to a radar site in the Redwoods of northern California where the Klamath River pours into the Pacific Ocean. Our small radar site was located on the cliffs overlooking the ocean. It was very beautiful with large pine trees and redwood trees. The radar ran 24/7. There were three shifts, a day shift from 8:00 a.m. till 4:00 p.m., a swing shift from 4:00 p.m. till midnight, and graveyard from midnight till 8:00 a.m. Each of the radar teams would take turns serving the three shifts each for seven days with time off between shifts. This gave me a lot of free time during the day when I was on the swing and midnight shifts.

I got a part-time job in the small town to the north called Crescent City. I changed logging truck tires and pumped gas at this station. I learned to break down the large tires, fix the flats and put them back on the large logging trucks. Some nights the base would get a call for airmen to come to the loading docks and help load barges with logs to be taken down the coast. I did this regularly. I also helped a plumber in the town of Klamath, California, just south of our base.

That winter at Christmas time in 1955, a huge rainstorm back in the mountains, way up, in the headwaters of the Klamath River, caused a terrible flood to come through the town of Klamath. Nineteen feet of water washed the town into the Pacific Ocean. We were asked to take over with martial law and protect the flooded homes from looters. We helped clean up for the next few months. Our unit got an outstanding unit award from headquarters.

Besides working on my off times, I also became very interested in reading different books from the base library. The library had a whole array of different kinds of books. I had no deadlines, no tests to take, and no book reports. I began to enjoy reading for the pleasure of it. During this same period, my mother gave me my own set of scriptures and some church books for Christmas. When I would go home on leave, I would go to a bookstore and purchase a "Cliff Book" about a subject that looked interesting. I had no particular plan but just began to enjoy reading about everything. I tried to take a correspondence course in basic math, but the text was poorly written and too confusing for me. I did not complete this course.

After a year at this site, I volunteered to be reassigned to a site off the coast of Oxnard, California. The particular island was one of four channel islands named Santa Rosa Island. Though I had grown up in southern California, I never knew these islands were out there. The duty shifts were the same, but there were no towns or businesses to get work during my off times. That is when I really bore down on my reading, studying, and painting. I also spent many hours exploring this island. I found ancient Indian bones, beads, and artifacts along the high cliffs. *The Island of the Blue Dolphin* was written about this particular island.

My Continued Quest to Learn

By now the reader is probably wondering if I am going to give my whole life story. I am not. It is 2015. I am 78 years of age. I am a retired university professor. I have done the traditional research and writing that is a requirement for university faculty. I have three degrees, a B.A., an M.Ed. and a Ph.D. I am also a licensed Marriage and Family Therapist. I only mention that to let you know that I overcame my reading and math difficulties. I did this in the beginning through simply reading many things. I learned to read by reading.

I learned math through learning how to use math in research. Math used for a purpose. Handheld calculators saved me. The calculator did the tedious, mundane work of calculation while I used the results to answer the research question I was pursuing. What I needed to learn was what statistical procedure would answer my research question. This was strictly a conceptual problem more than a memory issue.

Concluding Comments

Parents, get to know your children and their interests. Help them to see how vital the "tool subjects" are in our real world. Help them in those early lessons of breaking the reading code by making a game of it. Read, read, read to your children out loud for a few minutes in a comfortable setting each day. You might have a family ritual of reading to your children at bedtime. Fathers, be a part of this. Have a whole array of books readily available for your children. Take them to the library if you can't afford books. Ask them questions about what they are reading as they are reading. Slowly go from picture books to books with fewer pictures to chapter books.

Teachers, your task is overwhelming. In the typical public school, you might have at least thirty children. You have them in your stewardship for 180 days of the year for 300 some odd minutes a day. They all have their specific needs, fears, and hopes. Your task is to meet all those needs, strengths, and deficiencies of each child while teaching them to capture the required curriculum of the district, state, and even the federal government. So typically, the isolated, self-contained teacher tried to have at least three reading groups in those early days. Historically, students were identified in the bright Sunshine group, the average Blue Birds, and the slow Turtles. And so it went. The children were labeled from the beginning of school, and the differences between the children expanded throughout their school experience. The bright progress in spite of the teacher, the average plug along in the required curriculum, the slow fell farther behind.

I have spent many years working with children in classrooms who have difficulty learning. These experiences were in both private and public settings. In the most successful learning environments, I have encountered teachers that have "divided to conquer." Sometimes this means one-on-one teacher-pupil teaching and other times small groups. In all cases, the successful students are given immediate feedback on their learning responses. In the key skills of reading and math, successful teachers do it differently. They don't have the children guess the correct answers. They use modeling, prompting, and immediate feedback in those early lessons. They *teach*! Children read and write for a purpose: to send and receive understandable messages. They learn that reading, writing, and verbal communication have one purpose: for understanding. If understanding does not occur, your reading, writing, and speech have not been effectively communicated.

Thank You, Dr. James Young!

Given my experience, I have read that in the United States, 15 to 20 percent of the population has dyslexia. It is common knowledge that most methods of teaching this population do not remediate the needed skills. It is a necessity that the appropriate methods are employed.

Dyslexia can be observed and diagnosed by an aware educational psychologist with the support of a well-trained teacher. However, that being said, I have had students who have not had the opportunity to learn to read. They can't read, but they do not have dyslexia! There is a definite difference between the student who has not had the opportunities to learn reading skills and those with a cognitive processing deficit.

Also, it has been my experience that no matter what the reason for the lack of skills for learning to read, using a multisensory method will teach the student these skills.

For the student with dyslexia, the method will include one-on-one time with the teacher and the student, and taught with direct instruction. The appropriate multisensory program is designed to include explicit and systematic instruction in phonological awareness with phonetic and spelling patterns.

A well-designed reading program will address the needs of 80 percent of the population who are learning to read. However, let us take a serious look at the 20 percent. Therefore, it is my opinion that the reading problem should be diagnosed so that correct intervention can be implemented. **Listen, observe, and think about the problem.**

Uncle Lloyd, Aunt Nona, Daddy Allen, Argie Ella, Mother Edna, Grandma Effie Argie, Grandpa Leslie, Beulah—Aunt Boo. This picture was taken in 1937.
More than just a picture!

This little girl, Argie Ella, was looking at her Daddy's finger and pointing with interest. This interest told the world she was visual and connected with her environment. She remembers the emotional connections with Daddy and Mother. Brains are amazing as they continue to reach for information. Emotions are incredible as they reach out for understanding. Study this picture for body language and facial expressions. This picture was not professionally staged; it expresses the real and interestingly accurate way they lived their lives.

4

Happy Me:
Before School Days
The Years were 1935, 1937, 1939

The Year Was 1935

I remember the patterns in my baby basket, then called a bassinet. They kept my attention. To this day, I can recall the weave. Another time, I saw Mother swinging a spatula over the basket while talking to her friend. Oh yes, I can also hear the sounds and smells of cooking. Before I could walk, Mother sat me on the ground next to the house, and again, I remember the patterns in the plaster on the outside of the house. Feeling the texture of the plaster, I would rub my fingers over the white painted surface. I can see the irregular patterns in my head. Being outside was the best! When I was inside, the design of the old wool Axminster rug grabbed my imagination as I looked underneath it for make-believe people. I don't know why *Mrs. Meanie* lived under that rug. One day, a carpet tack with its black head was found by my toes, and I was trying to make it a new friend. My mother said, "Sister, don't put that in your mouth! You can't play with your new friend with the sharp head." My whole world had an intriguing twist of goodness.

The Year Was 1937

Daddy would carry me around on his strong and broad shoulders, holding on to me with his bigger than big hands, so I wouldn't fall. My game was to duck as we went through the doorway.

Daddy would say, "Let's go ride Morgan," and away we would go. Out in the country, he taught me to ride his horse. After a day of riding

Morgan, we would drink pumped well-water from an old rusty cup. When I was two years old, Morgan and I led the Fourth of July Parade. No fear! On that red, white, and blue day, I have no memory of Daddy being near, only Morgan. I claimed him as my horse! Morgan was my life. I still love and want a horse. Being outside was my happy world.

The Year Was 1939

My next door neighbor and I were four years old. Friends! I would feel the New Mexico dirt all over my body as my truck ran along and off the child-made roads. We placed sticks for trees here and there. Days filled with fun. My friend Benny Ray and I would run across the street to his grandmother's home to snack on treats, climb trees, and look through the leaves. These things were my heaven on earth. Trees! Mother would come and snatch me away to go so far as across the street, to go home for something, which I can't remember as necessary. And one time, she even scratched my head, "My head itches, how about yours?" Mother touched me, so nice. I longed to be touched. When I wanted to be *touched* and was not, I cried. I believe our souls long to be touched even when we push away. I have experienced this with students. Touch the heart!

Days filled with dancing on the lawn, which was dirt with patches of grass, days of sunshine and warmth. I found arms of joy in picking and sharing colorful flowers. My great-granddaughter does the same thing. Abby!

As Daddy carried me outside to see the moon, my first words were a sentence, "I see the moon." It was exciting, even though I knew words, I wanted to talk to the big people with lots of words. It took a while to figure that out. I did not make the usual parroting sounds. No sounds or single words of language until I spoke in full sentences. My head had a difficult time using only a single word. I knew that I could understand the concept—idea with one word. However, I felt that I needed to use lots of words so that others could understand me. I still use lots of words.

Life was unfolding as I wrapped my heart around a life that was good.

5

Unhappy Me:
Public School Days
The Years were 1941, 1944, 1945, 1950, 1954

The Year Was 1941

After school I pulled myself up and down the hills from Sully Elementary School kindergarten to our company-owned home; I could hardly wait to get home. The tears I held back in my eyes flooded my heart. The Santa Rita Kennecott open pit copper mine, large as it was, couldn't contain the feelings of disappointment that filled my soul as I told myself, "I never want to return to that place where *monsters* live." The place where I was going to *amount to something*. My caring mother had prepared me for the occasion in a lovely new hand-sewn dress, white socks, and brown leather shoes, with a pimento and cheese sandwich in my hand. It was supposed to be an exciting and happy time for me. Pleased to be all dressed up for school! Then came the day the *monsters* changed everything. My future!

I raised my hand. The teacher called on me. Replying as taught and always saying the name of the person to whom you are speaking, "Teacher, may I take the roll to the office?" The stinging reply pierced the silence of the room, "Don't you ever call me *Teacher*. My name is Mrs. Travaro!" And the sound was not muffled but loud, clear, and well-defined. She meant it! I could not remember the name Travaro but *Teacher* worked perfectly in my mind. For the school year, she was *Teacher*.

And the *monsters* didn't stop there because they seemed to be all over the place. When do we eat? Was it before reading or after reading? The playground bell would ring for students to run and not to be late. Those who seemed to be my friends would make it into their seats before me. They didn't run with me but ahead of me, way ahead of me. I didn't like to run; if I ran, I missed seeing my world. Couldn't school be outside where I could smell the wet dirt, look at the weeds around the flagpole, feel the wind in my hair, and hear the sounds from the grasshopper's wings? I wanted to have freedom from the schoolroom walls and the little desks that wedged me tightly in place.

Oh, yes! I would have places to hide on the side of the hill from the boy who tried to kiss me under the coloring table. Mr. Parry, the maintenance man, rescued me and my crying eyes by taking me out of the classroom when Keith had tried to kiss me under that table. He was only a cute little boy, but I viewed him as another *monster*. I hated to be at school. I wanted to go home to watch Daddy bring the coal for the stove, and I longed for a taste of Mother's cooking. I never told them that I didn't like school. My secret and not telling!

The fire drills came often and then came more drills; war drills trained us to hide if the warplanes should happen to come over the school. Outside the class we would go, hurry and trip over each other with hearts beating fast because the bombs may be coming; we squelched down and stayed hidden until the bell would ring to call us back into the building.

One day, a delightful horned toad peeked out from a scrubby old bush. He looked at me, and I studied him. Oh, no! That bell rang to call us in! I wanted to stay outside because outside was more inviting than being in the classroom. The world was full of "hurry up" and just in time for another *monster*. Confusing book of sight words, *Dick and Jane,* and the phonics drills, I was expected to remember all! Other kids caught on, but I could not for the life of me remember those sounds and how did the teaching of both sight words and phonics drills relate? I wanted to go outside and see the world of trees, flowers, rocks, and sunshine with horned toads.

Well, something really, really super happened! Johnny was the smartest student in the class, and everyone knew Johnny because he knew

28

everything about everything. The teacher asked him a question. He couldn't find the answer in his head, but I knew the answer. See, I am smart!

After school that day as I was walking home, Johnny caught up with me and told me how smart I was, even though he knew I couldn't read. I wish I could find Johnny to say, "Thank you, Johnny." He made me feel like I was okay. He never talked to me again. Smiled!

It was a celebrated occasion when my parents took me out of school to go on a trip. It gave me an excuse not to know those words. They just didn't make sense! And I was such a good actor that Mother didn't know I wasn't learning to read. When we went to the store, and the can label read *beans,* I would see the picture of beans on the can and then I knew that the word was *beans.* When Mother would say, "Go get a can of beans," I would go. Everything was a picture, or in other words, I was learning words by seeing them not by hearing all the sounds.

The consonant sounds were difficult because I had to get them in the right sequence. I always seemed to be getting into trouble because I couldn't get things in the correct sequence. Mother didn't know! The same thing happened with the piano; I faked it all the way, making up songs. Children and adults learn ways to compensate, either for good or bad.

The Year Was 1944

Oh! Nobody told me about more *monsters.* My 3rd grade teacher's words echoed through the Sully School classroom in the mining camp of Santa Rita, New Mexico, "Argie Ella! You will never graduate from the 8th grade, let alone high school." I stood there with the sunlight shining through the large glass panes of the old building, feeling like the sun had just gone out. Where could I hide? Remembering the gray stalls, I did find the school bathroom to hide in sometimes. I can still smell the bathroom. I cry every time I allow myself to think about that moment. It is still painfully real!

What is that old and repeated saying? "Sticks and stones will break my bones, but words will never hurt me." Words hurt! I will never graduate, not even 8th grade! Oh, it is hurtful what we say while trying to motivate someone to do better. Why do we do that? It doesn't work. I will never forget how I felt that day while the other kids watched as I sat down. I felt like I was going to wet my panties.

As I stood there that day in the classroom trying, trying to read the word AWFUL, I could not bring to memory how to say the word, even though I knew what it meant. And, ironically, that is how I was feeling at the moment . . . just AWFUL. I was never asked to read aloud again until I was in the 8th grade. The teachers were sure that I could not read, and I could not until I had gathered enough sight words that I could put it all together. I could not remember the sounds and sequentially bring them together to make a word. The vowel sounds were the *monsters* on the printed page. As I learned those things, they left my head and where did they go? Why could not I just spit words out like everyone else? Why was I different? What was wrong with me? I studied hard, did my homework, and always made it home on time.

Mother read to my brother and me. We loved *Nancy Drew* and the *Bobbsey Twins*. I could understand them, but I could not remember the details of the stories and repeat the plot. I could tell you what happened in the story but not the details in order. Sequencing everything I did was hard! However, I could take the messages from the books, abstract the lessons and apply them to life. Yes, I was learning needed and useful information.

On the way home that sad day, I designed a plan to cope with my head. I would tell my mother that I couldn't see. Mother took me to the ophthalmologist in Silver City. Heaven knows that I couldn't say that very strange sounding word nor understand it. He asked me all kinds of questions, put one glass "Coke" bottle bottom looking thing after another up to my eyes, trying to figure out what could help me see. I was telling him stories about what I could see or couldn't see. My glasses ended up as a joke. Now, I really couldn't see. Little did I know that seeing acuity was not the problem. The problem was how my brain was working: cognitive processing.

When I went back to school, I told the teacher, "These glasses are not working for me, I still can't see." I had learned how to avoid being embarrassed by teachers by creating an intervention. Smart move!

Thus, I was a child with a cheerful smile reduced to an emotionally sad and lonely little girl, feeling hopeless, *me*. However, I was born with a resilient and determined spirit. No matter how challenging my situation of tears and heartache, ***it was written on my heart to keep trying and not give up.***

The *monster* of "no hope" can defeat the spirit. It will keep telling your mind that life is not worth it, to give up and go back to bed. The *darkness*, darker! The savor for life was gone. Please, oh please, jump up and write down the *light* side. Once I wrote, "It will be all right because I had no fear as a two-year-old riding my horse Morgan in a parade." Well, not only riding Morgan but leading the parade. Fear not and do something!

The Year Was 1945
Now back to those horrible elementary school years, why did I feel defeated just because I couldn't read? Well, if I had known what I now know, my early years would have been joyful as opposed to being impacted by disturbing questions, "Who am I, and what is wrong with me?" "*Why?*" My life could have been one of enjoying my sensory gifts as I strengthened my sensory weaknesses. I wonder if that is what every tear will be, a drop of water that brings the rainbow.

It felt like a slap in the face, and how can I look my little world in the eye with a face that does not smile? I knew that I was smart, even though others didn't. I heard there was going to be eight grades before high school. It would be a relief for the eight years to go by since I wanted to be that happy girl again. Only eight years!

It was something like this: no one knew I was sad because I had learned to act my part as "happy," and I happily played with my friends. The one I really wanted to be my friend and I liked best, Ann, made fun of my singing because I couldn't remember the words. While I was swinging one day, I was pushing her, and she kicked my nose. Broke it!

In the middle of the school year, they gave us those achievement tests that decided who would be moved up a grade or skip to the next grade; my very best friends left me behind. Four of them! Gone! I remember the day of decision; I went home and into the bathroom, so my mother wouldn't see my tears, sat on the toilet, cried and stayed there for a very long time thinking about how *dumb* I assumed I was. I was troubled that I couldn't read because I couldn't make sense of the phonetic patterns and the sounds never made it into my head. If they did, they didn't stick around. Also, it was said that I was anything *but* the best in arithmetic. I couldn't figure out the order of the numbers. However, I seemed to think about other things very well. This dilemma became a horrible challenge. My tears were hidden. I didn't want my mother to know my secret . . . I was *dumb*! However, I do remember taking some comfort from an awareness that other things in school seemed to go better.

I was smart, even though some kids and the teacher didn't know I was smart. The teacher would say things like, "Argie Ella is sweet." Now, you and I know that is not a rewarding message about your skill level in academics. There were moments of relief when I knew I could quickly solve problems in my head when the teacher was talking about life and how it works. My parents had taught me well about manners and had given me examples from their lives; they showed *common sense* and the *work ethic*. I knew the answers!

When I knew the answers, I was afraid to say anything because I had no confidence in how to use language to respond to questions. So, all I said was "I don't know." Just thinking about this makes my heart beat fast and my eyes fill with tears. Not being able to communicate what I knew was torment! And believe it or not, it is still very challenging to express to my world what my mind knows, and what my heart is saying. The gift of language is a gift extraordinaire. This gift is not my gift. It is easier for me to write my mind and heart than to speak it. When I write, I can go back and change words to say what I want to say. Thank goodness for the computer! And the spell checker is great, but it misses some of my words. Break the language code!

Now back to my world of 1945, I could remember the faces of everyone, where they sat, what they ate, when they cut their hair, where they lived, and with whom they lived. Yes! I could remember the color of the dress that the teacher had worn on the previous days. I knew who missed class. I knew so much, but I couldn't read!

And that's not all! I didn't know how to converse with my friends; they would talk, I didn't talk; it was sequentially confusing. However, if given a studied or familiar subject, I could talk for a long time; this speaking is using my strength of *spontaneous language*. I was afraid that someone would ask me a question and I would need to use my *demand language*. That kind of language is difficult for me. I believe that *spontaneous language* is my brain looking at the whole picture, but my *demand language* looks at the parts. And the way my brain works is by looking at the whole picture, not the parts. I intentionally force it to look at the parts.

I remember how important it was to have a place for *this* and *that* and everything in its place; then I could find what I needed. Mother liked it when I would iron my clothes on my little ironing board and clean under my bed. I became compulsive to survive my unorganized brain. Get rid of "stuff." My brain does not know how to sequence unneeded "stuff." A place for everything! Powerful!

It wasn't hard to find my way home. I could *see* little things along the way and remember them the next time. Colors were fun! The colors of the moss on the rocks, the bright colors of flowers with their delightful fragrances, and knowing where the barking dogs lived, helped me find the way home. The rocks and the hills, up and down, helped.

I didn't like to cook, but I *loved* the smells of cooking; the tastes were fantastic.

The dresses Mother sewed for me made me feel like a queen when I went to church. One Sunday at the Community Church, I wore my new Children's Day dress. It was made of a cotton material called Pique. I can still see and feel the patterns in the fabric: white with small flowers. Lovely. My world was a mosaic of colors, textures, and patterns.

I loved splashes of color with the sun shining through the waves on the oceanfront and the leaves of trees. My world was so enjoyable when I wasn't at school. I lived for what I could see, touch, and smell with my sensitive heart. Ah so! I wish I had known that I had an intelligence or gift for things other than those things called *reading, writing, math, language,* and *sequencing.* You too have gifts!

The Year Was 1950

Auditory processing *Monsters* in my head were real. My elementary school reading teacher, you know the class that had *monsters* chasing me, was teaching me by sounds or phonetic patterns, but I couldn't keep the sounds in my head. She could have strengthened the visual side of my head with appropriate sight-words, known as the look-say method, and I could have learned to read. She was using a phonetic method, but it was the wrong one for my brain. Another method of phonetic instruction would or could have worked. By the 8th grade, I had finally gathered enough sight-words on my own to convince them that I could read.

I learned to see each word as a picture with meaning. I found out that my Daddy's Bull Durham smoking tobacco had the words *Bull Durham* on the little bag. I associated the words with the meaning. My Daddy rolled his own and used Bull Durham tobacco. For a while, I concluded that all tobacco was called Bull Durham, and when I saw the word *Bull*, I would see it in my head and say it. I thought *tobacco* had something to do with a bull. Seeing words associated with meaning is the way I learned every word. My spelling words were seen in my head before I could write them on my paper. While I was looking for the right word to say, I would have to see it in my head first. I absolutely could not bring it out of auditory memory.

When I learned the concept—idea of the word *inundated,* I could not remember with my auditory memory if the word was *inundated* or *unindated.* Thus, I could not depend on my auditory memory to be correct. To remember how words are said, they have to go through my visual memory of seeing them in my head before I know how to say them. If I do not use my visual memory, I don't learn the words. Well, that is *me* and how I learn.

These are the things I had and *still* have trouble processing:
1. Hearing similar sounds in words: bad, tad, man.
2. Hearing similar sounds but unable to create sounds.
3. Organizing the motor sequence of sounds.
4. Hearing similarities of sounds of syllables.
5. Hearing the right sounds in consonant blends.
6. Hearing consonant blend but unable to create sound.
7. Hearing the correct short vowel sounds.
8. Hearing short vowel sound but unable to reproduce sound.
9. Hearing rhyming and repeating the pattern. Nightmare!
10. Differentiating between rhyming words. Difficult!
11. Remembering the word but using a word with same meaning.

You got it! When a person is intelligent and cannot do these things, life is a nightmare. And I conclude that even with less intelligence, these stated things are nightmares. I know many tears have been shed over the awareness that something is not right: auditory memory, sequencing, and motor challenges! Challenges have increased, as I have seasoned or one may say become older. I have become more aware of the need to compensate for deficits. It happens faster than you think. Yes, faster!

The Year Was 1954

When some sideline kids called me the Onion Queen, as I rode the float as Homecoming Queen, I wept. Then I remembered that I was not an onion queen, and they were wrong. My first reaction was that I looked like an onion. Changing the view will start a new beginning. Who am I? Not the Onion Queen! Change your thinking, and you will change your behavior. For as he thinketh in his heart, so is he.

Think positively. Think of one thing you have that a one-legged person doesn't have. Positively keep saying, "I will give." Perhaps, a kind word or a smile! Do something for someone that you would like for someone to do for you. Having validation is like unto breathing, and dying will come to those who are not validated. I learned early in life to validate myself. I clean! I do something for someone. I acknowledge someone. One day, I told someone that I liked seeing them look at the trees as they walked and two days later, a card arrived. "I just knew it was past time to write you a short note . . . I just wanted to thank you for your friendship. You are a loving and caring person." A win-win moment Treating others like they are knowingly precious will help all feel valued.

We are all islands with the sea around us. Not only do we need unseen anchors stabilizing our boats, but we also need a life raft to keep us afloat. That life raft can be as simple as an unexpected smile. **Try it! We all need to know that we are real and not a bump on a log.**

Does it matter? Yes, it matters!

6

My Brain Gift:
Wired Differently, But Why?

I am reminded of one time when I heard Dr. Galaburda lecture and answer questions; someone asked, "If you could fix the brain, and it wouldn't have dyslexia, would you?" He answered, "No." Taking the gifts of dyslexia away from the world would silence the world.

Dr. Kevin Currie-Knight has been a Teaching Assistant Professor at East Carolina University's College of Education. He teaches classes about the psychological and social foundations of education. I have been excited to learn from Dr. Currie-Knight's insights and appreciate his brain. I greatly value his presentations and expertise. Take a look!

Dr. Currie-Knight wrote the following in the article entitled *Don't Assume I'm Smarter Than My Contractor*. (Dr. Kevin Currie-Knight 2015)

"Whether we mean to or not, we constantly reinforce the message that only the stuff kids are taught in school counts as serious learning. Extracurriculars are fine, but what really counts is in their textbooks and homework.

We send them to school precisely because we believe that's where they'll be taught the most important subjects. We grade them on those things and in many ways we measure their worth (at least while they're in school) by how well they do on tests and school assignments."

This article was originally published by The Foundation for Economic Education and may be freely distributed, subject to a Creative Commons Attribution 4.0 International License. This license requires credit to be given to the author. I am grateful to Dr. Currie-Knight for his insightfulness. I agree with him.

I am reminded what Currie-Knight said about what the Educational theorist John Holt wrote about schooling in his frankly titled essay *School is Bad for Children*. *"Oh, we make a lot of nice noises in school about respect for the child and individual differences, and the like. But our acts, as opposed to our talk, say to the child, 'Your experience, your concerns, your curiosities, your needs, what you know, what you want, what you wonder about, what you hope for, what you fear, what you like and dislike, what you are good at or not so good at—all this is of not the slightest importance, it counts for nothing.'"*

John Holt also said, *"It is a rare child who can come through his schooling with much left of his curiosity."* I concur that this is true today. John Holt originally wrote this article and the *Saturday Evening Post* published it on February 8, 1969.

Likewise, in *Shop Class as Soulcraft,* philosopher and auto mechanic, Matthew Crawford, forwards the dichotomy of how we have evolved in our schools and society between knowing and doing. He is one of my favorite philosophers. He exposes the damage done by schools that are canceling programs to make way for more **knowing and less doing.** He emphasized the crucial role of thinking in manual labor.

Institutions are convincing us that what we learn in them is of utmost importance, and what we learn out of them is of little consequence. I believe that *more doing and less knowing* **finds the path** *to more knowing!* **Daddy was brilliant. Here Daddy is with his grandsons, Chris and Brad.**

Celebrating brain gifts that schools do not always recognize are treasures that can be lost in the depths of not understanding the beauty of different talents. I say, "Wake up before we lose more of our beauty in the ocean of despair rather than in the reward of seeing the treasures on the shore." I have known and experienced the consequences. Please more doing!

Richard L. Masland, M.D., Department of Neurology, Columbia University, quoted Holton as follows:

"It is coming to be more widely agreed that an apparent defect in a particular person may merely indicate an imbalance in our normal expectations. A noted deficiency should alert us to look for a proficiency of a different kind in the exceptional person. The late use of language in childhood, the difficulty in learning foreign languages . . . may indicate a polarization or displacement in some of the skill to another area. That other enhanced area is without a doubt, in Einstein's case, an extraordinary kind of visual imagery that penetrates his every thought process." (Holton, G. 1971-1972, Winter. On Trying to Understand Scientific Genius, *American Scholar* 41:102.)

Dr. Masland shared, *"Jerre Levy has suggested the possibility that you cannot have it both ways, that the development of superior language skills, investing functions on both sides of the brain, is at the expense of the spatial skills of the nondominant hemisphere; and that, conversely, strongly developed spatial skills are at the expense of the language function."* (Levy, J. 1969)

Now, I appreciate my particular brain. It serves me well. I understand the gift. *Me*. When I was in the 2nd grade, my teacher was less than charitable toward me when I didn't seem to catch on to reading or math. As I reflect back on those classroom days, can I believe that I graduated from high school and later from university with honors? Unbelievable! My Daddy lived his life to show me that you have to be smarter than the machine on which you are working. When someone forwarded the message, "You can't do it!" Smarter than the machine, I did it!

In 1957, I submitted an application to American Airlines for a job as a stewardess. I was selected and succeeded very well in the six weeks of rigorous training where the courses were of college-level difficulty.

Subsequently, I served as a stewardess for nearly three years and was being groomed for a job as a supervisor. I worked hard and was successful. Resigning from American Airlines was a painful experience, but my decision had been decided. It was more desirable to be married and have children than it was to continue with the job that I loved.

Even though my brain is wired differently than most, for a long time, I didn't know *why*. I have always tried, tried, and tried again until something works out. Through my discouragement, I have learned lessons. **Hopelessness has paved the road to faith**. There have always been those who will send the message of despair. *Hope for the best while looking through the lens of reality* because something good may come along; if it is not blurred, with doubt, your lens will allow you to see.

Once I prayed for a miracle, I found that the miracle was the changing of me. The one for whom I prayed, my grandson, brought a precious gift, one of understanding. He passed away at age fourteen from a disease that day by day changed him. Brigham's happy and joyful spirit influenced everyone who met him. He was thrilled with having the precious experience of life. Brigham hurt.

Through pain, I have learned lessons of empathy for others. The Hawaiians have a word I have grown to understand, Ho'oponopon. Ho'oponopon is the practice of reconciliation and forgiveness. I forgive that which has brought me pain. I am grateful for the pain I have experienced with my cognitive challenges. I am also grateful for the pain I have endured through feeling the pain in the lives of others, as well as my pain. These have been customized lessons for me. I have learned that through *pain,* I have learned to have Empathy, Hope, and Faith. For me this is Charity. Ho'oponopon! Love Hawaiian philosophy!

I desire that together, our slippas will reward us with lessons that will bring *Hope*. **We are all unique and have special gifts. Share!**

7

Using My Brain Gift
I Did It!

The following is an excerpt from *More Than A Ticket   Memoirs Flying with American Airlines from Props to Jets* by Argie Ella Hoskins. American Airlines knew me as a talented stewardess. I did it with what gifts I had, not what I did not have. And that is what mattered!

They had no awareness of the challenges I had experienced all my life with cognitive processing. They knew that I was bright and attractive with a warm and giving personality. They did not know my brain held a secret *monster* and a beautiful gift—dyslexia. Well, that is what it seemed to be from all that has been written. Some would say that I have that *thing* called dyslexia. I know that my challenge with learning far exceeds the popular notion that my brain is a brain with "dyslexia."

I quote the American Speech and Language-Hearing Association: "*Dyslexia* has been used to refer to the specific learning problem of reading. The term *language-based learning disability*, or just *learning disabilities*, is better because of the relationship between spoken and written language. Many children with reading problems have spoken language problems. The child with dyslexia has trouble almost exclusively with the written—printed word. *The child who has Dyslexia as part of a larger language learning disability has trouble with both the spoken and the written word.*"

I have a language impairment as it pertains to both receptive and expressive language processing, and it has been a puzzlement. Along with that, the fear of demand language and the reward of spontaneous language has been a mystery. If you ask me a specific question, I can't think of the answer. If you give me the same subject without questions to be answered, I can talk about it all day. I never fear being asked to speak at public meetings until question and answer time.

Conversation is awkward. What idea should I talk about *next?* I have many ideas. Never an end to what I can intelligently talk about, even though I find myself repeating the same things over and over again. I think it is because I am never sure that I am being understood, so I am trying it again, in the hope that it is making sense.

When I had my final personal progress interview with my supervisor that was to pass or not pass me—that is, to earn my American Airlines' wings or not. Chris Debraggio, my supervisor said, "You are shy and don't talk much, but we need some stewardesses who are *coy* and quiet. You know what our passengers need. You will be fine." I grabbed the dictionary: *Coy* means having a shy or sweetly innocent quality that is often intended to attract attention. Well, I did know about Southern charm. I made it in spite of the language—conversation challenge. In fact, I remember in one class, they taught us how to converse. Relieved!

To top it off, I also have a massive sequencing challenge. It has been a nightmare. Sequencing challenges emerge everywhere from little daily tasks, such as -- turn the other way, left or right, on which side is the fork placed, etc. Crucial acts and big life decisions, such as how do I organize my world with putting first things first! And the huge one, such as socially what *next* in a relationship! This list might even include life-saving acts. Woe is me! Is it my turn to jump down the evacuation slide? Which foot first or does it matter? Which side of the wing will the window rope be on, and which direction do I turn the latch to open the aircraft door? Minor things!

Over-learn and I mean over-learn. No wonder with fear in my heart, I got 100 percent on test after test. I was viewed as the perfect student. Some gals would be happy with 95 percent. Not me. I had learned how to compensate for my sequencing challenge. I call it Argie's sequencing disorder. Real!

It has been difficult to understand my intelligence, confused in some areas and apparently high in others. Tests and observations show that I am in the superior range of intelligence in some areas and certainly lacking in other areas. My verbal intelligence is my weakness. One who has held the rank of Full Professor in two significant universities has often reassured me of my high *global* intelligence and that I am not *dumb*! Revamped my view of reality.

It has been very perplexing for me to feel validated. I keep looking for validation. Do I socially fit? Where and how? At times, I have allowed my weaknesses to control me. And there are lots of people out there who have the same problem. How do I know? They have told me. **Doubt and fear will block the flow of positive energy.** Look up, not down.

No one, I mean no one, will know what I owe to American Airlines for giving me the opportunity to prove myself in complex and sequential ways that required personal and social skills. My book *More Than A Ticket* speaks to what it takes for a person to become successful in a larger and sometimes uncomprehending society and find ways to communicate thoughts, needs, and feelings best while discharging one's responsibilities. I worked very diligently on the task. And it was work!

With my sequencing challenge, I learned to *stop* my spinning brain, *look* at what I was doing, and *listen* to my thoughts and words before taking the next step. The next step says, "Now, you are ready." *Compensating for a weakness requires a studied intervention that serves to change a given behavior.* Placing not sequenced thoughts into an order for a given action is the template for a desired behavioral outcome. I learned how to do new tasks; I understood the process of cognitive awareness.

I had to know what the problem was before I could intellectually compensate for the problem! While flying as a stewardess, I intuitively came to understand my brain and how it functions. After I became a special education teacher with additional training in brain functioning, I learned to understand my brain.

As a special education teacher with over thirty years of teaching experience, I have tested many students and identified their learning styles and other challenges. I designed interventions for remediation, followed by focused instruction, student discipline, and hard work.

Those who have some awareness of dyslexia and the impact it has on the learning process may not be aware of dyslexia's upside and some of the extraordinary gifts it brings. I am referring to gifts, such as intuitively seeing a picture or a concept—idea immediately as a whole and then seeing how details fit it together. Another gift is the ability to connect dots rapidly. Gifts, such as being more curious than average, thinking in pictures instead of words, or thinking in words instead of pictures, being intuitive and insightful, and having more than the ordinary awareness of the environment, have been both thwarting and endowing. I see the dust on the furniture and grains of sand on the beach. My vivid imagination enables thinking outside the box. I can utilize my brain's ability to alter and create perceptions. I think and perceive multi-dimensionally.

Usually, I experience a *thought* as a detail that becomes viewed as the whole picture. Seeing details with their intricacies are more than just details. I have to push the details together to see the whole picture. With this comes seeing the beauty of details. Profound! And there are others!

Please Don't Call Me Dumb! addresses those with cognitive challenges. After not understanding their beautiful gifts, they can make friends with their brains. **I did it! You can do it.**

Questions my brain asks, "What do I do? Where do I go? How do I get there?" My answers have been in the doing, and most of the time it has been doing it over and over to be correct. I have tenaciously worked very hard with applied focus, attention, and direction. Failure before success!

I was honored to be a stewardess on the Boeing 707 Inaugural Jet Flight from Los Angeles to New York on January 25, 1959. Historical!

My book *More Than a Ticket Memoirs Flying with American Airlines from Props to Jets* **tells a story of the Golden Age of flying—a time I enjoyed when passengers were treated as guests, and everyone dressed in their Sunday best.**

Children have the strength to move beyond their parents' weaknesses and to forgive.

Life is challenging; you will hang in there with your brain gifts. I love these brains! First question when I meet my maker, "Tell me about the uniqueness of brains and how they were created?"

8

What I Learned from My Four Sons:
Resilience and Validation

I have thought about *Resilience* and *Validation* and how each concept is compelling as they relate to each other. These will be addressed because of changes in the family's environment. Never easy.

We moved to a small and rural area of Arizona with our young family of four sons. My husband liked the town. He was validated for his service as a contributing member of the school board. His job at work proved to be rewarding for a while, and it was validating. I was active in the town's social and service clubs. There were several that kept me busy. We enjoyed the lovely weather and pure water to drink, along with the local food sources, which provided organic this and that, to feed our growing family. The locals rewarded me with accolades of *you are a giving person*. I loved this little community. My husband and I were validated.

Now for the children and what they were getting out of the move and the new experience, *I was blinded to their aching hearts*. Different story! I assumed that in general, they had incredible experiences that would endear them to the whole community and broaden their view of the local culture. But I was wrong! It was a surprise when, years later, they told me they hated living in that *charming* town. Baffling! After I had done a lot of pondering, I understood why this charming town was not charming for them. My heart broke. I had not validated the *why* of their values. I had assumed too much.

We had taught our children values not found in many of their peers; however, they had some good friends. By and large, they were not validated. I may say that they were not accepted or recognized for their values. How they dressed, walked, talked, and played were foreign to the local culture. And I, their mother, was always saying, "Just try to understand the situation and fit in." Their hearts were breaking, and we, their parents, were not listening. At their early ages, we failed to walk in their shoes while expecting them to walk in our shoes. Wrong fit.

There was a disconnect between my heart and my children's hearts. I was sure that I had taught them *resilience* or the ability to recover and how to use it. I had not! They felt like outcasts and were bullied. Where were we, their parents? The children didn't have the language to tell us what their personal battles were and that they needed support to survive emotionally. Physical battles of abuse from some kids were more than they felt they could tolerate, but they did survive silently without resolve.

My mother had shared with my brother and me that life isn't about what happens to you, it's about what you do with life when things happen. It matters not how many times you are down and out; you have to pull back up and keep the energy moving forward. How did I miss passing this along in a powerful way to those for whom I cared? My tools were seasoned and strong, but I had not given my children the tools.

Thank goodness my personal life had been well-expressed but without the caring, connecting, and understanding words to explain. It was a shallow experience! Just living an example without the *why* words had not taught the needed lessons of resilience and validation. I felt that my example without explanation was what was necessary and essential, but example alone had not explained the lessons. Words, along with an understanding heart, are imperative. I had created loneliness, not support.

Sometimes, I had missed an opportunity to teach when the window was open; a path which will not be walked again, a view which will not be seen again, or a feeling which will not be felt again. Unique opportunities are treasures either embraced or lost forever. Look for the roads to teach a better way and to learn a better way. Walk with understanding!

We talk of *Resilience*. What does that mean? *The desire to keep going* in spite of the obstacles of discouragement and moments of conflict and frustration? That feeling of "I can go on!"

How? It has been my observation and experience to highlight the most important of important concepts. Catch the dismayed person in a positive act of desirable behavior and positively reward the action. V*alidation* of appropriate action is the breath which lifts the weary traveler. V*alidation* is survival, and without it, we die. If my world is full of denial, disagreement, disapproval, and rejection, I *am not okay*. I wither and die like the animal without water.

The question asked, "What is positive *validation* and where do we find it?" It is, among other things, stamps of approval. It is a feeling of *I am okay;* I am lovable with needed feelings of acceptance, affirmation, endorsement, recognition, and authentication. Yes, the message is that life is worth living. We need to look at the *positive* face of validation because that is where we are nourished and sustained to live emotionally. We all need to feel and hear validation.

Where do we get our *positive* validation? We get it from honest living, service to others, hard work, and from others who care and are trustworthy. Knowing we are good and have a relationship with a higher power validates who we are! Work has been my validation!

Well, some acquire *counterfeit* validation and feel that *negative* validation is better than no validation at all. Negatively manifested actions, such as immoral affairs, drug highs, and the list can go on and on as expressed in the world of TV, tell us how we must be to be "all right."

It is important to have regular opportunities to have open and honest conversations with our children about what they are thinking and experiencing. At other times, they need to know what we are thinking and feeling about what *we* are going through, not only with them but without them. The question must be addressed as to how we should or if we should share that which is happening to us personally in a given situation. **I feel that children need to know how parents are solving unhappy circumstances and celebrating happy moments.** In that new and small community, I should have shared the process of my journey and how that could have been of value in their lives. Now, I wish they knew the depths of my sorrow for my mistakes and how I have lived through those depths. Also, I wish I could go back, show, and tell them how I was sometimes happy even in stressful situations. My resilience brought me through new and uncomfortable moments. By doing so, I have found myself being validated. Important!

At the time, I had not stepped through the process of *empathy* for the children's experiences while they were struggling to be accepted and validated by this new community. Children need an understanding about the consequences of appropriate and inappropriate behaviors within their world. I should have encouraged them and continued to validate the good and sound decisions which they were making, even though others may not be following the same standards. Life is what we make it. Good or bad! Look beyond the surface of every situation.

Having revisited what made my children hate our town, now I could do a much better job of seeing they obtain *validation* for who they are, rather than telling them to fit in. Know who your children are and how they feel. They are unique and exceptional. Ask the *why* questions.

While I was talking about *validation* with a friend, she shared her experience with *validation,* a way to validate appropriate behaviors. My friend, Angelia, shared what she had experienced with her daughter. Angelia learned the wisdom of never saying, *I love you because of all the right choices you are making.* She shared that she loved her daughter, not her behavior choices. Angelia said, "Jan, I love you. You are my daughter, and you will always have my heart." "I do not approve of your shoplifting behavior. I will not reward you for deviant behavior. I will only reward you for acceptable and appropriate behaviors, so let's take the stuff back to the store and fess up." Children need to see and be told with understanding what behavior means.

Good for Angelia. It took courage for her to walk into a store with stolen goods and a humiliated daughter. Her daughter's shoplifting behavior stopped. Validate that which is good. Behavior! I have been privy to many such situations.

And, of course, as parents, we need to be careful always to do what is appropriate and not talk ourselves into thinking that another time will be a better time. The opportunity to take action is now, not when the child wants another time. "But mom, I am sick, got to go to school, my friends are waiting, or Mom, you don't understand." We cannot support negative behavior in others or ourselves for our convenience. Don't wait!

I watched a mother teach her four-year-old daughter how to steal from a store. This attention actively encouraged theft and is child abuse! I was standing in line behind her. What did I say or do? I needed to ask more than "How old is your daughter?" or "What a cute child." I needed to teach more than validation! Honest principles are necessary, and I must be committed to explain in the moment thereof. Entitlement is not positive validation. Speak up!

To be told that I am wrong and wrong again without hearing the message that I am okay and have done something right is devastating. I know more than one wife who sent the message to their husbands that their husbands could *never* accomplish a task correctly. No matter what! It was like cutting and cutting again at the heartstrings. One and then another marriage was over! In one case, the wife was trying to make herself and her husband *perfect* by focusing on the negatives. She destroyed her relationship with her husband. He had an affair to justify his own sense of worth. She felt justified in leaving the marriage. They each made significant contributions to the divorce.

Yes, validations should be positive messages, "Your feelings make sense, and I understand why you are thinking the way you do. I know there are reasons why you think the way you are thinking." A positive message has to be heard for the survival of a relationship, "You are not a bad, wrong, or stupid person for feeling the way you do." *Validation* is when I feel good about who I am, even if we have differing opinions.

Validation is *not* a message which is twisted, such as "Just live with it

51

and if you don't, you are wrong to be thinking the way that you are thinking." This message moves with a pointed tone that says, "How stupid you are!" and it is a sharp criticism that becomes a weapon to destroy and to discredit the other person. They feel sorry for who they are!

Some people do not understand the need to validate others or even know how to validate another. They give messages to everyone that no one is as educated, as smart, or as experienced as they. Such egocentric views, though designed to be self-validating, turn out to be precisely the opposite for everyone. Relationships gone! No validation, no marriage!

Smile and help someone feel important with the message, "Your feelings are worthwhile." I add, our feelings are often unconscious. A smile breaks through the barrier, "You smiled, and I am worth it."

Validation is a gift to be given freely and without reserve for others to feel loved. Someone needs your validation. Give it! I believe it is important to build *resilience,* and it must be nourished with *validation.*

**There is little time to connect with others. Communicate with the heart.
Every moment in time is precious and should be given studied care.**

9

Divorced and Single:
Could be you!

I had to do something to educate myself, so I could be home as much as possible with my children. During the day, I worked as a motel reservationist, served meals at the resort restaurant, and at night learned to be the night auditor. Hours away from home felt like the polar opposite of being home "as much as possible." This kind of life was grinding on my mental and physical health. I loved my children and desired to change the situation which felt like a rock pulling me off a cliff, like a termite eating at my roots while I continued to smile and act like things were all right. They were not all right, so I moved from Patagonia to Mesa and went back to school while working three jobs and accepting family support. I was solving my problems. Even more stress!

Several employers have hired me through the years, and I have had a wide variety of job titles. Some jobs, I liked, and some jobs, I could hardly wait for the day or night to be over, but I appreciated all of them.

In spite of the following reminders, I succeeded! And you can as well! Could this be you?
Here are memories about my challenges with jobs and social roles. Do you find yourself anywhere here?
1. Have an awareness of others' emotions, intent, energy, and needs.

2. Struggling in school to achieve an academic goal.

3. I am always easily distracted and annoyed by noises.

4. I try to order my world not to be distracted by any stimuli.

5. Appearing to be unaware of whatever is happening.

6. When I misuse or mispronounce words, it is embarrassing.

7. I have excellent recall of events that have been experienced.

8. Hearing the words, "You are not listening," when pondering.

9. I never forget faces, but names are difficult.

10. My most difficult challenges: difficulty with verbal instructions.

11. It is hard for me to recall conversations not tied to experiences.

12. Remembering the sequence of events is next to impossible.

13. I am easily and emotionally overwhelmed.

14. Low self-esteem, am I okay?

15. I am either extremely disorderly or extremely orderly.

16. I am so glad that I had fingers for counting. I had to hide them.

17. I have had difficulties making decisions concerning life.

18. Changing my direction in life, as to which way to go, is hard!

19. Difficulty with directions: left or right, up or down, north or south.

20. Difficulty being aware of time, being late is another **me.**

21. Mixed up **me** is my constant need to bring order.

22. Physical health and fatigue magnify the impact of everything.

To top it off, having an extra dose of intuition has helped me make up for the massive challenge of not being able to sequence everything from **soup to nuts.** I say, "How on earth do I put everything in the right place and at the right time?" For example, everything from placing sounds, letters, syllables, and words, to organizing the many steps of getting on an airplane, all are sequencing nightmares. There you have it, **for the life of me. Perhaps for the life of you!**

Here is the life of me. Believe me. It has not been easy! From the beginning of my life, I have worked very hard at making things work, which means little play and keeping my eye on the ball, and I work again. A favorite country and western singer, Johnny Cash, sang the message of my heart, *Up in the morning and out on the job, Work like the devil for my pay . . .* (Gillespie, Haven and Smith, Beasley) I am grateful for what I have learned. Alas!

Education

1954	High School Diploma	*Difficulty with written tests*
1954-1955	College	*Difficulty with written tests*
1955-1956	College	*Difficulty with written tests*
1957	Stewardess College	*Difficulty with written tests*
1961-1962	University	
1980	B. A. degree, *Magna Cum Laude,* 3.7 GPA	
	Major: elementary and special education	
	Minor: social studies	
1980-2007	Obtained many additional college credits and attended many workshops.	

Certification

Elementary Education (1-8) and Special Education (K-12)

Arizona State University (Tempe, Arizona)

Employment History before B.A. Degree

1954	Soda Fountain and Cashier (New Mexico)
1955-1956	Secretary, Engineering Department (New Mexico A&M)
1956	Clerk for El Paso Natural Gas (Texas)
1957-1959	Stewardess American Airlines (Illinois and California)
1959-1961	Scheduling Sec. & Receptionist, Placement Center (Utah)
1961-1962	Registrar's Office, University (Tempe, Arizona)
1975-1978	Assist. Manager of Int'l School of Languages (Arizona)
1976	Receptionist & Secretary
1976-1978	Auditor, Front Desk, Accts. Receivable, Hostess, Waitress
1978-1980	University Cataloger & Maid cleaning private homes

The Year Was 1980

Needing a job that would allow me to be home as much as I could with my children, I went back to school. I graduated from Arizona State University in 1980.

Employment History after B.A. Degree

1980-1982	Regular Education 4th grade teacher (Arizona)
1983-1989	Resource teacher (Utah)
1989-1990	Unit teacher (Utah)
1990-1991	Resource teacher (Utah)
1992-2002	Teacher & reading specialist (Utah)
2002-2004	High School teacher (Hawaii)
2004-2005	Elementary School teacher (Utah)
2005-2006	High School teacher (Hawaii)
2006-2007	Elementary School teacher (Utah)
2007-2008	Reading Specialist (Hawaii)

Professional Affiliations

Council for Exceptional Children, Vice President, Utah Chapter

International Dyslexia Association

Community Service

Past Worthy Advisor, Rainbow Girls

President of Friends of the Library

President of General Federation of Women's Clubs (Patagonia, AZ)

Church Service

Teacher and Leadership Positions

Honors

Beta Phi Chapter, Kappa Delta Phi

Extra-curricular Activities

Cheer Leader: High School and College

Homecoming Queen, Sun Carnival Princess, Military Ball Queen

Student Government

Mother Edna passed away. I remember well our time together as we traveled the road to know each other's minds and hearts. Often we wanted to throw rocks at our brains, but we would later rejoice in knowing without knowing that we had beautiful and unique spirits. We were humbled. We had a closeness I treasure! The relationship has been emotionally rewarding. We knew each other well and desired to understand the *why* of our minds, so we could help others. We would cry for those who would ask *why* and not know their bright minds. With devotion, we committed ourselves to share and do what we could do!

10

Helping Students Survive:
Edna Hoskins and Daughter Argie

Edna Lawson Hoskins received a diploma from the Woman's Institute of Domestic Arts and Sciences, A Division of International Correspondence Schools, Scranton, Pennsylvania. Domestic Arts in Dressmaking and Designing with Pattern Drafting.

I was starting to teach the 4th grade in a regular elementary setting. Having graduated with honors from Arizona State University with a dual major in Special Education and Regular Education, I knew my subject matter well but still did not understand the *whys* of my brain. Whirling in the middle of a nightmare of emotional confusion, playing the part of a well-rounded, energetic, and intelligent person, knowing that I was bright, I forged ahead. Doesn't everyone have unanswered holes in their head? I was making my way through life with tears in my heart. I knew that my brain was different from the majority of the laughing people around me.

There was something I needed to know that I had not found in the textbooks or current research at the university, so I could be a competent special education teacher and write Individualized Education Programs for struggling students. The *whys* of my brain had not been answered? I accepted a teaching job in regular education. I knew that I could figure that thing out for all the students in my classroom, no matter how their brains were working. I could teach them to compensate and survive.

Mother and I both had struggled in school. We sat down with our thinking caps and started writing. Mother would tell me about her horrendous experiences in school, and I would wade through my nightmares of wandering through the world of being in school.

As I reflect back on those choice conversations with my mother while mopping up her tears, as I shed my frustrations, we came up with some beneficial *interventions* which I have subsequently shared with teachers and parents. We relived the lessons that we had stepped through and thankfully survived with unseen scars that were clouded with emotional and moving webs. We started to write after we mopped up the tears.

Students Surviving the Regular Classroom: Suggestions for Teachers and Parents from Two Specific Language Disabled Adults
Mother Edna Hoskins
with daughter Argie Ella Hoskins
Public School Teacher and Educational Consultant

As Mother and I sat down at the computer, we recalled our painful childhood experiences of being cognitively challenged with *sequencing problems,* as well as being socially awkward. We came up with a few suggestions that could have helped us better survive as children in the classroom. The first thing that came to our minds was that we could not work under *time* pressure. Pressure to accomplish a job correctly is one thing but giving *time* to finish a job is most important. Please do not say, "Right now!" We would not be able to organize ourselves using the proper sequence to get the task accomplished. Allow us to work at our pace to think through the steps necessary to do well. That being said, we started our list.

I have stated the learning **challenges** with letters **bolded;** then the *deficits* have been *italicized,* followed by instructional suggestions in a regular font:

1.   **Task: Difficult to accomplish a given task**. *Organizational, Sequencing, Visual Memory, Auditory Memory, and Tactile Memory deficits.*

Give the individual a small amount of work to complete and then give small amount again. This step-by-step approach will assure the success of attainable short-term goals.

2.   **Learning: Can't learn without seeing, hearing, touching and sometimes smelling things.** *Visual Memory, Auditory Memory, Tactile Memory, Organizational, and Sequencing deficits.*

For the initial learning of a concept, you give the individual concrete manipulatives with simple step-by-step instructions. For example, teach numbers with objects that can be seen and touched: number 1, one block, number 2, two blocks, etc. Learning math concepts on the concrete level with manipulatives is a must for building a foundation of success on an automatic level. I was successful as a math teacher using manipulatives to teach basic skills. I know hearing yourself saying the numbers is also necessary. Numbers represent real things. **TouchMath** is a program that teaches with manipulatives—things you can touch. I found it most successful. I recommend it.

When our foster daughter was in elementary school, the teacher had the students paint rocks. Some of the rocks had happy faces, some sad faces, angry, mean, sleepy, and whatever they wanted to paint to show an emotional expression. They used the rocks to show how they were feeling. This expression was such a good idea. I remember one child didn't know how a happy face looked. Another teacher was tired of hearing the tattle tales after recess. The teacher had a *tell it to the bear* stuffed bear in the corner of a room where the students could go and tell their recess story to the bear, not the teacher. It worked. The students just wanted to tell their story, and it turned out that the bear in the corner worked out well. Anyway, use things that you can see, touch, smell, and move around to teach for understanding on a concrete level before moving on to the abstract.

3.   Choices: The individual cannot make decisions easily.
Organizational, Sequencing, and Self-confidence deficits.
We need to help direct the problem-solving process. Again, take baby steps, so children can learn to step their way into making choices without being overwhelmed. I had a granddaughter who would not take a letter to the post office. The first step was getting out of the car before me. Next step was walking to the post office door with me. Another step was opening the door and walking into the post office. The following day, to the post office we went, she went through the door and right up to the letter drop, and her little hand pushed the letter through the slot. She was immensely pleased. Be patient!

4.   Social Skills: The individual finds it hard to work with other people due to needed social skills and language processing problems. *Self-confidence and language deficits.*
Janet Lerner, Ed.D., stated: "A deficit of social skills implies a lack of sensitivity to people and poor perception of social situations, thus the deficit affects almost every area of the child's life. This is probably the most debilitating learning problem the child can have." Relationships between learning disabilities and juvenile delinquency have been well documented. Treatment is not easy. Parents need to involve several disciplines and coordinate the treatment. Look under every rock.

For me, the **social challenges** were **language centered.** I just can't find the right words to say the right things. I would like to have had the opportunity to role-play to learn how that conversation skill works. All I could say was "I don't know." I did know but couldn't remember how to carry on a conversation. Scared to death! To help children with this language challenge, give daily opportunities to practice the skills of conversing with an interesting dialogue. Do not humiliate when they cannot find the correct word—they usually find another word with the same or almost same meaning. Over and over again with a constant effort, find every opportunity to use language. Be creative in orchestrating ways that students can interact with each other. At first, make it only one word, then two, then three, and soon into a sentence. What my students liked to do was for me to start a sentence, and they finished it. You can have lots of fun with that idea. Lots of laughs come when each student adds their word, be it an adjective, verb, adverb, or whatever you or the class decide to add. Students who have a challenge with recalling the right word or will not talk, have them draw a picture of what they would be saying in a conversation. Making an effort to help others feel they belong is a learned social skill which needs to be practiced. It will be achieved more easily for some than others.

5.   Math directions: Can't process auditory information and questions. *Auditory Memory, Comprehension, Organizational, and Sequencing deficits.*

The student must be provided with a structure that is sequenced step-by-step which will help recognize patterns from the basic to more advanced. Auditory directions should be designed for the individual. Start by speaking slowly and make it short for attainable goals. For example, avoid such complicated directions as "Take out your math book, turn to page eight, do the odd numbers on the front, and the even numbers on the back." Individuals need to have directions repeated quietly again after they have been given to the class. Have the individual repeat and explain the instructions to you for clarification. You can go to the board and write numbered steps to be completed. Have the student sit near the front of the room. All students with reading or language problems should be considered high-risk for math challenges. Math and reading problems have sequencing, visual or auditory discrimination problems. Same brain!

6.   Voice: The voice is high-pitched, forced, shouting, or mumbled. *Auditory problem, Attention deficits.*

The voice can be noise for some individuals. To this day, I will say to those with whom I am visiting, "Could you speak slowly, articulate and don't shout?" How does your voice sound: mean-spirited, friendly, soft, loud?

7. **Auditory processing, not a hearing problem but a cognitive challenge:** *Auditory Discrimination and Auditory Memory deficits.*
Seat the individual near the area where the instructor is speaking. Speak clearly, make eye contact, or look at the bridge of the nose. Eye contact can be distracting. For some individuals, it is difficult to distinguish between similar sounds, e.g., pen, pin, pan. Mother and I had a very difficult time with hearing and remembering vowel sounds, along with which syllable comes first. The teacher should keep voice at a moderate and even level. Some students experience soft sounds, as though they are amplified; sounds like the scratch of the pencil. It is important to seat the student away from other students when noise is an issue.

8. **Environment: Mother and I could not have a cluttered area for getting a task accomplished.** *Organizational, Selective Attention both Visual and Auditory deficits.*
The environment which we establish for accomplishing task completion is necessary. Have the individual work in an uncluttered area, free from visual or auditory distractions. Some individuals can work in a stimulating environment. However, others cannot sustain attention with visual and auditory stimuli in the environment.

Learning to *categorize* is a valuable skill. The umbrella over everything we do is to internalize the skill of *everything has a place and everything in its place*. Then we don't have to deal with clutter. When I say free from distractions, I mean free from all stimuli.

9. **Writing: Hard time copying from the board.** *Visual Memory, Visual Motor, Motor, and Sequencing deficits.*
If the individual has difficulty copying from the board or far point, give

the student a desk copy from which to copy. Often, this student will have a right-left orientation challenge, not knowing, from which side of the paper to start writing. Also, teach the individuals to organize the paper on which they are writing by folding it into boxes and turning the paper sideways to order columns. Tape the paper to the desk to position it correctly, and give visual prompts for right-left orientation.

We use handwriting to be able to write legibly and at a rate that is required for accomplishing a writing task. It is one of the best ways to ground the student to focus on a task. Those who are gifted with motor skills and visual intelligence catch on fast.

I know that with the technology which surrounds us, there is not the same need for handwriting as when I was a young student. So I hear, "Why do we bother and why does it matter?" Because there are children who need the orientation of learning the skill of directionality, I say, "It matters." Maybe not all children need this, but the ones who do, need it for life skills. There is a direction to writing.

With our current technology, perhaps we do not need to know how to write in cursive. However, as an art form for those who are visually gifted with motor strengths, this opportunity to express a talent could be a building block for self-esteem. And again, I have stated and in a better way; write cursive, one letter at a time going from left to right and with each letter flowing into the next; this serves to strengthen directionality kinesthetically. It is more than learning; it is neurologically connecting the balancing factors of the brain. Everything you think and do is keeping the neurons working in your brain. *Neurological connections in the brain are paramount to learning, which in turn creates new neurological connections.* Everywhere in our lives, the presence of computers with the keypad design is creating new talents for growth and knowledge as we learn to use them. The computer fails to take the place of learning cursive writing which uses our kinesthetic sense to wire the brain for directionality and balance.

When thinking of remediating handwriting deficits, I have used an

Orton-Gillingham method. I have been trained in this method and certainly have appreciated the training. *"The highly individual character of the organization of skills and disabilities in a given child emphasizes again the need of full analysis of each case and an approach to treatment without fixed methods but rather as an experiment."* (Orton and Gillingham 1933)

Typing sometimes proves useful as an alternative method for any communication. As students' productions improve, they begin to take pride in their accomplishments. They work hard, so the quality of their compositions becomes better. They receive commendation instead of blame from teachers and receive better marks in related subjects.

Speaking of writing, while teaching special education classes, the skills that students learned in cursive writing were valuable. The students learned the most valuable of valuable lessons—*discipline* of staying on task. The debate continues as to whether to teach cursive writing or not to teach cursive; I am for teaching the skill considering the grounding principle of *discipline*. It is one of the best ways to ground the student to focus on a task.

I teach the lowercase letters first. The alphabet has two languages: lowercase letters and uppercase letters. With cursive writing, teach the alphabet and then words. From words, we go into sentence structure. For the more advanced students, the flow of learning how to use proper writing skills slips into diagramming sentences. Valuable. Combining the learning of how to write with how to use good writing to learn other things is important.

When Mrs. Hardin taught the class how to write cursive using the Palmer method back in 1944, I felt that I was in the war zone of World War II. My body said, "No, not again!" I did not want to write in cursive or ever write again. I did not have outstanding motor skills in writing. I showed visual intelligence with large or gross motor movement as an endowment but not fine motor skills. Discipline was the hallmark of Mrs. Hardin's life. "You will secure a job if you have beautiful handwriting and without it, it will be difficult." Think of that as a threat to little me when I knew that women did not glean many jobs except when they became nurses, teachers, secretaries, and those who went to war. Many were going to war, so each day as Mrs. Hardin walked the aisle, I shuddered. The reward is that my handwriting is beautiful, even though I shake with age, my writing is outstanding. Thank you, Mrs. Hardin, you taught me how to discipline myself, even though I had a motor challenge.

10.   Reading; poor word attack skills but understands content:
Design a program for each student, a plan for those who can understand the content when hearing it read to them. When the content is relevant, allow the material to be read to the individual. Let students express their ideas for someone else to write down or have them put their thoughts on a recorder. Teach them how to use the recorder.

Remediate reading skills separate from developing understanding of content. When reading is difficult, the individual can sit in the reading group and follow along by listening and responding on a comprehension level rather than a skill level of reading. When the anxiety level is reduced, the individual can learn better.

Another idea encourages proper rate or pacing along with focusing on directionality. Sometimes this works for some of my students; the teacher and student sit together with the student placed slightly in front of the teacher, so the student can hear how the teacher is reading. The student's finger is moving under the words with the suggestion that the eyes are moving along with the finger. If the student has a difficult time keeping up with the rate of reading, then the teacher can change the rate while moving the finger for the student. Making the rate comfortable and not creating anxiety is important to building confidence in the reading task. Remember that this is not the time to correct reading mistakes but is the time for patterning rate and directionality.

11.   Reading Distractions: *Visual figure ground problem, and selective* *attention deficits.*

When reading, the student will use a marker to block out all but one line to reduce distractibility. When necessary, all but one word can be blocked out. When doing math have the student use a marker to cover all but one math problem. Other distractions are whatever one considers noise. The noise level needs to be at a low level. Keep the dog out while homework is being done, along with whatever else is distracting.

12.   Tests:

The individual can be given tests orally over the content material, such as spelling tests, book reports, theses, and research papers. Reports can be illustrated to bring out essential concepts. Give short questions without lots of words for the student to process. Make them simple and to the point.

Test-taking suggestions: Knowing I must give time for those essay questions at the end of the test, I think about how much time I have to take and finish the test. When I take tests, I have learned not to perseverate on one question, as I must avoid my tendency to not move forward, leaving all the other questions at the expense of one question. I quickly read the entire test and do the easiest questions first while placing a mark by the most difficult questions to be studied later. If some questions are more important in regards to the value of the question, I give them special consideration. As I calm myself and carefully read everything, I look for "key" words which would give me a clue. At the end of the test, I will look at the most challenging questions and give them an educated guess. Knowing that the test will not be given the way my brain learns and processes information, written tests increase my stress level. I over-study and over-learn everything to be learned. And that is how I obtain a high-grade point average. It is a matter of spending enough time to claim the reward. When an individual cannot read the test questions or write the answers, give them orally. Some children cannot work under time pressure. Mother and I felt strongly about this.

13.   Self-esteem:

Do not focus on weaknesses in front of a student's peers. Visit with the student privately. A careless statement can destroy self-image. For example, "Jolene, I'd like to help you a bit with these problems. I'll be with you in a minute." A better way to offer support could be, "For those needing assistance, I will be available shortly."

I have heard that an awareness of self is what differentiates humans from other animals. Be that true or not, to judge our value with someone else's given awareness and to be identified with that value can cause emotional pain. Some of us are more sensitive than others about awareness. Cursed with this, we find ways of protecting ourselves. I have a friend who has built emotional walls to protect himself from this awareness. He is blocked to the point that he won't allow his feelings to *get out* or feelings to *get in*. To avoid the judgment of others or self-judgment, we blame, we anger, we work, and work some more. I know someone who brags to the extent that others are very uncomfortable around him. Several people, whom I have known, have turned to drugs, alcohol, or both. And there are always the excuses that follow. Humans do try to protect themselves from hurt, sometimes positively and sometimes in a negative way. The negative approaches will twist and trap. Presenting ourselves to the larger society in a positive light will engender respect from others. However, this is an ongoing challenge for most of us if we wish to avoid the pitfall of pride and self-deception. Being careful about what we say to others and ourselves is of crucial importance in building self-esteem and the good feeling of being a valued person. The next item which has to do with relationships will expand upon this idea.

14.   Relationships:

Relationships have the power to connect and build a foundation for lasting and caring friendships. Cuddling relationships build bridges for communicating and connecting with your child and the adults in your world. Eye to eye contact is essential, and appropriate touch is an excellent facilitator of closeness and the communication of caring. For those who are distracted by eye contact, train them to look at the bridge of the nose. I am one of those who cannot look at the eyes of others (distracts me); I look down at something else. It is important to feel the warmth of caring for others and being cared for by others. It says, you are important, and that translates to mean, you *belong*. I have heard a psychotherapist, who serves the community as a Marriage and Family Therapist, say that this does not mean just *having a listening ear*. It means to powerfully "Cuddle Your Relationships" in a way that is active and thoughtful. Families that stay together through the storms of life *Cuddle their Relationships* consistently, not just when someone is wounded but on a regular basis. Consistency builds a sense of belonging and thus self-worth. From self-worth comes self-esteem.

Why is self-worth important and what does it have to do with learning to learn? I do not quote just for the sake of quoting. I believe what I quote, and here is a good quote from Albert M. Galaburda, MD, Harvard University Medical School, Director of the Dyslexia Neuroanatomical Laboratory at Beth Israel Hospital. *"Despite the fact that Dyslexia and other learning disabilities may be increasingly associated with medical conditions, the handling of the problem is still in the hands of educators, parents, and psychologists. A direct corollary of the statement that learning disabilities are accompanied by learning superiorities in other fields is that the medical suppression of a learning disability may result in the suppression of a specially welcomed gift. Medicine is still far from being able to change the disability without altering the other special abilities. On the other hand, early detection and early application of special teaching methods continually prove to be highly effective in helping the learning disabled individual. These educational programs are aimed at teaching individuals how to handle tasks that are difficult for them. Unfortunately, almost nothing is done to develop the special abilities that many of these children have from the time they first arrive at school. A learning disabled child is reminded on a daily basis of how difficult life is, of how arduous it is to achieve satisfactory results while all the other children seem to be having an easy time, and of how impossible it is to excel. During those early formative years, the learning disabled child is reminded only of his inferiority with respect to the rest of the children. It seems reasonable at this time to weigh the benefits of teaching a dyslexic child how to read and write at an early age against the indignities suffered by the child during learning. Instead, the child first could be taught to develop those skills for which he is likely to be better than the rest of his classmates. In this matter, self-esteem could be built early to help the child cope with the difficulties to come."*

Then Galaburda refers to a story in the book by Suzanne H. Stevens, Classroom Success for the Learning Disabled. She also wrote one called The Learning Disabled Child, Ways That Parents Can Help. *"The story is about 'Al' for whom society failed. It is a story about a sensitive educator who understands the value of developing self-esteem in disabled children who nevertheless have special abilities. The world needs these special abilities. Society must find a way to bring them out lest they are lost in a sea of shame and failure."*

Language and the Developing Child, by Katrina de Hirsch, states that the most important factor in helping the child who is having trouble with learning is a psychological support system tied to the developing child. Again, we hear the need to establish belonging and worth. This survival need is in all of us; we are valuable and valued.

I appreciate the mind of Katrina de Kirsch. She taught me something that I knew but didn't understand well: oral language difficulties contribute to reading disabilities. As the child develops, maturity plays a part in the ability to compensate for deficits. She shared that those viewed as having trouble " . . . *do not necessarily present a specific pattern of dysfunction, nor do their difficulties stem from a single root.*

71

There are many other roots associated with psychological and physiological factors, the child's genetic endowment, including his vulnerability to stress."

Helen and Martin Weiss say in their book, *A Survival Manual*, *"The need for support, encouragement and 'sense of self' because they always bag 'the short end of the stick' is the basic underlying need expressed most often by teenagers. They want and need adults to have faith in them so that they may have faith in themselves. We believe that one teacher can 'light one candle' and spark a flame in the mind of such a student by making him feel important and valued as a person and that this can 'turn on' a winner. We have seen this happen frequently. So our aim is to increase awareness that there are many styles of learning which we must encourage despite our traditional attitudes."*

The reason I have taken the time to address self-esteem is that all the appropriate teaching interventions in the world will not work if the child feels worthless. Valuing the individual is paramount. I can drill, over-teach with multisensory, and all the excellent methods which I use and recommend can make a change; however, if the individuals feel that they are *nothing,* then nothing is going to happen to solve the problem at its cause—worthlessness. The problem will only worsen.

At one time, I wrote all the ways we could use the letter "C" to emphasize the need to have a close and caring relationship: *Close, Caring, Connecting, Committed, Crossroads, Conversations, Considerate, Can, Correcting, Consistency, Count, Candle, Careful, Closure, Courageous, Compromise, Creative, Call, Calm, Caution, Companionship, Change, Chat, Cheerful, Choose, Celebrate, Celestial, Closure, Colorful, Continue, Communicate, Compassion, Complete, Confidence, Connected, and Cuddle* your relationships. I could go on and on. Stick these *word concepts* in your Mary Poppins carpet bag; you think about their meanings and have them ready to pull out quickly and often. It would be well to use them for all relationships.

15.   Feeling insecure academically: *Unsure.*

Individuals who are feeling academically insecure need to be given credit for what they do that is correct, rather than focusing on what they fail to do. They need to be given encouragement and praise for whatever is correctly accomplished. Highlight the correct problems and do not demoralize with a red pencil. When an individual is rejected for any reason, design efforts to include and support a spirit of belonging.

16.   Distracted by other stimuli in the room: *Auditory distraction, Visual figure-ground problem deficits.*

When Mother and I are reading, we cannot concentrate if anything is going on near us. **Mother and I liked to work alone.** When an individual wants to work alone, respect this and allow the person to work alone. It is difficult to have the stimuli of others around you. Create opportunities for strengthening weakness without demanding an immediate result. Gradually step the student toward a more complex social interaction.

17.   Short attention span: *Sustained attention deficit.*

Many things make it difficult to bring and sustain attention. Not only the child with dyslexia has a short attention span, but many students without dyslexia also have a difficult time. Eliminate all distractions. Reward for staying on task for a certain amount of time. Start with small amounts of time: reward and set timer for a longer time. Focus!

> **Move forward with a flow of positive energy to build success. Another day to start the finishing of a goal. Within reach of time, I believe there are no dumb or lazy, just those who have been misnamed or misunderstood. Some individuals designed in extraordinary ways are pleading to be understood. Beyond the surface of awareness is a quest to be sought-after and appreciated.**

Lynn is a teacher in every sense of the word. She has always been a support and inspiration for all who have interacted with her. For me, she has been the *best of the best*. Year after year, she has lived that which she teaches. Her natural curiosity has hiked up and down the roads of life, turned over rocks, and played in the sand. Lynn's footprints in the lives of her children and students with their parents are inspirational. Everyone she meets is a friend who knows they have met a teacher. When you experience Lynn, you know what her students loved and remembered. They were in her class where their minds were unfolding, and they were different from that moment. A teacher makes a difference. Thank you, Lynn.

11

Regular Education Teacher:
Classroom's Best Practices
Lynn Walker, Classroom Teacher

Lynn Walker earned her Bachelor of Science degree in 1983, Masters degree in Educational Leadership in 1996, Masters with English as a Second Language (ESL) in 2004.

The following story is shared by Lynn:

In 1982, when I started teaching in a public elementary school, I was given valuable tips from my new teaching partners. One of the tips was: Before school starts, pull the cum—cumulative folders of all your new students, so you will have an idea of what you will be dealing with in your new class. So believing that the other teachers had the key to success, I pulled the "cums" which had past grade information from former teachers. I read files, past comments, looked at grades, and made notes of behaviors, to help me see what kind of problems these kids were dealing with and, more importantly, what kinds of problems with which I would be dealing. I had them categorized and labeled. Boy, I was off and running, ready for the first day of school. After a few years of doing this, when the categories and labels never seemed to materialize, I thought, what a waste of valuable hours. I think I will just wing it. I found out that I never really had those belligerent, slow learners, those who would never read, those who could not concentrate or sit still, or those who were chronic troublemakers, or those who just seemed to have no future in education. I was beginning to think they were padding my class with unique students of all levels, excited to learn, polite, with many different learning styles, and numerous personalities. Thank heavens, they were not all the same. I was definitely more excited for school to begin.

I felt like I worked really hard to set up my classroom in such a way that it would enhance learning. I tried to remove distractions.

When a concept was taught and basically learned, I would have students go to the board to teach certain problems. There were always different methods and different kinds of verbal instruction. The students would ask questions of their *student teachers*. Sometimes it was another student who would turn on the light in a fellow student. What a self-esteem booster for the students. I soon learned that my students had different learning styles; they processed information differently, but not *dumb*. I had to learn how they learn, and let them know that they all were capable of learning. We may just have to take a different approach for different students. It did not require labeling or classifying. One of my 5th grade students liked to stand when he did his work. His mother apologized and mentioned that his past teachers had really tried working on the "problem." He just could not concentrate and get past work already done. They had thought about a resource setting. I mentioned to her that he was extremely smart in all areas, and his standing did not bother the class or me. He was doing exceptionally well. Let's just watch what happens. Just recently I received a card from this young man's parents. He graduated from college with two degrees, then went to medical school and is now a country doctor in Idaho. This situation is only one example of adaptations that were sometimes needed to help a student be successful. They were *strategies that led to improved student outcomes.* In science, with many resources available, students studied a topic with a partner or two, and then they would present to the class what they had learned. They could talk forever about their newly acquired knowledge. Usually, they could answer the other students' questions. In these situations, we all learned together. One example was a student whose parents let him shop on his own at Radio Shack, and he, on his own, built a model of a city block with functioning stop and go lights for cars and train lights and signals. His parents were in awe. This child was their *nonfunctioning student* who was so proud of his work and couldn't wait to explain it to the class. My students knew that they were capable of accomplishing anything they desired. The sky was the limit. My students were always excited to report on something, or someplace that they had been, or something they saw that related to the curriculum. Everyone, at all levels, could participate in this activity. School and learning became relevant. It is sad that we *measure the student's worth by how well they do on tests and school assignments.*

I gave each one of my students a spiral notebook to use in class. Sometimes I assigned a topic, but the students knew they could write to me anytime they wanted. They could write about a concern or need, questions, likes and dislikes, a way I could help them, something they wanted to see happen, an interesting tidbit, something they were curious about, or some experience in their day or life that they just wanted me to know. I wanted them to know that everything in their life was important to me as it was to them. The student might be too shy to share in front of the class, but the journal was safe. These journals were private and not shared with the class unless the student agreed. I would always comment in some way to let the student know I understood, that it made sense, a good for you, or just thanks for sharing and your message was important.

Students learned that it was okay to risk. I had a banner right in the front of my classroom that said, "If you can't make a mistake, you can't make anything." The students knew that there were no *dumb* questions.

My students had many different talents. Each student had a way to enhance the learning experience. We learned in many different ways, and the concepts learned became a part of our life's experiences.

DRA, Direct Reading Assessment testing in the schools, helped me to find challenges that the students had in *reading, writing, spelling, speech, memory, grammar, direction, and concentration.* It was a one-on-one experience for each student to help us know each other. It was a great assessment that could be administered two times a year to watch the progress. If studied correctly, it pointed out challenges in cognitive processing. It was a worthy assessment.

With the new test and assessment way of teaching, a teacher can no longer spend a lot of extra time with the whole class, working on new concepts. Now, you work fast and stay on a schedule. We were told that we had to be within one day of our teaching partners or assessments would not be valid. We had to keep moving. The idea was that 20 percent of the students would not master the skill anyway so just keep moving. It was the *one size fits all*. Everything is based on test scores, not whether students are learning and happy in that learning, or that learning is relevant and useful. I have seen some great teachers punished because of low test scores, something that will never measure real learning. Summed up beautifully in Argie's quote, *"We must stop asking how smart people are and start asking how people are smart."* Argie was quoting Dr. Howard Gardner.

Another experience is an individual who felt *dumb* and hopeless at times in the educational experience. He was labeled a chronic behavior problem, which followed him through all grade levels. He was excluded from numerous school functions which compounded his feelings of hopelessness. The problem was managed, but no solution was addressed. This problem, with other defeating situations, helped him to become vulnerable to negative and aggressive behaviors in his self and society. He was labeled a *juvenile delinquent* who will never amount to anything. This person is extremely bright, fun-loving, and tender but ended up in prison. He struggled with ADD, but he did not want to stay on medication because that told him that he was definitely *dumb*. There was lots of confusion, and it took awhile to see that this person had some unique ways of thinking and processing. He did not like others telling him how he should perform. All the punishments and remarks in elementary school set him up to fail. He believed he was *dumb* and would never be successful. He would have to find a different way to succeed. Many years later he found ways to achieve positively. He is functioning well. He has found ways to succeed and turn that into helping others feel success.

I have learned many valuable lessons over the years from my students. After thirty-two years, I see that all students have challenges, but I know that more importantly, they all have strengths, unique gifts, and a desire to learn. I did not need to go through cum folders to help my students. I just wanted them to know that I was there to help them, guide them, and hopefully instill in them the love of learning. I tried to see the whole person. They did not need to be categorized or labeled to be taught. Sometimes there are lower expectations for children who are labeled than children with identical behaviors who are not labeled. They needed to have a safe and orderly work environment with boundaries and rules. They needed to know that they were valued. They needed to know that each one of them could be successful and that all of us, working together and helping each other would set a healthy climate for learning that would follow them through their life. In thirty-two years of teaching, I had no *dumb or lazy* students. I had students who came to school, ready and eager to learn. Together we explored the best ways.

Thank You, Lynn!

Given my experience, I wish I had had a teacher like Lynn. She had the intuitiveness to know what to do with the uniqueness of students. Lynn was not looking for *what is wrong,* but *what is right.* Given an attitude that none of us is perfect and we will work out our challenges together, she created opportunities to strengthen the *wrong* with the *right.* As quoted by a student after having children of his own and meeting his former teacher, Lynn, "I worked so hard in your class, but I had so much fun." You work hard, feel success, and have fun; thus, she changed the activity patterns of her students in productive ways that benefited the whole class with their diverse abilities and personalities.

Lynn never allowed students to use the word *dumb* or *stupid.* However, students find a way of labeling themselves. We do that to ourselves. Why?

Lynn did not give up; she was an *open box* teacher with ideas that pulled the best from her students. She encouraged the students to push through the learning experience to feel success and not feel *dumb*. I call this encouragement the undoing of pre-conceived labels.

Society dumps labels on all of us. Students are labeled by weekly assessments. Classroom teachers are labeled by their end of the year test scores. Schools, districts, and states are labeled as functioning or nonfunctioning. Society is still using the *one size fits all.* You and I know that this mindset does not allow for the uniqueness of the brain. Again, I would like to repeat what Lynn shared; everything is based on test scores, not whether students are learning common sense life skills and happy in that learning, relevant and useful. Are you learning? Are you happy? Are you stepping through life's journey with adventure?

Challenges of working within unrealistic guidelines imposed by outside control can create problems. All persons involved want to have better control of education, desiring to solve problems with their stewardship and to be able to go to the local school authorities, if needed. Excellent teachers retire early, quit their jobs, or continue for more education to hopefully find the answers to the dilemma of helping *all* children. Little wonder there is a shortage of teachers.

All students need a classroom teacher with a caring and *"you can do it"* attitude. Teachers make a difference. That is if they are allowed to do so, within a system that understands the heart and situations. They say it is not the need for labels, materials, or personally more money; it is the need for *smaller classrooms* and time to get to know the students.

A moment in time came back to me while reminiscing about the children who call *me,* Mom: blessed with four sons. I married again; thus two more sons were added—one passed away from a drug overdose. The drug world was brought in focus for me to shake with fear. Soon, I realized the prisons are full of grown children who have not found a place in society. With that focus came the realization that this population did not know how their brains work, nor did parents, or society. I wonder how life would have been different if someone, somewhere, would have introduced them to the power of their unique brains and how to use them. They needed parents and a teacher like Lynn who knew how cognitive processing works.

Addressing this subject, I will continue to share. I spent hours training and helping a mother understand processing uniqueness. She did not apply what was shared. As an adult, her son is in prison. Unhappy ending! I know that he does not understand that he has a brain gift which is hidden from himself and society. He has a *deficit which became a disability* since he did not learn to compensate for the deficit.

While I was teaching, I had many students with a challenge called reading. Again, I spent hours with parents introducing them to how brains process information. They took the information and used it to make a difference. They are now functioning members of society and using talents to make a difference. Some of these students didn't need my resource room after our conversations. They had a *deficit which did not become a disability* since they learned to compensate for the deficit. We all have deficits that make us imperfect. Happy endings!

The following case is from my journal. Names have been changed. I will call the student Allen. Again, Lynn, I think of you, and my desire that some teacher like you would have helped Allen.

Journal entry from my years of teaching
December 2nd
I demonstrated for Allen's mother a given assignment and how he would complete it for a positive reward. He would start off the day with a Green card—positive beginning that he would take home at the end of a successful day for his mother to reward for the appropriate behavior. She said that she liked the idea. There would be a Yellow card as a warning that his behavior needed to change or the Red card that said *no reward*. He could earn his way back if his behavior became *solidly* appropriate. This

card statement was the plan in a nutshell. After taking the plan to the educational team for consideration, I started working the plan.

December 3rd

12:30 – 12:40   I showed Allen his assignment sheet for the day and explained in detail what was expected. This sheet had the continuation of assignments from the previous day and he understood it very well. His response was, "Too hard. I *can't do it.*" I told him to do one problem and we would talk about it. Allen looked at his math but didn't want to do it. He said he wanted to do his timed-reading. I explained to him that it was his choice as to which assignment on the sheet was to be done first, and I reminded him that he starts every day with the Green card which was a positive start. He did the assignments.

December 6th

Allen announced that he did not want to do any work. I explained what would happen after doing one assignment; he could run in the gym, which is right outside my door. He did it. After completing two assignments, I gave him a happy note to take to the principal or the office to receive positive feedback. After Allen completed another assignment, he came back to the gym, and so forth. The hope of an immediate reward effectively motivated Allen: constructive work. He responded positively! Finished assignments. The plan was working! Before this behavior plan, he was not doing any assignments and throwing tantrums.

At this point, I should explain that in addition to using the cards as part of behavior management, I also gave students "play money" which they could trade for goodies. In addition to rewards for completed assignments, when I caught them "being on task," they were rewarded. Also, when students completed a given task we ran races in the gym. Free time activities included water coloring, working with clay, reading, drawing, and "talk story" with a neighbor. The plan was effective, and students were productive. Yahoo!

December 7th

Allen said he wanted to go home, grabbed his coat, and a Yellow card. I reminded Allen of the agreement that he would not be permitted to return home before the end of the school day. Without raising my voice, I quietly repeated the rule and invited Allen to resume the task at hand. He picked up a chair and threw it. Picked up another one and threw it. I flashed the Red card for Allen to see and sent the other children out to wait in the gym. I closed the door and tried to calm Allen down. He picked up another chair and threw it. I reminded Allen that he was earning the right to go to the office to "stop, think and reflect." He repeated that he wanted to go home. I then escorted Allen to the office, but he refused to go in the room. I went into the office to tell the staff what was happening. Allen repeatedly kicked the office door. The secretary couldn't find the principal, so she went out into the hall to talk with Allen. At that point, Allen was making his way toward a stack of Caution Cones on the Kiva and started to kick them. The principal appeared and took over; I returned to the other students and didn't see Allen again until 3:10 p.m. when I visited with him before he went home.

The principal reported that he had called home. He and Allen's mother reaffirmed the agreement that Allen would not be permitted to return home until school was out. Allen went to the "think" room, where he read a book, fell asleep and wet his pants. I believe that Allen now understands that he can't go home when he requests the same.

Following day

To the principal's office and fell asleep. When Allen awakened, he wanted to return to my classroom. It should be noted here that once or twice a week, I take my students to a regular class where they read aloud from their books to other students. When Allen returned from the office, he joined us in the other classroom. During the reading, Allen's behavior was appropriate; however, he wanted to quit reading on several occasions. After he read, we returned to my classroom, where Allen asked for a

Green card to take home. His mother has designed a big reward for "x" number of Green cards brought home. I sent him home with a Yellow card to acknowledge his improved behavior at the end of the day. In retrospect, it appears that a Red card would have more accurately summarized the events of the day. However, he redeemed himself very nicely. Perhaps, a card of another color like Blue could have been sent home to show that Allen had experienced the process of redeeming. This Blue card would be a good idea. I plan to take this question and suggestion back to the team. We need both a method for acknowledging a change from bad behavior to improved behavior while at the same time having a symbol for the predominant behavior of the day. Sending the Yellow card home may have reinforced the bad behavior, or the lack of Green card may have created hopelessness. This plan is a team effort on the part of the parents, student, principal, school psychologist, and myself. I designed this plan, used it, and it was working until it fell apart because the same energy was not carried out at home. Multiple distractions! Too complicated for Allen's fractured family to be consistent with any behavioral plan.

The following days got better and better as Allen knew that I was following a plan and was consistent with my behavior of following through. No matter what! However, the home behavior was falling apart and extending into the neighborhood. The local law enforcement had gotten involved with complaints from the neighborhood. The family was falling apart; a community agency recommended a referral to a hospital behavioral unit. This situation left me feeling sad since it was the family who needed help and consideration, not punitive action. They needed parenting skills and family therapy, not for Allen to be institutionalized. The mother was doing her best with what she knew; she needed help! Where was the appropriate understanding and intervention?

It is my observation that before Allen went to the hospital inpatient unit, he was on task and manageable in my classroom *all* the time. The first day back from the hospital, I found Allen asleep on the floor in the hall which I reported to the office. The school nurse came down and assured us that this was just Allen getting used to his new medication. The classroom teacher has regularly reported that since Allen's return from the hospital, he has consistently fallen asleep in her room. She has said she believes he is over-drugged. It appears that Allen has to be in constant motion to keep from falling asleep. I never had these problems with him before his hospital stay. Since the first day he came back from that experience, I have constantly asked the parents and the social worker for a tracking form from the doctors, so I can track his behavior. No form!

Allen has been drugged beyond his ability to respond appropriately. It appears that his filters for determining appropriate behavior are limited. His behavior has deteriorated since he went to the hospital. I am trying to figure out what to do with the previous school plan that was working.

An alternative explanation could be that Allen's behavior is actually under his conscious control and that he has learned to mobilize power and excitement through his negative and sometimes bizarre behavior. He does seem to have established a cycle of obstinate behavior to go to the principal's "think" room, wet his pants while taking a nap, and then returning to the classroom in a mellow mood to hopefully pick up a Green card to take home. This behavior suggests that Allen was fully aware of the colored card system and was willing to use it for his own ends. However, at this time, after the hospitalization, it has become evident that the colored cards became ineffective regarding help for him to stop his acting out behaviors. With his bright mind, Allen has learned to manipulate his world to meet his needs which include the avoidance of work and assuming responsibility for his inappropriate behavior. He invariably blames the problem on someone else. He has a broad deficit in problem-solving and communication skills which has become a disability.

We continue to work with Allen and do our best to help him learn to manage his behavior while we document the behavior. Hopefully, an accurate diagnostic formulation with a more effective intervention plan will emerge for all who are involved with Allen. At this point, I strongly suspect that Allen was better off before *medication* started at the hospital. Allen has conceptualized that he is not able to control his actions. He has been forced to listen to the wrong voices which are telling him that he is sick and can't change without medications. I know that he can control his behavior when he desires. I am frustrated because no one in the larger system is asking his teachers what was going on in their classrooms before the hospital stay. My classroom!

No one outside of the school has asked the school for its observations about Allen and his interactions with the school and within the family. **Is it the child or the environment?** There is a breakdown in the system. Systems can become fractured. Help! It is my opinion that the medical social worker and the school social worker needed to collaborate on a treatment plan which would include the input from all relevant societal resources. My husband who spent three years as a school social worker is in full agreement.

It has been difficult for Allen to change learned behaviors. However, through a given and **consistent** routine with the goals that our team carried forward, he has been in better control of his behavior. When in control, Allen felt *safe* and seemed to be more concerned about the *safety* of others. I relied on my relationship with him. He would not disappoint me because he trusted our relationship. The question remains, how do we create a caring relationship? I believe that setting limits or rules in a relationship is the first step. *I will not cross this line, and you will not cross the line,* and there are consequences for a given behavior. The consequences must be powerful enough to change attitudes and behaviors. Next, the established feeling that comes from knowing no matter what the individual does, you *care for the individual but not for inappropriate behaviors.*

My strong message to parents is to support your children; you need to be at the **crossroads!** I know that it makes a difference to learn what it means to be at the *crossroads.* It may mean changing the behavior of parents so that they can find the crossroads. Parents may desire to change

86

but need help to be effective. We all need to look at how we are contributing to the dysfunction of others. I tearfully have had to do that for myself. I said it! It was difficult!

Having written this summarized version of Allen's story and viewing it as history, it is my firm belief that in our larger society, we overuse medications to manage behavior. In Allen's case, it would most probably have been a less costly and a more effective societal intervention to send a clinical social worker to spend several days living in Allen's home to observe the processes of daily living as they were being played out. Impossible, the way our current systems are setup! The treatment team including parents and professionals could then formulate an active treatment plan which would consist of the totality of the resources. Allen would then have not been in control by manipulating the system with its limitations. In my opinion, **Allen's behavior was a learned behavior, and the labels which the system attached to him do not explain or address causation. Hopeless!**

Allen's story is not isolated. I have sat in meetings with a team brainstorming and walked away with few answers to bite into the depth of the situation. We continued to need more information.

It is essential that regular education training addresses the needs of *special needs* students along with regular education students. If all students are to be successful then students, parents, and teachers need to understand the meaning of discipline, work ethic, and the brain.

I would suggest that we as educators start thinking in terms that not all school problems are child-centered. Moving a student from place to place is not as productive as once considered. The possibility is that the school system itself should look for a change in the school's behavior. I am somewhat discouraged to hear that it is too frequently assumed, that it is the child who needs to change. Let's look at the total picture for answers to difficult situations and not look at the child as the *exceptional* one to change. It is worth rereading Lynn's contribution.

My experiences have taken me from the Mainland to Hawaii, back and back again several times to teach. No matter where I teach the conversation is the same, *sharing and caring.*

12

Special Education Teacher:
Know the Student
Successful Programs

One of the objectives of the special education teacher is to recognize the student who has learning disabilities. Disabilities are exhibited with a disorder in one or more of the basic psychological processes involved in the understanding of language, or in using spoken language, or written language. Here are the psychological processes: auditory and visual perception—receptive language, organization of the integration of language, memory, expressive language, motor response.

Learning disabilities are not primarily caused by any of the following: low intelligence, emotional disturbances, lack of parenting skills or lack of educational opportunity. I have observed that these can cause a difficulty with learning but not cause a learning disability.

Along with Specific Learning Disabilities, I find some of the other classifications: Autism, Deaf-Blindness, Deafness, Developmental Delay, Emotional Disturbance, Hearing Impairment, Intellectual Disability, Multiple Disabilities, Orthopedic Impairment, Other Health Impairment, Speech or Language Impairment, Traumatic Brain Injury, and Visual Impairment, including Blindness. For example, if you are deaf, it doesn't mean you are also Specific Learning Disabled. If any of these conditions adversely affect educational performance, it is our given responsibility to help students develop the skills, attitudes, and confidence essential to becoming independent learners. A student is considered to have more than a deficit when the deficit hinders the development of skills to become an independent learner. The road to becoming an independent learner is through interactive assessments intertwined and integrated with plans for interventions and accommodations.

This process includes but is not limited to the following:
1. An assessment is given each student for learning disabilities and cognitive impediments to learning.
2. An assessment is given each student for individual learning styles.
3. Assessments are provided to find the impact of other factors which influence student's ability to learn, *viz,* the student's environment, personality, unique brain functioning, and any social or emotional problems which might be of concern. Assessments need to be in collaboration with members of the team.
4. Needed observation for behavior at home and school.

Based on the assessments and intervention plan, my goal is to help each student overcome or compensate for impediments to learning. The goal is to develop fundamental learning skills which are requisite for full integration into the regular classroom.

Following Federal guidelines, I have regularly written goals for Individualized Education Programs. As I classify the student for services, it is always on my mind that we have different brainprints, and it is best not to label, however, if needed, create a plan for remediation based on uniqueness. The challenge is to take the unique brainprint and design an intervention which would fit the needs to be remediated, using the student's strengths to turn the weaknesses into strengths.

While I was studying at the university, many times I visited with my father-in-law. Sometimes the conversation would turn to his wisdom, and I would hear him advising me to think of the brain as a tool to be used to get a job done. He, being an attorney, was very experienced and bright, but he said certain areas of his brain did not process, as well as others. We all could have a label as something or another, but as some Hawaiian students would say, "No labels. No need!" or just "No need!"

Take the strengths of the brain and use them. The idea jumped into and through my mind. There it was in my brain the whole time with what my Daddy would say, "Use the strongest chain to pull a weak car, not the weakest chain." You do not use *weak* to fix *weak*. Thanks, Daddy!

Yes, if you have a visual strength, the brain needs the visual strength to learn the concept. If you find you have an auditory strength, the brain needs the auditory strength to learn. If you have a motor strength, the brain needs the motor strength to learn. Wow, the multisensory method of teaching with all the senses at play is for getting a job done. Oh yes, I say, "Please don't forget to use the kinesthetic—movement and the tactile —touch to strengthen."

My heart vibrates with gratitude for those rationally minded teachers who came before I taught and had skills to inspire the learning of great minds. With advances in brain research and educational application, we deepen our understanding to teach *all* students.

The Education for All Handicapped Children Act or Public Law 94-142 enacted by the United States Congress in 1975 required all public schools accepting federal funds to provide equal access to education. Public schools were required to create an individual educational plan, with parental input, that would accommodate the educational experience. *PL 94-142* contains vision that disabled students be placed in the least restrictive environment allowing for the maximum possible opportunity to interact with unimpaired students. The student will return to the regular classroom setting when the skill level is learned. Separating students from the regular classroom may occur when the severity of the disability is such that instructional goals cannot be achieved.

The law was passed to meet these goals:

1. Ensure that special education services are available.
2. Guarantee that services to disabled students are fair and appropriate.
3. Establish specific management and monitoring requirements.
4. Provide federal funds.

In 1990, *PL 101-476* changed the title of the special education law to *Individuals with Disabilities Education Act*—IDEA, also known as the

91

"Person First" law. As stated, the law was to recognize children first and the disability second. This change was to revise and extend the programs of special education and inclusive education.

Materials: As a Special Education teacher with years of teaching experience, I have tested many students and identified their learning styles along with their challenges. The next step is to design interventions for remediation, followed by *focused instruction* and *hard work. I know that there are many approaches to teaching reading, but about 80 percent of the students can learn to read no matter what method.* Perhaps even more. We must find the plan which works for the rest of the students. It must be multisensory.

The inferential learning of any concept, cannot be taken for granted. Multisensory language instruction requires the direct teaching of all concepts with constant student-teacher interaction and supported by parental involvement. Direct instruction is essential for success.

Orton-Gillingham: In my opinion, the Orton-Gillingham programs significantly outperform the sight word approaches. This method of teaching has been used since the 1930s. As developed by the teaching principles of Samuel Orton and Anna Gillingham, this method is language-based instruction with emphasis on multisensory materials, structure of English language, sequence of skills, skills tied to skills for cumulative outcome, cognitive rules for decoding and encoding, and flexible teaching for individuals, groups, classes, and for ages from preschool through adulthood. I have enjoyed success with this approach to teaching reading. It was not easy for me.

When as an elementary student, learning on my own by using the sight word or look-say method, I was overwhelmed. I now wish that my teachers had been teaching with the *Orton-Gillingham* methods. Perhaps, I *would* have learned to read before I was in the 8th grade. The phonics method my teachers were using didn't work for me. It was not multisensory. However, it was *auditory* or *orally* taught without using other senses. The students learned by hearing. For a person who has a serious auditory memory challenge as I do, the phonetic program has to be multisensory in structure and intensity. Yes, more than one sense!

Some phonics programs will not work for the likes of me. I learned to read by sight words. One word at a time was not very effective.

Knowing what didn't work for me as an elementary student, I have been determined to find answers that do work. As far as I know, a screening test that would have helped my elementary school teachers understand my unique brain, not used in 1941. I wish my teachers would have had the privilege of knowing about and using the Slingerland screening test designed from the Orton-Gillingham approach.

Beth Slingerland died in 1989. She brilliantly adapted the Orton-Gillingham method of teaching children with reading challenges such as dyslexia. Beth founded the Slingerland Institute in 1977. It exists today as the Slingerland Institute for Literacy. This guided approach is structured, sequential, simultaneous, and designed to be effective, yes, not only in special classes but general education classrooms as well. I am grateful for my training in this method. It is intense and rewarding for me as a teacher. It teaches academic competence with the energy of effective work habits and the focus of self-discipline. Teaching work habits and self-discipline takes a dedicated team: teachers, administrators, parents, other professionals as needed, and students. Learned habits!

Slingerland: This method is of the Orton-Gillingham origin. It is important to note that research has shown that the Slingerland approach works not only with children but also with *adults* who have challenges in how to read, spell, and write. I appreciate my training with the Slingerland method. Using this method has served me well in being successful with many students. I figured out how to fit the method to the students' needs. In designing an intervention plan, it is essential to know the brain strengths and not guess at the program that fits. Developing interventions for the uniqueness of the brain is hard. With this comes the unique nature of environmental factors which expose themselves to both negative and positive faces. Taking all that into consideration along with the training of the teacher, and energy of parents in combination with the desires and motivation of the student, we can move forward.

I have successfully used the Slingerland Screening Test. It is widely recognized in classrooms and research projects. No attempt has been made, however, to develop "standardized" national norms. My purpose for screening children has been to find those of average to superior intelligence in need of particular help to compensate for their cognitive processing differences. I used this screening with students before being trained with the Slingerland method for teaching.

The Slingerland Institute for Literacy is a nonprofit organization that trains teachers to instruct students who are struggling with reading, writing, and spelling skills. It matters not the reason for the deficit; the method is used for all types of learners. This multisensory method is accredited at the Teaching and Instructor level of Teaching by the International Multisensory Structured Language Education Council.

Touchphonics: Another method which I endorse and with which I have had impressive results is Touchphonic which was developed by Dr. Robin Steed. I helped with the research as this multisensory method developed. As Robin studied the brain and explored the research, she designed a teaching model. Robin knew more about the brain and how it responds to sensory input in the learning process than anyone I have known.

Principles of multisensory methods are paramount. Sweeping through the brain, using all learning pathways simultaneously, is a powerful approach: multisensory teaching. This direction is to be determined by actively engaging the use of visual or auditory, kinesthetic or tactile, and all the brain pathways to enhance learning. Along with this, sequence the elements of language from easiest to more difficult.

Reading Recovery: During my later years of teaching, I found that

Reading Recovery served the needs of struggling 1st graders. At this point, I also found satisfaction in teaching students who were not in Special Education. Marie M. Clay was a clinical child psychologist whose study of young learners during their initial, formative years of literacy acquisition embraced a complex theory of literacy. Her passionate search for theoretical explanations focused on building an understanding of both the specific perceptual and cognitive behaviors involved in reading and writing. Her knowledge of how the brain integrates the complex processes of reading aided her in designing interventions to bring the child back to the developmental track for literacy acquisition.

Learning to read is a major challenge for a significant portion of children who appear to have normal cognitive and behavioral abilities. However, my experience has pointed toward other methods for students who need a more intense and ongoing method.

The following suggestions I pulled from my experience. We would not teach two different languages at the same time to someone who is having a tough time learning one language. If something is going on in the head or brain that has a hard time learning one language, I will not confuse by simultaneously teaching two languages. About 20 percent of the population has a difficult time with the process of learning one language as it relates to reading. I can say that reading is a language challenge. For some people, even their native English tongue is a foreign language. I have had students who not only had a comprehension challenge but finding the correct word to explain a concept was difficult.

We might consider that the lowercase letters of the alphabet are one language and the uppercase—capital letters of the alphabet represent another language because they have a different look. Uppercase letters mean the same thing as capital letters. At first, I will teach only the lowercase letters. I will not introduce the uppercase until the lowercase is on an automatic level of retention. At this point, I will start teaching the uppercase *as needed*. For example, when we write a sentence, the first letter of the first word in the sentence always needs an uppercase or in other words, a capital letter. There are other times when we use the capital.

I know that having a difficulty with another language is true because I have experienced it with some of my students. I have had students who were called to serve in foreign countries and came home prematurely because the stress of learning the foreign language was overwhelming. It is indeed something to consider when learning another language.

I associated with a person who was having a horrible time learning another language. After the well-designed attitude of determination and hard work, he learned the second language the same way he had learned his native language. He learned it through living with the people who spoke the second language, not through a given method with a book in front of him and teachers trying to teach him. It is amazing what the brain can do when challenged with desire, along with focused and disciplined determination.

Argie's Learning to Read Method: Sound definitions: Phonics is a method for acquiring reading which associates letters with sounds. Phonetics is the linguistic study of individual sounds. Phoneme means the smallest phonetic unit of sound: vowels and consonants.

I designed a method for teaching vowel sounds from my learning experiences as a child. I used this method when teaching those with an **auditory memory** disability.

Jeneal and I made sandpaper covered letters for students to trace with popsicle sticks, fingers, and feet. Students learned the alphabet letters and sounds. Tactile: touch with texture.

Short vowel sounds were my first learning to read challenge because I have no auditory memory of the short vowel sounds. I am deaf to these vowel sounds. I try to remember the sounds I have heard and produce them but they aren't there. I hear the sounds, but I can't remember them —auditory memory deficit. My heart cries!

Mother and I created a chart for each short vowel sound. At the top of the chart was a red letter representing the short vowel sound. Under

96

the letter was a word with the consonant, vowel, consonant phonetic pattern, with the vowel letter in red. Under the word was a picture of an object representing the word. The object became the keyword.

An example would be to have a picture of a "cat" with the word "cat" printed on the picture. This picture was my visual prompt because I need a visual prompt to learn. Also, I learn by seeing a picture in my head with the sound in an image, not by hearing and remembering the sound. I am a visual learner, not an auditory learner. For me, taking this given information, couple it with pictures, and sounds of a word is a start of learning to read. This way worked for me. Rocky road!

First, I teach readers the short vowel sounds. I have a picture of a cat with the word "cat" written on it with the vowel highlighted in red color; the word "cat" is a keyword. I use this keyword as a template for decoding and encoding the sound patterns for all the short vowel words; this is for the consonant, vowel, consonant pattern.

To learn the vowel sounds, I teach students to slowly stretch the word out by sounding each letter and then to say the whole word—stretch out each sound of the letters, **c a t**, then say whole word—**cat**, and again (sound) **c a t**, (word) **cat**. The students use their arms to show stretching: (sound) **c a t**. I use the visual, the sound, and the motor movement to stretch the word: **cat**. Encourage the student to see the image on the wall chart.

Next step, I take the middle sound out of **c a t**, and practice the short vowel sound of "**a**". Next, we put the short vowel "**a**" sound in the word bat. Now, we stretch each sound of the letters, **b a t**, then say the whole word—**bat**, and again (sound) **b a t**, (word) **bat**. We continue with the word fat. I use my vowel keywords as templates for other words with the same phonetic patterns. I teach all the short vowel sounds with this method: a, e, i, o and u.

Next step, I move to words like fan, can, etc. I use this same phonetic pattern from known words to nonsense words like zat, gat, etc. At the same time that I am teaching phonetic patterns, I teach sight words: I, the, and, etc. Soon students will write stories like: I can bat and run.

I use the vowel sound in a keyword to sound out new words. I can look at a word, see the phonetic pattern of the word, and bring up the correct vowel sound. I use the keywords in my visual memory. I can process rapidly; however, most of my words are learned as sight words as I learned them as a child; every word eventually becomes a sight word.

The consonants are not a problem for me unless not heard when spoken, or they do not follow an over-learned phonological pattern. Words like *handsome, arctic, often,* etc. are words which need to be learned by sight and stored in visual memory. Short vowels have been *monsters* and still are. I have needed a lot of keywords. And a lot of sight words!

Long vowel sounds are not difficult for me to hear and remember. For teaching spelling, I use the book by Nina Traub, *Recipe for Reading.* It teaches what is necessary for sound and symbol relationships of letters and letter groups linked to phonemic awareness. The word lists have a sequence for what needs to be learned next. This is a valuable book. I can look at a spelling test and know if the student is a phonetic speller or a visual speller.

Now, I read faster and gather concepts rather rapidly. I can also take the ideas and transfer the information to other situations very quickly. That said, I can't read in front of others with ease. I can read the material privately and out loud, after which I can talk about the content with ease. I remember time and time again when I left my glasses at home—I would not have to read when called on in Sunday school class. Remembering how to say names in the scriptures: nightmare. However, I invite the opportunity to do special readings. "Practice makes perfect."

Given my experience, I know that the most effective methods are multisensory. I am grateful for being trained in many methods. Students have learned to read. Over-learning patterns helped with sequencing. Success! The reward has been observing the learning process. Thanks to my students for *working hard.* You did it!

13

I found the *Why*:
Tears of Grateful Relief
End of Personal Quest

As a Special Education teacher, my brain was still whirling with *Why* and my heart was still feeling lonely with *Why*. Yes, I knew the pain of feeling *dumb* and yet knew that I was smart.

Why could around 80 percent of the population learn in a different way than I? *Why* did I know that I was different, but I did not know *why* the difference? I could answer questions orally but had a very difficult time with recalling and writing answers to test questions. Teachers were impressed and commented on my responses, but I felt there was something *wrong* with my brain! When I need you, where are you my language brain?

My hidden secrets that haunted me were in my brain. I spent hours crying as I had nightmares about communicating with other people. I sometimes didn't want to live with this *why* in my brain. It was like seeing the sunset and not being able to share the beauty. It was smelling the rose and not being able to share of the fragrance. It was feeling happy and not being able to share. It was touching a stove and not being able to describe the pain. It was touching the cottontail bunny's tail and not being able to share softness. It was hearing the song of a bird but painfully not being able to sing a song. *It was knowing the concept of a word but not being able to recall how to find or say the word that represents the concept.* I was in prison. In my head, I found a vast world of known concepts, but words to explain concepts were not found in my mouth and if found, confused. Confusion with both the words going out of my head and words coming into my head was like a bad dream. And communication was everywhere. Orally communicating was and still is *maddening!* In my head, I can talk with my silent language. I understand my silent language. How can I use language so that you understand what I am saying? One son said, "Mom, who really understands what others are saying?" Take time to understand!

How can I accurately bring to memory things that others cannot? How can I feel what others cannot? How can I empathize when others cannot? How can I reason where others cannot? How can I discern reality in a way that others cannot? On the other side of the coin, as a child sometimes I couldn't recall the word or words to explain a concept; I still can't. Where is that language path? Hopeless! And where do I fit in a conversation without words that convey the depth of the meaning that I understand in my head?

And then evening after evening, I sat in a university classroom listening to a teacher, Dr. Robin Steed, lecture on the brain. She was explaining cognitive processing. Interesting to learn how the different parts of the brain fit in particular ways to gather and disseminate information. She shared that there are strengths and weaknesses in the way the brain processes information and how the brain uses the different ways of thinking. Uniqueness!

This new information was making sense to me. Perhaps I am not dumb, just different with my strengths and weaknesses. Suddenly, I started thinking of my brain in another way than how I had been thinking of it. I had thought it was my intelligence that had let me down. It wasn't! The feelings of relief started to build as I was learning the *Why* of brain processing. Tears filled my heart.

Another question I was asking and pondering seemed simple, "What does this have to do with reading and teaching?"

Robin returned from the Orton Dyslexia Conference and eagerly shared what she had been learning about the brain and reading. Robin was instructing a graduate class on reading, and she was talking about the complexities of brain processing and how it guides the **reading and**

language process. She was talking about the complicated relationship between the technicalities of brain functioning as they come to bear on reading and learning. **She was talking about my brain.** AHA!

This same brain processes everything we do. And this sets the stage for what I know about cognitive processing. My brain has a very difficult time with everything I do concerning *sequencing,* as well as anything to do with *auditory memory.* I have a cognitive challenge, and it is all right because this is *me.* I am intelligent, and I will compensate. There are those who call it dyslexia; I call it an *auditory memory* challenge with the overarching s*equencing* challenge. And this condition is spread over the many areas of living and not specific to reading and language. I now know the *Why!* I had found the *Why* that is my hidden and crippling deficit.

After several classes where I sat silently, I slowly, with tears of joy and relief, made my way to speak with Dr. Steed. How do I tell this knowledgeable, caring professor how she held the key that I had been searching for the past forty-nine years. I finally knew the *Why!* The *Why* I do what I do while sadly and happily stumbling through life. At the same time, intuitively knowing how smart that stumbler is while stumbling through learning experiences.

Knowing what I learned in that class was a pivotal experience. It was with a grateful, determined, and studied approach that I knew that it was my time to take the *Why* key and turn locks; the key would unlock knowledge to help others. Others who have the same puzzle with a nightmare of questions about how their brains process information continues to be my mission to bring knowledge, understanding, and hope. Knowing that each brainprint is just as unique as each fingerprint, we paint a picture. A window opens! You can find the special *you!*

Having a desire, I know that each of us will find an *Individualized Education Program* with interventions which can be ongoing throughout life. Our weaknesses can become our strengths, and our trials can become our gifts. I am grateful!

This experience was truly that pivotal moment in my life. As I walked through the door, the light of understanding was clear, bright, and beautiful. Robin, thank you for bringing the information that I needed. Thank you for showing me a path that gave me a mission. Understanding! Now, I knew what this had to do with reading. I understood the answer to my *Why*, as I began to become acquainted with my brain. I was starting to understand that human brains are as unique and individualized as our human fingerprints. The opening of a new window brought peace to my soul. I did not have the wrong brain. **I have the right brain for me**. Robin **helped me find the glue for my heart. Find your unique kind of glue.**
Thank you, Dr. Robin Steed!

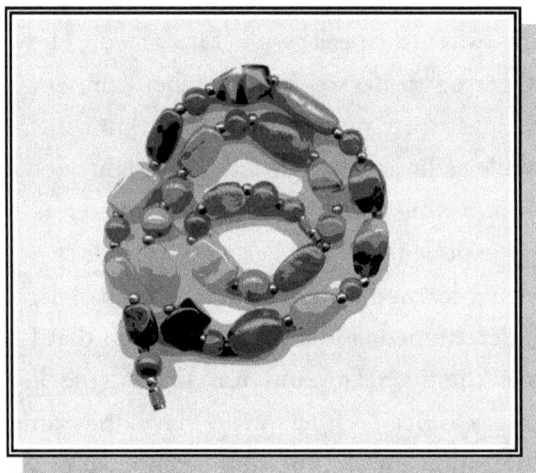

One day, I opened my mailbox. Robin had left a note. "Take a rough stone, polish and a treasure you will find.
Take a person, polish and a treasure you will find." Same day, a necklace! This unexpected gift was an ironic moment. A month before I had expressed a want for this necklace. My son Chris had tenderly wanted to give it to me. No money! And here it was!

14

A Reading Diagnostician:
Dr. "Robin" Steed, University Faculty, Designer of Educational Program

As I prepared for my adventure to Hawaii, another powerful influence came to my mind. Dr. Robin Steed's influence had led my brain to many valuable deductions and applications. She educated me far beyond the usual teacher and student relationship. The prepared journey has taken me successfully through countless hours of changing lives: many students, their parents, and teachers. I am thankful for my ever learning quest. The following information was given to me by my mentor and subsequent friend. We agreed that observations of academic behaviors were key to successful remediation.

Every Teacher – A Reading Diagnostician
Techniques that are practical for a classroom teacher to use in diagnosing for the prevention, correction, and remediation of reading difficulties, are mainly the using of informal tests and observational procedures.

I. Personal beliefs are the basis for my suggestions:
    A. Students are over-tested on standardized tests without any subsequent diagnostic analysis.
    B. No diagnosis without follow-through remediation being planned and put into practice.
    C. Some of the best diagnoses can be made by trained classroom teachers using informal tests with useful observations.

D. Teachers have a great deal of diagnostic material that is not utilized. Teachers need to learn to use everything available.

E. Need for early screening to prevent failure.

F. Discover each student's particular difficulties and plan a reading program designed to remediate the difficulty, rather than changing to another program or materials when a student fails.

G. All students with severe reading problems need to be taught using a multisensory approach.

II. Suggestions for diagnosing student's reading problems:

    A. Any reading test given should be analyzed for low achieving students.

        1. General things to observe:

            a. Word recognition problems

            b. Comprehension difficulties

        2. Error analysis:

            a. Perceptual errors (visual and auditory)

            b. Phonetic errors

            c. Syntactic errors

            d. Semantic errors

    B. When a student reads orally, see if a pattern of difficulty appears.

    C. Analyze any writing the student does.

    D. Observe student in a writing activity.

    E. Note attention span and ability to follow directions.

    F. Tape some oral reading activity.

III. Informal Tests to Give:
  A. Placement test for instructional level
  B. Informal inventories and Criterion-Referenced Tests
  C. Oral reading tests
  D. Specific skills tests
  E. Copy from the board (far point), from desk (near point)
  F. Body awareness of left and right
  G. Listening comprehension
  H. General Intelligence
  I. Slingerland Screening Tests

IV. Kindergarten and 1st grade screening as a preventive measure:
  A. Visual and auditory perception
  B. Visual-motor integration
  C. Concept development
  D. Rhyming
  E. Beginning Phonics
  F. Sound blending
  G. Receptive language
  H. Listening comprehension
  I. Lowercase letter names
  J. Lowercase letter sounds

As I study the words of Robin, I can see that she was a pioneer in my days of teaching reading. She has passed on to her reward, but her legacy lives on and on. I have sat at her grave, leaving my regards and appreciation. With tears from my personal loss, I think of those, many indeed, who have benefited from her wisdom, and I am thankful for the joy of having had her in my life. One day, she gave me a necklace that represented my dedication, for and on behalf of her efforts. Treasure! Robin was grateful to those who supported her mission to change lives and make the world a better place.

Dr. Robin Steed asked me to join her to show faculty members from the Department of Educational Psychology and Special Education, with whom she was working, how her reading program was developing. I was happily very nervous. While I was using Robin's exciting and carefully designed reading program that she was pulling together from years of study and observation, she often visited my special education classroom to observe the progress being achieved by my students.

Dr. Steed was in the process of developing a reading program she named *Touchphonics* that became very successful. For me, the favorite part, of her materials, was her textured letters—bodily-kinesthetic intelligence rewarded with learning. I helped her with the research by using this program with some of my special education students. Through the manipulation of letters, the student links sounds to recognize a pattern and then generates words to build a foundation and then moves forward to the reading content. My life as a reading teacher was unimaginably rewarding.

My students would use four modalities: visual, auditory, kinesthetic and tactile. They were learning to read! And who were they? Struggling readers, identified as Special Education students in public school and those in homeschooling.

Students classified with Attention Deficit Disorders found grounding for their attention by touching the letters, and those who did not have adequate language skills could use limited language. One of my students with Cerebral Palsy could point to patterns while I placed the letters.

Later, toward the end of my high school teaching in Hawaii, my high school administration asked me to go to the home of a student with autism so that he could be taught without being distracted by other students. At home, he did not experience the noisy and confusing environment of being on campus.

As it turned out, although he didn't talk much, he particularly related to me, and we became friends! Relationships will change the *noise* of stress into being contented and self-assured. He smiled as he rewarded himself with a new word.

Dr. Steed's *Touchphonics* program was valued by the student's aide and me. I taught the aide to use the reading program, and when I left the island, I gave the reading program to the homeschool aide.

It was pleasing to Dr. Steed how I used her textured letters to create the patterns for coding and decoding, but the letters were very expensive to make and somewhat rigid. Later, she replaced these letters with a different material that was more friendly to use. Still being used! The three-dimensional, textured, plastic, colored, and coded letters could be used to create patterns for teaching core reading skills. Along with learning to read came the skill of spelling. Learned patterns are gems to be treasured and appreciated for a lifetime of enjoying the written word.

Dr. Steed was pleased with the system she developed and the impressive results. She felt it was time to show the results to her university faculty. She was opening the door for research. Obtaining permission to take one of my students with me, we were on our way. This particular student had been in an accident and still had a large nail in his head. As a struggling student, he couldn't read. One of the professors for whom Dr. Steed was having me demonstrate the reading program was Dr. James Young.

I did not know the university faculty who were watching me teach. I was scared because this was not only important to me but more important for Dr. Steed to establish an acceptance for her difficult and challenging task of developing the program; a program that she desired the university to support for research purposes. This reading system developed and designed by Dr. Robin Steed was tested and proven in the reading laboratory at Brigham Young University for over six years. The system dramatically increased reading skills. Students previously weak in phonics gained one or two grade levels in fluency in twelve weeks.

Touchphonics meets the phonemic awareness and phonetic research standards of the National Reading Panel. It is designed to be a balanced literacy program. The goal is to achieve an automatic and fluent level of reading while understanding the content. Dr. Steed believed the human condition improved with the acquisition of the skills which she was addressing.

In the year 2002, the Touchphonics Reading Systems was acquired by Educators Publishing Service and the product can be purchased by contacting them. Robert Hall established this business in 1949. I have bought lots of valuable teaching materials from them, along with helpful books. He and his wife were also members of the International Dyslexia Association.

Thank You, Robin!

For years, my face was smiling, but my heart was crying as I asked over and over again the question—*Why?* I finally found peace due to what I learned from Dr. Steed and those associated with the International Dyslexia Association. I found that I have a gift.

15

Dyslexia:
International Dyslexia Association

The International Dyslexia Association—IDA actively promotes educational interventions for dyslexia. Having been to their conferences I walked away with a ton of information to wrap my head around, I highly endorse their goals. The International Dyslexia Association publishes the following: *"International Dyslexia Association actively promotes effective teaching approaches and related clinical, educational intervention strategies for individuals with Dyslexia. We support and encourage interdisciplinary research. We facilitate the exploration of the causes and early identification of Dyslexia and are committed to the responsible and wide dissemination of research and evidence-based knowledge. The purpose of IDA is to pursue and provide the most comprehensive range of information and services that address the full scope of Dyslexia and related difficulties in learning to read and write . . . in a way that creates hope, possibility, and partnership so that every individual has the opportunity to lead a productive and fulfilling life, and society benefits from the resource that is liberated."* For further information contact the International Dyslexia Association. I believe this organization is the *best of the best* for learning about the brain and how it relates to language processing. Contact them!

At one time The International Dyslexia Association was called the Orton Dyslexia Society. They called this condition Specific Language Disability. Some children are born with developmental difficulties.

Results of abnormal development:
1. Individual will not be able to bring inter-understanding (sequential

conceptualization) of oral language. Me!

2. Individual has a difficult time bringing up what is known subconsciously. Me!
3. Individual has a difficult time organizing thoughts. Me!
4. Individual has a difficult time with phrases and sentences. Me!
5. They cannot generalize grammatical patterns. Me! And me again!

Oral expression with the auditory representation of a visual concept is difficult. Comprehension is difficult to express. Therefore, self-esteem plummets. Individuals can conceptualize on a higher level than their developmental oral expression will allow.

With most people, these tasks just happen. With a Specific Language Disability person, the patterns of language have to either be taught or learned through trial and error. Some people are never taught; however, through native intelligence some individuals develop interventions to survive. Through my experience, I know this to be true.

Given my experience, I know that an appropriately designed intervention depends on knowing the severity or degree of disability. Other factors to be considered are intelligence, desire to succeed, educational value system within the person, and a variety of other conditions, such as the individual's emotional system of support and social environment. General intelligence, as indicated by an IQ, is not a causal factor in Specific Language Disability.

I am grateful for bright minds with dedicated energy who continue to set an excellent standard for research, education, and caring about the cognitive processing of brains such as mine. Pushing the training information for teachers is vital. I look forward to the day when this information is common knowledge. My language deficit was a puzzle until a university professor, Dr. Robin Steed, shared what she had learned from the International Dyslexia Association. And I in-turn have taught others about and how to compensate for developmental difficulties. **Thank You, International Dyslexia Association!**

16

Dyslexia:
Dr. Samuel Orton, American Physician, Neuropathologist

Samuel Orton was born in 1879 and died in 1948. He was an American physician remembered for his pioneering work on the causes and treatment of dyslexia. Dr. Orton was not the first to study learning disabilities, and he obviously did not have access to modern brain scanning equipment. Orton made contributions to our understanding of dyslexia, even though he did not have the support of interested persons, such as we have today, researching the many levels and aspects of the brain. Dr. Orton opened my world.

I know how it feels to be searching for answers, which seem to be unanswerable. Surrounding oneself with others who are searching for the same answers gives one a sense of needed support and clarification.

Orton's interest in reading disorders was said to stem from his daughter's difficulties in learning to read. (Wingate, 1997, p. 150) Orton was a pathologist in Massachusetts, where he worked with adult patients who had documented brain damage. Their difficulty with language functioning and reading tasks led him to study why some children with apparently intact neurological functioning had similar challenges with language processing and reading. He also discovered that those with reading challenges whom he tested at a clinic in Greene County, Iowa had average or above average IQ scores. Orton tried to explain the same difficulties in children whose brains were not damaged. He rejected the notion that it was brain defects that caused the problem.

"Orton's study of reading difficulties in children led him to hypothesize that those individuals have failed to establish appropriate cerebral organization to support the association of visual words with their spoken forms." (Orton, ST, 2519)

In other words, some brains during the developmental process fail to establish a cerebral organization, at least concerning what we refer to as hemispherical dominance. Therefore, what we know as a deficit, if such deficits interfere with the individual's adequate functioning, the deficit becomes a disability. The association of visual words with their spoken forms become the culprit. We know there are areas of the brain with hidden secrets. Thus, Dr. Orton forwarded his idea of multisensory teaching, which integrated movement with the sensory pathways of visual and auditory, for outstanding results. Multisensory would facilitate the learning of concepts by serving all brain connections regardless of brain dominance.

Gillingham & Stillman elaborated upon reading and spelling methods that Orton developed. They emphasized building the following linkages: visual-auditory, auditory-visual, auditory-kinesthetic, kinesthetic-visual. Gillingham and Stillman believed, *"It is essential to establish each linkage with patient care, even into the thousandth repetition."* (Gillingham & Stillman, 1936, p. 36)

The Gillingham & Stillman method considered the sound equivalents for every letter of the alphabet to be taught, followed by sound blending. Tracing of letters to maintain left-to-right progression rewires the brain to program over the reversals. Spelling associations between sounds, letters, and words established a teaching method. Sound discrimination was stressed.

"Anne Gillingham, a follower of Orton used modality combinations in her teaching. They included (1) visual-auditory: translation of visual symbols into sound; (2) auditory-visual: translation of auditory symbols into visual image; (3) auditory kinesthetic: translation of

112

auditory symbols into muscle response for speech and writing; (4) kinesthetic-auditory: movement of a passive hand by another to produce a letter form; (5) visual-kinesthetic: translation of visual symbol into muscular action of speech and writing; and (6) kinesthetic-visual: the muscular feel of the speaking or writing of a letter, in order to lead to association with the appearance of that letter." (Myers & Hammill, 1976, p. 263-264)

Samuel Orton's observations concluded that a syndrome, a group or cluster of symptoms, is characteristic of a specific condition. He named it, *Strephosymbolia*, twisted symbols.

Following are the characteristics Orton observed. Dr. Orton would have had an uncomplicated time diagnosing me.

1. Inability to recognize taught sight words. [I learn from my environment as I recognize words associated with meaning.]
2. Reversal tendencies. [Figuring out what part is first: b or d, or which way: w or m.]
3. May spell with visual strength but auditorially weak.
4. Speech and language retrieval. [Mental *monsters* for me.]
5. Delayed speech patterns. Sequence chunks of speech. [Confusing!]
6. Poorly written skills. Grammar, syntax, and construction. [Me.]
7. IQ. [I have seen challenges in individuals with a high IQ.]
8. Neurological organization skewed, spatial and directional confusion. [Me! And me again!]
9. Poor reading comprehension. [I have had to read and read again.]
10. Difficulty in sequencing. [I call it *Sequence Confusion*.
    I think this is the overarching deficit; it can become a disability.]

As we study the history of research to understand the challenge with reading or language processing, there were those from medicine, psychology, social work, and the field of education who studied the research of Hinshelwood and others from outside the United States.

Samuel Orton was a key figure in the United States. His research and experience differed from others, in view of the well-established fact that *"somewhat over 10 percent of the total school population had reading disabilities."* With this population came all *degrees of severity.* From my experience, I believe this to be true. In my opinion, as with almost everything, finding *real reasons* and then for the populace to endorse them, is a steep hill to climb. Why? It seems that everything needs to be researched and proven over and over with a comprehensive and in-depth view. Marketing the truth is not easy. It should be common knowledge and applied with dedicated energy.

Orton believed that acquiring the skill of reading was a complex activity that involved more than *one* area of the brain. He reasoned that reading disabilities were often inherited, and I certainly concur. Along with other things, Orton observed, researched, and concluded that *mixed dominance* was a primary symptom to be considered.

I would like to suggest that we look at mixed dominance as a possible sequencing problem. Which hand do I use? Which side comes first? Yes, which way do I write my "d" and my "b" because I am not sure of the proper direction as to face each letter after the vertical line has been drawn. I could remember by saying "c" and drawing the "c" and then the vertical line, and there was my "d" which comes after the "c." I know that is complicated, but it helped me. As I sang the alphabet song "a", "b", "c", the "d" came next. Yes, the song was sung in 1941. Music helps!

As I have mentioned many times in this book, a sense of directionality and problems with sequencing in human activity become a significant challenge for a wide variety of people with problematic cognitive processing. They are frequently included as symptoms in many of the diagnostic categories. This valuable information contributes to our understanding, as we plan for teaching skills addressed to learning disabilities. We plan and prepare for accommodations.

Might a sequencing problem be a mixed dominance problem? Just thinking! I have not yet turned my attention to this question to see what the research literature might reveal; however, **I have repeatedly observed that the problems with sequencing are ubiquitous.** And I have observed and stated that my reading problems had a significant sequencing challenge. And that is why I learned to read by the sight-word method. Dr. Orton, you have no idea how I would like to visit with you.

Orton later emphasized that the teaching of letter sounds was not enough; there was a need for sound blending. *"We have repeatedly seen children referred to us as reading disability cases with the statement that the phonetic method had been tried but had failed. In these cases examination has revealed the fact that while the teaching of the phonetic equivalents may have been fairly complete, the next step, that of teaching the blending of the letter sounds in the exact sequence in which they occur in the word, had not been attempted or had been poorly carried out. It is this process of synthesizing the word as a spoken unit from its component sounds that often makes much more difficulty for the strephosymbolic child than do the static reversals and letter confusions."* (Orton, 1937, p. 162) Argie Ella this is you!

Orton was forwarding the idea of multisensory teaching and, of course, stressing the use of sound, sight, or kinesthetic. Anna Gillingham and Bessie Stillman wrote a book, *Remedial Work for Reading, Spelling, and Penmanship*.

I have used ideas, which were generated by Dr. Samuel Orton, with every program that I have ever used since learning of his brilliant research and observations. Many programs have been created using the Orton-Gillingham approach.

I used this concept of multisensory teaching when I helped out in regular 2nd grade classrooms while assisting the teachers during their break time. I would leave my Resource room for my break and serve two regular education teachers. The students enjoyed having their whole bodies working to learn. They liked the music component added for interest. It worked! Yay!

Have you wondered if you have dyslexia? Perhaps or perhaps not?

1. Do you not enjoy reading because you read slowly and need to read again for comprehension?
2. Can't spell. I have heard that about 80 percent of us do not spell well.
3. Things of detail, like remembering names and dates, are somewhere else but not in the head?
4. Do you have a difficult time recalling and pronouncing spoken words?

One root of the problem could be that you are problem-solving other things in your head, making connections, and you are not focusing on reading, writing, and arithmetic with the mental energy needed to conquer the task. You are solving other problems with your imagination and intuition. See how bright you are! You have a gift.

On top of that, you can see the whole vision of how the building or whatever should look; however, you need to study the details to score the job well done. First the whole picture then the details. You have heard that *the devil is in the details,* which means that the whole picture may seem simple, but the details may be complicated and cause problems.

Diagnosing a problem area or areas is a difficult problem or procedure because not all have the same challenges or need the same interventions. Success for one may not be success for another.

Finding answers and asking more questions.

17

Dyslexia:
Dr. Norman Geschwind, Behavioral Neurologist

D r. Geschwind died in 1984. It was the consensus that with his passing the world of neuroscience would suffer a substantial loss. He was without a doubt an impressive pioneering American behavioral neurologist. Geschwind's role in neurology and neuropsychology will be the shoulders on which others will stand as research on the brain continues. Dr. Geschwind was neurologist-in-chief at Beth Israel Hospital and a professor at the Massachusetts Institute of Technology. He was an impressive presence in the field of research as related to the structure of the brain and human behavior.

Dr. Geschwind studied dyslexia and how the two hemispheres of the brain have functional differences. Studies concluded that left-handed people were more vulnerable than right-handed people to such ailments as learning disabilities, stuttering, migraine headaches and so-called auto-immune diseases. Auto-immune diseases are where the body attacks its tissues. **These studies say that it is not left-handed people only.** He made a lifelong study of language and cognitive functions.

Geschwind studied differences between left and right hemispheres. *"It certainly seems reasonable to hypothesize that this great anatomical difference accounts for the dominance of the left hemisphere in the language in most people."* (Geschwind 1972)

I remain an interested follower of the idea of "learning and digging deeper" and "teaching and digging deeper." The story is not complete. I have observed my student's behavior in both cases; I find that I am in concert with the concepts which were speculated by Geschwind. (Annals of Dyslexia Volume XXXII, 1982)

"During the last few years of his life, Geschwind became interested in the developmental learning disabilities and set out to uncover their neurological substrates. His keen clinical acumen led to his noticing that mothers of dyslexic children often reported left-handedness, atopic illnesses, and thyroid disease. He then studied in London and found a significant increase in the incidence of stuttering, dyslexia, colitis, thyroid disease and myasthenia gravis in the population of strongly left-handed individuals. Follow-up studies expanded these findings to include other illnesses as well and found associations between laterality scores, learning disabilities, blond hair, and occupation. Furthermore, this work led to the finding in immune-defective mice of developmental brain changes and learning disorders. Geschwind's work evolved from the re-establishment of classic thinking to the forging of new frontiers, thus reinforcing the idea that in order to make progress it is necessary to know the useful past. As did his early writings, Geschwind's last work remains an invitation to the world community of neuroscience to test his hypotheses for right or wrong, always in the spirit of the lively science he so much believed in." (Albert M. Galaburda 1987)

"The term learning disabilities is a loose term . . . . These conditions are present in large numbers in people who, despite normal or superior talents in other areas, have difficulty in acquiring one or more specialized skills." (Geschwind 1983)

Finding answers!

18

Dyslexia:
Dr. Drake Duane, Neurologist

Dr. Drake Duane was reared in Detroit, Michigan. He earned his B.A. degree at the University of Michigan and his Master's degree at the University of Minnesota. Dr. Duane is a graduate of distinction and a member of the Alpha Omega Alpha medical academic honorary from Wayne State University College of Medicine in Detroit, Michigan. Completed his residency in Neurology at the Mayo Graduate School of Medicine in Rochester, Minnesota. At Mayo, he co-founded the Learning Disabilities Assessment Program and the Didactic Neurology Training Lecture series for residents, receiving the Teacher of the Year Award from the residents at the Mayo Graduate School of Medicine. He is Certified by the American Board of Psychiatry and Neurology.

Drake D. Duane, M.S., M.D. has helped to transform the lives of hundreds of patients who suffered from the challenges of learning, behavioral, and movement disorders. We know that early identification and intervention is the road to success for the challenged. Dr. Duane's compassionate approach paves the road for improvements. Self-image is one of the facets he addresses with his unique interest and study. His humane approach to early identification and treatment interventions provides measurable improvements in learning, behavior, mood, and self-image. Dr. Duane is currently a psychiatrist in Scottsdale, Arizona and affiliated with multiple hospitals in the area, including John C. Lincoln North Mountain Hospital and Paradise Valley Hospitals. He is past president of the International Dyslexia Society and International Academy for Research on Learning Disabilities.

Dr. Duane co-authored an article on *Antibody to Acetylcholine Receptor in Myasthenia Gravis* that is of great interest to me. *"In summary, anti-receptor antibody, similar to that found in animals with experimental autoimmune Myasthenia Gravis, is detectable in patients with Myasthenia Gravis. Anti-receptor, but not antiacetylcholine site, antibody is detected in most patients with Myasthenia Gravis but not in persons without Myasthenia Gravis . . . ".*

What is myasthenia gravis? The definition by the National Institute of Neurological Disorders and Stroke:

"Myasthenia gravis is a chronic autoimmune neuromuscular disease characterized by varying degrees of weakness of the skeletal (voluntary) muscles of the body. The name myasthenia gravis, which is Latin and Greek in origin, literally means "grave muscle" weakness. With current therapies, however, most cases of myasthenia gravis are not as "grave" as the name implies. In fact, most individuals with myasthenia gravis have a normal life expectancy." "The hallmark of myasthenia gravis is muscle weakness that increases during periods of activity and improves after periods of rest. Certain muscles, such as those that control eye and eyelid movement, facial expression, chewing, talking, and swallowing are often, but not always, involved in the disorder. The muscles that control breathing and neck and limb movements may also be affected."

Over the years, Dr. Duane has developed concerns about and a specialized interest in problems with cognitive processing and learning disabilities. He has thoroughly evaluated and treated children and adults with these challenges and studied their impact on the emotional status of patients. Dr. Duane serves those with both developmental and acquired disorders. His expertise serves him very well with various communication challenges. Duane is also knowledgeable about coordination, and involuntary movement problems. These concerns are noted in a long list of the societies and organizations with which he affiliates and boards on which he serves.

The year was 1985, and the Orton Dyslexia Society's annual conference was in Chicago. I was teaching at Highland Elementary School in Highland, Utah and was very, and I do mean very, excited to board the plane taking me to Chicago to sit at the feet of some of the most brilliant minds in the world to learn more about dyslexia. One such mind was that of Dr. Duane. I had a brief conversation with Dr. Duane. After a short visit he excused himself. As he stepped on escalator going down, we were still visiting. I said, "I know there is more than one kind of dyslexia." His response, "Let's talk about that." And later, we had an opportunity to talk.

In the following year of 1986, I was energized and organized to obtain an invitation from the Slingerland Institute, along with the support of the university's Department of Education for Dr. Duane to come to BYU to give a lecture. He told a story illustrating the beauty of thinking out of the box. A medical student was having a difficult time passing written examinations which would have made the difference in the outcome of his brilliant career. Dr. Duane visited the school and opened their eyes to another way of testing this individual. They tested his medical knowledge with an oral examination and soon, after making this adjustment, they could see that they had done a service in forwarding the education of an outstanding person.

Dr. Duane probably does not know this but a couple attending his lecture shared their insights. Their lives were literally changed by what they heard from Dr. Duane as he opened the window of understanding that dyslexia was real. This lady with a Master's degree was aware that her husband was not *dumb*, but she didn't understand how or why he processed information in such a different way from her. Dr. Duane's lecture deepened her understanding and, as such stories sometimes end, "They lived happily ever after!" Here we see that a Neurologist can be a marriage counselor.

Years ago Dr. Duane inspired me with these words: *"The problem of language, particularly reading retardation in otherwise apparently intellectually intact children and adults, has over the years received the attention of several disciplines. Neurology, psychiatry, psychology, speech pathology, pediatrics, ophthalmology, and special and general education have approached this area hoping to provide improved subject identification, comprehension of the cause of the deficit, and provisions for a rational and successful mode of therapy. However, communication among these disciplines has often suffered because of the perspective and terminology peculiar to each."* Once Drake Duane said, *"The key to life is language."* For me, it is also the core of knowledge!

Thank you, Dr. Duane!

I am confused because at this point there is not a ground for common knowledge among the disciplines. I know because I have kept in touch with the many disciplines. Confusion of language!

More questions and more answers!

Thoughts from Margaret Rawson
Past President of the National Orton Society
Currently, International Dyslexia Association

Dyslexia
The differences are personal
The diagnosis is clinical
The treatment is educational
The understanding is scientific

Margaret sent me the following:

Teaching, as well as learning, is a multi-dimensional affair. While we, ourselves, are keeping the structure of the language in mind, we need also to remember the learner's need for a program that is at once: *Structured, sequential, cumulative* and *thorough*. It is to be kept constantly in mind, also, that we both want education, for understanding, to make the principles clear, and training, or practice, to make the elements stick and the processes automatic. The skills are to be learned through all the avenues of learning open to the student — visual, auditory and tactile-kinesthetic, in interaction (our familiar multisensory approach). But although we use all the input and output modalities, we do it with the full realization that clear vision, sharp hearing, and controlled muscles are the necessary servants. *Yet the mind is the master.* It is, in the end, not the eye, the ear, the voice or the hand but the brain which learns both to read in order to understand, and to write that others may read. And so we teach the language as it is to the child as he is — a human nervous system with a unique configuration, a thinking, learning person. This will take all the knowledge, skill and wisdom we can muster in the years it takes to become professionally competent, an endlessly fascinating lifetime challenge.

Margaret Rawson

Bulletin of the Orton
Society, 1971

Margaret B. Rawson
Foxes Spy
7924 Rocky Springs Road
Frederick, Maryland 21701

This artistic rendering was on the envelopes penned by Margaret. I enjoy the remembrance of a treasured relationship.

Humbled by knowing the people I have been privileged to meet and having the opportunity to glimpse their giant shoulders has brought me inspiration. I am especially grateful for Margaret Rawson and Dr. Drake Duane.

Mrs. Margaret B. Rawson
7924 Rocky Springs Road
Frederick, MD 21701

1-13-86

Gaylie Savage
195 W. 700 No.
American Park, UT 84003

Dear Gaylie Savage and Argie Shumway—

Here's a hasty reply to your nice letter of 1/8.

The 13 Points I referred to are the neurological ones described by Geschwind in his Annals of Dyslexia paper in 1982. It's also available as Reprint #98. The 14th is outlined in the enclosed typed item. The "What Is Dyslexia" that I probably mentioned (I don't remember) was doubtless the all-over-the-place flyer, also enclosed, since Geschwind didn't write one by that name. "Point 15" was a very hypothetical suggestion of mine that perhaps the equal, and large, planum temporale sections so surprisingly cosistently found in the dyslexic brains so far might reinforce Orton's often scorned theory about ill-established hemispherical dominance as an explanation of some dyslexic phenomena. It seems possible, at least.

There's been quite a bit written about social behavior concomitants, but I don't have the references at hand. You might look up Tanis Bryan and Susan Vogel, and see whether they lead to veins worth mining.

It was good getting to know you. May we meet again soon!

Sincerly,

Margaret B. Rawson

19

Dyslexia:
Dr. Albert Galaburda, Professor, Researcher

Professor Albert M. Galaburda from Harvard University, USA is an outstanding and caring person who has amassed more than just the following credits: the Emily Fisher Landau Professor of Neurology and Neuroscience; Harvard Medical School Co-Director of the Mind, Brain, and Behavior Interfaculty Initiative; Harvard University Chief; Division of Cognitive Neurology.

Boarding the plane to Chicago for the 1985 annual conference of the Orton Dyslexia Society, I found myself wondering what I was going to learn. The speakers would be the most brilliant minds in the world who were researching and studying the brain, along with those in education, and how all that fits into what I would like to learn about dyslexia. I will add this pungent comment. When coming back from Chicago, stepping off the plane, I said, "It is true!"

As I listened to Dr. Galaburda, it occurred to me that, for him, talking about the brain was like playing with Tonka toys with him running the trucks through the brain and discovering wonderful things. After I heard Dr. Galaburda speak, I took the opportunity to have a one-on-one conversation with him. He graciously said that he would appreciate me donating my brain for research. Of course, documentation that I have both dyslexia and a brain will not be difficult to establish.

Dr. Galaburda delivered a passionate paper entitled *Dyslexia: Advances in Cross-Level Research*. At that time, he was affiliated with the Charles A. Dana Research Institute, Division of Behavioral Neurology, Department of Neurology, Beth Israel Deaconess Medical Center, Boston, MA. This institute was part of the Harvard Medical School. He was Chief of the Division of Cognitive Neurology, Researcher at Beth Israel Hospital and Professor at Harvard University.

Galaburda's paper is filled with information; it would be interesting for anyone's personal study. The most salient point of the paper reads like this: *"The mind of a dyslexic contains other structures besides auditory and linguistic processes and representation, which include visual, motor, somesthetic, (of, relating to, or concerned with bodily sensations <a somesthetic image of the body created by the brain from sensory inputs of touch, pressure, cold, heat, and pain>) memory, attention, motivations, and other executive functions, the roles of which are not known in Dyslexia."*

I recently found an article about Galaburda which validated that which I wrote several years ago in my book *More Than a Ticket Memoirs Flying with American Airlines from Props to Jets.* To quote my book, *"But my brain held a secret monster and a beautiful gift—Dyslexia."* With today's understanding of dyslexia or specific language disability, I know my challenge exceeds the popular notion of what dyslexia is as it pertains to both receptive and expressive language processing. The fear of demand language and the reward of spontaneous language has been a puzzlement. If you ask me a specific question, I can't think of the answer, but if you give me the subject, I can talk all day about it. I never fear being asked to speak at public meetings until question and answer time. To top it off, I have a massive sequencing challenge, which has been a nightmare, blocking my organizational desires. Sequencing challenges emerge everywhere from little daily tasks, such as *turn the other way, which is the left or right? Say it again, do it again, still another way* to big life decisions, such as *what next in a relationship?*

It has been difficult to understand my intelligences, confused in some areas and apparently high in others. My years with American Airlines gave me the opportunity to prove myself in complex and sequential

126

behaviors, which also required personal and social skills while achieving much! Not *dumb*!

With my sequencing challenge, I learned to stop my brain, look at what I was doing, and listen to my thoughts and words before taking the next step. The next step says, "Now, you are ready." Compensating for weaknesses requires a studied intervention to change a given behavior. Placing non sequenced thoughts into an order for a given action is the template for the desired outcome. I learned how to do new tasks because I understood the process of placing things in order. While I was flying, I intuitively came to understand my brain and how it functions. After becoming a Special Education teacher with additional training in brain functioning, I learned to appreciate my brain.

As a Special Education teacher with many years of experience both in regular and special education, I have tested many students and identified their learning styles, as well as their challenges. I designed interventions for remediation, followed by focused instruction and student discipline.

The New York Times published on January 13, 1987:

"Studies by Dr. Galaburda at Beth Israel Hospital in Boston along with other neuroscientists have shown that in brains of dyslexics, the language areas in the right hemisphere were as large as those on the left, and the right hemisphere also contained a greater than normal number of brain cells. Researchers theorized that a more developed right hemisphere would be able to rival the left hemisphere for control of the language function, creating tension within the brain and distorting the reading process."

The Australia Association for Research in Education published Professor Albert M. Galaburda's article *What's New About Dyslexia?* I found a truism regarding Dr. Galaburda's statement, ***"Not all dyslexics are the same."***

I know *all dyslexics are not the same*. I have had students in my classes who have the Orton cluster of symptoms for dyslexia except for one or more symptoms, as well as including myself with all but one symptom. I would have never learned to read phonetically. Learning by sight was my strength. By the time I was in the 8th grade, I had gathered enough sight words to be able to read. Learning words from cans of food, signs, and greeting cards, etc., was how I learned to read. The phonetic *monsters* at school, thank goodness, stayed at school. I did not like school.

Continuing with the article *What's New About Dyslexia? "There is a lot more about Dyslexia research and one of the most exciting parts of it is that it dovetails nicely with biological research on other learning and developmental disorders. So, there are lots of people working to make things better. Moreover, there are lots of people making sure that the research is good."* Galaburda emphasized getting children into programs that will lessen the impact of their neurobiological brain situation while spending time developing their particular genius.

As a teacher, parent, or individual, I have choices as what to do with the research. The last I heard was that the researchers were looking for a risk gene. A gene that points in the direction of predisposing a person to have what is called dyslexia.

I have long respected Dr. Galaburda for his research. *"These genes, interestingly, point to pathways involved both in the structure and function of brain cells (neurons). They involve both neurons in the cerebral cortex and neurons in the deeper structures noted above. In some cases, the neurons may be noisy and unable to represent fine sound distinctions."*

"There are clearly differences in the ways the brain functions when faced with a language task in dyslexics compared to good readers." (Dr. Albert Galaburda)

Given my experience, I know that this phonetic linkage is what doesn't happen in my brain; I am unable to represent fine sound distinctions, remember the sounds, and put in order the sound sequence. I have called it an auditory memory deficit. Since 1980, I have been saying that there are different kinds of dyslexia. I have observed it with my students. With that being the case, the interventions have differed by pulling on the strengths to remediate the weaknesses. I believe that not only the interventions are different, but the brain is designed to make up the differences.

Thank you, Dr. Galaburda!

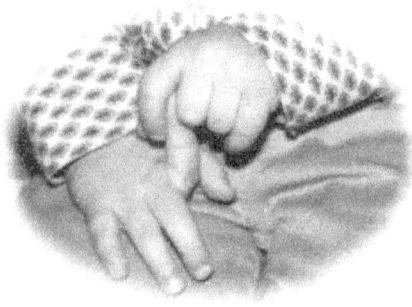

Bradley studying his world. What now! "Which intelligence do I use?"
He is a computer engineer for a university. Would he change his
brain or redesign it? No!

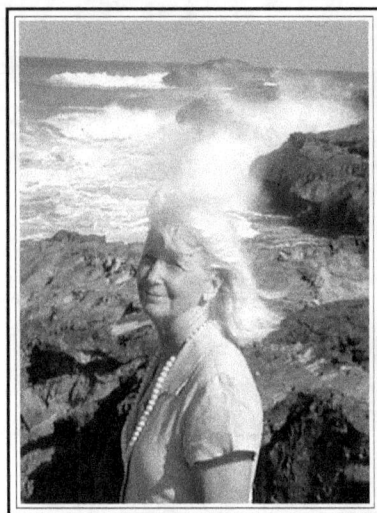

I am grateful for the unfolding of understanding.
The vastness of intelligence is overwhelming.

20

Multiple Intelligences Theory:
View of Intelligences
Dr. Howard Gardner, Professor of Cognition and Education

H oward Gardner is the John H. and Elisabeth A. Hobbs Professor of Cognition and Education at the Harvard Graduate School of Education. He holds positions as Adjunct Professor of Psychology at Harvard University and Senior Director of the Harvard Project Zero. Gardner received a MacArthur Prize Fellowship in 1981 and the University of Louisville's Grawemeyer Award in Education in 1990. He has received honorary degrees from thirty-one colleges and universities, including institutions in Bulgaria, Chile, Greece, Hong Kong, Ireland, Israel, Italy, South Korea, and Spain. He has twice been selected by Foreign Policy and Prospect magazines as one of the 100 most influential public intellectuals in the world. In 2011, Gardner received the Prince of Asturias Award for Social Sciences, and in 2015 awarded the Brock International Prize in Education.

Harvard Graduate School of Education: Another Window Opens
Thank goodness, we see the light where intelligence is viewed as the combination and integration of several different threads of intelligences. The Multiple Intelligences Theory continues to be researched, resulting in a widening picture with more information in understanding how cognitive processing works. Crucial!

Dr. Howard Gardner has introduced a new way of looking at and understanding intelligence. I am excited about what this new approach has brought to our thinking. Let's ask, "In what ways are you smart?"

I say and believe that without a doubt as we seek ways to better the whole of our human condition, we must find the **details** in the picture called **better** by achieving a place for each human gift and then reward the gift with respect and dignity. The gifts are Multiple Intelligences. Think about what we expect of others. Look for the details of individual gifts not what we want others to have as gifts or what we want them to become but rejoice in their special intelligences.

Howard Gardner said, *"It is of the utmost importance we recognize and nurture all of the varied human intelligences, and all the combinations of intelligences. If we recognize this, I think we will have at least a better chance of dealing appropriately with the many problems that we face in the world."*

"It is important that we as a human community recognize the many faces of human intelligences and with that awareness, we bring a deeper and profound impact on the challenges which we encounter in the world. Better communication will come from understanding what and how the brain is processing information. Of course, this is only a chunk of the whole picture of problem-solving. The established community is complicated."

The study of how the brain is constructed and how that structure processes information has been a fascinating conversation for centuries. For me, the human brain is the most complex phenomenon in the known universe. We are aware of some things about the brain. According to the Smithsonian National Museum of Natural History, the brain gobbles up energy. Your brain is 2 percent of your body's weight but uses 20 percent of your oxygen supply and gets 20 percent of your blood flow. So, we understand why oxygen is essential to our functioning. Bring on the oxygen! My oxygen is used to know about the brain and what to do with it.

Finding out how the brain processes information through threads of intelligence is key to **learning how to learn.** As a parent, teacher, and an individual, I have experienced what it means to learn how to learn. That was the theme of a workshop for teachers and administrators. I share, "This is a powerful insight that could change the whole world of understanding as to how we teach and how we learn!" As we discussed the concept, it came to me that it is exciting to know how that happens, how we learn. Oh, to understand how the brain receives and responds to information is enlightening. Our uniqueness as individual human beings can be seen in our fingerprints and especially in the *brainprint* and how our particular brain processes information. This understanding will make a difference in how we communicate with each other.

Then, one day, I heard about Howard Gardner and his theory. Howard Gardner, one of the pioneers, in Multiple Intelligences Theory defines intelligence as:

> *"The ability to problem solve as one encounters life;*
> *The ability to generate new problems to solve;*
> *The ability to make something or offer a service that is valued within one's culture."*

I agree with this quote: *"All students can learn and succeed but not all on the same day in the same way."* --- William G. Spady

Another quote finds me resounding: *"Our emphasis on accountability fails to take into consideration this single clear fact of life: children are different. Why, then, the authors ask, do federal and state mandates for accountability result in what teachers know will never work: a foolish emphasis on sameness?"* (Rex and daughter Trudy Knowles, Phi Delta Kappan, Vol. 82, Issue 5, 2001, page 390)

Present legislation in some states provides monetary rewards to teachers based on test scores. When there are "sped"—special education children in the regular classroom, and they fail to achieve because of the nature of their brain functioning, it means that the picture of success for the teacher is jaded. Teachers are punished financially. This injustice could be corrected by eliminating the scores of the special education students.

Given my experience, I know that it is a fact that teachers are rewarded for the learning achieved by certain facets of intelligence. It is considered teacher failure when those particular students score low on the tests, even though other facets of intelligence are not taken into account. Teachers are trapped in the mire of legislative discussion with unfounded opinions and policies which are archaic. It is ridiculous and without merit.

People have a unique tapestry of intelligences for a colorful and interesting blend which makes the individual fabric outstanding. Howard Gardner argues that the big challenge facing the deployment of human resources is how to best take advantage of the uniqueness conferred on us as a species exhibiting several intelligences.

My husband asked me the question, "When did this Multiple Intelligences Theory begin?" In the early 1950s, when he entered graduate school, he was hearing that there are many elements which together make up human intelligence. It was thirty years later when Howard Gardner, a Harvard researcher, was asked by the Bernard Van Leer Foundation to investigate human potential. In 1983, Gardner had the idea of "many kinds of minds" for several years prior to the publication of his book, *Frames of Mind.* In my opinion, this was considered the birth of the Multiple Intelligences Theory.

While I was studying and applying Howard Gardner's findings regarding Multiple Intelligences, I found success. It helped describe the world. His theory makes sense to me, and how I can use it in education. As a person, parent, teacher, and a member of the community, I say yeah!

Howard Gardner's findings have been a significant influence in my life. It has helped describe the world with a logic which has made sense. His theory, which is established in his work entitled *Frames of Mind,* has contributed in a significant way to my understanding of the brain. Once I thought of the brain as being a single creation of intelligence, which could be tested as such, sent to us through our DNA, and it could be trained based on that view of a single intelligence. Knowing the Multiple Intelligences Theory and teaching with multisensory programs has helped me to achieve a given outcome. In other words, it helped me understand the brain and what it can do. Hallelujah!

My brain has been opened to experience its strengths and weaknesses through the concept of Multiple Intelligences. Gardner's theory has perhaps had the most enormous impact on the field of education, where it has received considerable attention and use.

This theory is not without debate. Is there sufficient empirical evidence to support Howard Gardner's conceptualization? How can different intelligences be measured? I agree with the idea that testing could lead to more labeling and stigmatization: more harmful than helpful. Gardner challenges educators' traditional thinking about intelligence with the statement, **"We must stop asking how smart people are and start asking how people are smart."** I am suggesting serious consideration of the impact of Gardner's work.

There are other great minds forwarding the concept that the brain is complex with a continuum of many layers of intellectual functioning. That is to say that the many layers have a vast range of development, which can continue to progress or retrogress.

Howard Gardner: Multiple Intelligences and Education

This theory has been of assistance to parents and educators, along with a supportive team of professionals. This theory provides a conceptual framework for organizing and reflecting on curriculum assessments for successful interventions and improved behavioral outcomes. This theory has been significant; it has turned the thinking toward developing ways of teaching which might better meet the range of needs of learners in classrooms. Basic to this theory, I have seen results showing that all of us may be at very different levels with these various threads of intelligences and are developing depending on our intellectual strengths and weakness. This information has brought a new way of understanding how to teach.

The Multiple Intelligences Theory can be invaluable in developing teaching strategies. As it helps a teacher to identify a student's strengths and preferred learning style, it can serve as the basis for developing talents. This enlightenment creates an environment which allows several ways to teach, learn, and apply to living in a world where all gifts are valued. This hope brings relief to the minds of those who once did not understand their brains.

Speaking of education and how this Multiple Intelligences Theory works for serving students, Gardner argues that there is no one true way to measure intelligence. He said, *"I once thought it possible to create a set of tests of each intelligence – an intelligence-fair version to be sure – and then simply to determine the correlation between the scores on the several tests. I believe that this can only be accomplished if someone developed several measures of each intelligence and then made sure that people were comfortable in dealing with the materials and methods used to measure each intelligence."*

Framing information the way Gardner does, disrupts the old way of thinking by which data are measured as a global intelligence. The premise of Gardner's theory is that someone can be extremely bad at one thing but be the best of the best in another field. That makes sense to me. I have seen the ever so wide and deep range of cognitive abilities, sometimes called talents or gifts. Like my students in Hawaii, some couldn't read or write, but they could play football and surf like none other. Therefore, limiting the definition of intelligence is detrimental to our understanding of how the brain works.

At first, this view of understanding the brain could indeed appear to bring the death of formal education as it is today; however, it digs deeper to understand what we can do with what we have.

Given my experience, I know the challenge in designing an active Individualized Education Program as needed for each special education student. It is crucial to identify their strengths, in fact, an absolute must. I find that Multiple Intelligences Theory consideration requires deciding the most appropriate interventions to strengthen the weaknesses. I know that I have said this over and over. Imperative!

By its very nature, an Individualized Education Program that concentrates on the difficulties a student is encountering in a specific area, by focusing on weaknesses and neglecting the most developed intelligences, is only half of the intervention plan. For instance, a student experiencing difficulty in math may excel in spatial intelligence and have well-developed bodily-kinesthetic intelligence. To best teach the student, his Individualized Education Program should include interventions that focus on the mathematical skills and is supported by bodily-kinesthetic intelligence.

The theory proposes an approach that teachers have needed. Interestingly, before the theory, teachers did not realize what an available tool was missing from our Mary Poppins carpet bag. Missed opportunity!

Multiple Intelligences Theory goes further than developing remedial strategies and interventions. I have seen self-esteem soar as individuals began to understand they have gifts that had previously not been recognized. For years, I was only focusing on the weaknesses the student exhibited rather than with an emphasis on the student's strengths to remediate the deficiencies. The Multiple Intelligences Theory has found its way into the minds of educators. The theory has become especially of value when determining a student's placement in special education. Teachers identify the student's strengths and preferred learning styles through their awareness of Multiple Intelligences. **Hope** comes from understanding and the application of that knowledge.

I have interacted with well-trained and experienced teachers wherein it has been quite apparent that their students' success comes before their needs. Teachers give their time to teach information to cover the range of students' needs. I know these things from being in the teaching field, both in public and private school settings, for over thirty-three years.

While I was writing this book, I was visiting with one of the most loving, well-trained, creative, prepared for anything, and competent regular education teachers whom I have known. We were having a stimulating conversation as we engaged feelings of frustration, not unlike hundreds of others who could be talking about the same things; we gasped for air. As two retired and seasoned teachers, she and I shared some very treasured and salient thoughts that have emerged from all those days, weeks, months, and years of being parents and educators, as well as being two very different individuals. We have felt the hearts of many children, parents, and teachers breaking as they struggled through what for them was a world of educational and daily living confusion.

Day after day, from childhood to adulthood, one can have a sense of dumbness and hopelessness as a backdrop for problem-solving that can leave one more vulnerable to negative behaviors toward self and society. I have also seen those who have been very successful while still asking, "*Why* do I think so differently?" Sad to say, some who are bright and misunderstood end up in prison; neither they nor their world understood their cognitive processing gifts. All that, however, is only one significant piece of the puzzle as to what we do with and how we think with the uniqueness of the brain.

I am grateful to Howard Gardner for his theory about the multiple threads of intelligence and the influence it has had on humanity. Gardner claims that *intelligences rarely operate independently*. With a keen and clear awareness of our strengths, we have found the key to change and the dispelling of hopelessness.

I visited with a student who had been cutting herself. I asked the question *why* to which she answered, "I am *dumb*!" We continued to talk. She was not *dumb*! She was artistically brilliant but had no desire for reading. She hated reading and hated herself with no desire to live. She couldn't read or write thoughts down, but she was very gifted with dance and drama. For Heaven's sake, let her use her art to express her mind. She certainly had expressed her thoughts with all the tattoos on her. Sad story! As we visited, she found relief. Tears shed and knees bent over the *why* question. *"Why* do I feel *dumb* when sometimes I know that I am *smart?"* Understanding the whole person, not just a part of the person, is essential. Viewing a part of a person as the whole is absurd, and for some individuals, it can become devastating. Look for more!

Dr. Shumway, D.S.W. shared: *"These feeling can be extremely powerful and be mistaken by therapists as clinical depression or possibly other clinical diagnoses. We, thereby, induce a treatment plan that addresses only a portion of the problem. Look for other parts!*

When viewing the etiology of clinical depression, the most common contributions are genetics, social environment, and a backdrop of otherwise induced personal anguish with a sense of hopelessness. It is essential to understand and look for cognitive processing challenges. What is controlling the behavior? Not all learning disabilities include depression and not all depression includes learning disabilities. Study Multiple Intelligences!"

Learning ways the brain processes information brings relief and indeed hope. Understanding this information needs to be shared knowledge to be able to take decisive advantage of the brain's strengths. Appreciating the gifts of brain differences is a step toward accepting the human condition as a valuable and precious fabric woven with individual colors of interest. It is so nice that you and I can do some things better than other things. And thank the Heavens for not making us all alike. Let us rejoice realizing it is interesting to see the varied colors and beauty of fabric that is unique. Please see me with my particular patterns of cognitive processing as gifts, just as I see your patterns of cognitive processing as gifts. Beautiful!

These intelligences, according to Howard Gardner, can be used as constructive or destructive. This concept is most important to recall as the studies of intelligences are pondered.

Gardner initially generated a list of seven intelligences. *"His listing was provisional. The first two have been typically valued in schools; the next three are usually associated with the arts, and the final two are what Gardner called 'personal intelligences.'"* (Gardner 1999)

Dr. Gardner has subsequently added more intelligences to his listings, and I will take a look at those after these initial listings. Just remember that intelligences usually work together in complex ways.

I believe that most of us possess all of the intelligences to one degree or another. There is a continuum of functioning that enables each of us to excel in more than one area of intelligences.

Linguistic intelligence involves sensitivity to spoken and written language; the ability to learn languages, and the capacity to use language to bring about the desired goals of communicating. Language! I am astonished! Language is a significant piece of my confused brain puzzle.

As I listened to Dr. Robin Steed teach about the brain, I was more than attentive to her studied words. We use our linguistic intelligence when we have something to say in conversation with each other or when writing our language on paper. The process by which we voice our words through expressive language, and also the process by which we communicate through receptive language play upon this intelligence. What I am saying and hearing is revealed in this intelligence. Talent!

I know that I have struggled with this thread of my intelligence. I am still struggling with the expressive aspects of this intelligence, and my husband *admittedly* struggles with receptive language as he listens to someone's expressive language. There you have a real comparison of differences in cognitive processing. Yes, it takes a lot of words to figure out what each is saying. Wow! And this is a *first-class* dilemma. Can you see how this could affect relationships? I have heard many couples and individuals say, "He or she just doesn't communicate." See why!

While I was editing my writing, I asked my husband whether or not he

140

understood what I had just written. Help! He doesn't always follow, even though he is very smart. As my husband and I have discussed these principles and processes, we may have stumbled upon an entirely new way of conceptualizing an extensive and severe societal problem. It occurs to my husband and me that the divorce courts are filled with relationship problems, which are described and defined in one way by lawyers, different ways by linguists, and another way by social workers.

I sat in class while Robin was teaching about the brain and sharing with the class that the Broca area of the brain seems to bring the meaning of words and how they are related to each other. Is it a question or a statement and does it mean this or that? How am I receiving and interpreting what you are saying? And how am I answering with the correct meaning of words back to you? Am I using the right word with the right energy for the conversation?

As a teacher, I use language to go beyond recognition and spelling of the word, as well as for the understanding of the phrase, thus to integrate many aspects into the whole world of language. With this intelligence, some individuals can hear and understand words in their head before they read, speak, or write them down.

The left hemisphere of the complex brain does indeed clearly relate to details of logic in language processing. The right hemisphere brings to bear the rich emotional and creative side of our language, both in speaking and writing. When I write my stories, it is the right hemisphere that brings emotional interest, and this is more rewarding as a writer.

Logical-mathematical intelligence consists of the capacity to figure out problems logically, step-by-step while carrying out mathematical procedures, and thinking in scientific terms. In Gardner's words, it entails the ability to detect patterns, reason deductively, and think logically. This intelligence is most often associated with scientific and mathematical thinking. These people with logical and mathematical intelligence are good at scientific investigations and identifying relationships between different things. They can analyze complex and abstract ideas. Details!

Although the brain may cognitively be processing with less than logical response, it can be trained to think with details. Those of us who can think of the whole picture of a plan, and are aware that we think that way, can train our brains to look through the details of the idea and sequence the details through the whole picture of the idea.

Logical patterns have a sequence. Classifying objects is needed to train the brain to be logical. For me, the task to sequence the objects in a logical order was difficult but needed. Once I learned the skill, my attitude toward logic changed and math made sense.

Musical intelligence involves the capacity to learn the skills needed for performance, writing music, and recognition of musical patterns. It encompasses the ability to recognize and compose musical pitches, tones, and rhythms. According to Gardner, musical intelligence runs in an almost structural parallel to linguistic intelligence. It has been a challenging task to involve me in the learning of music; however, as I touch the language of music, it has yielded a rewarding outcome.

It seems that musical intelligence, like all aspects of intelligence, is unique to the brainprint. I look at musicians and listen to the various genre, and I see many aspects of a given culture in the mix. Again, I feel that being born with a generous helping of this intelligence can undoubtedly be enriching. The capacity to understand and appreciate music appears to be in the genome. Through deepening one's understanding of music, one can also cultivate an appreciation for music. There is a continuum of ability, which I have observed. I will not become a Mozart even with intense and studied effort. Developing one's talents is one thing but having unrealistic expectations is something else. It is alright not to play the organ.

Music has been a puzzlement. I can't carry a tune, but I can hear the music in my head, and I can hear my voice with the appropriate tone. Studying brain processing has been fun. I learned to play the piano, not by hearing the music, but by seeing the notes and learning. I can't memorize the songs in a way that facilitates playing them on the piano. "Oh, where did the songs in my head go?" The language of music comes out of my left hemisphere. Uh Oh! The rest of music comes out of my motor involvement and the creative part that understands rhythm. Like reading words, reading music . . . hard.

It took a long time to figure out how the music thing worked in my life. I love the rhythm in my bones, could dance all night. I was a cheerleader and could remember the words to the cheers. I remember back when as a child and without fear, I could lead the song at an assembly when I was in elementary school. Now! I can't carry a tune. Why? Fear and stress block brain processing. I didn't work through the fear of singing. I could have, but I didn't. My question as a teacher would be to look at the intellectual strengths along with other factors as to why the student is not learning. The learner is complex. Society has many lessons to learn about *how* to use what we have and what we have not. Digging deeply into the why is the road to success.

It appears to me that currently the music being generated is coming from the emotional and creative side of the brain. Listen to the message with the intensity of sound. It excites the soul. Music is powerful!

Bodily-kinesthetic intelligence brings the opportunity to use the whole body or parts of the body to solve problems. Gardner sees the mental and the physical activity as being related. This intelligence is an expressive intelligence, which can be displayed. It is shown well in sports, good at dancing, or in any activity that involves the movement of the body. Characteristics of bodily-kinesthetic intelligence are:

   Excellent physical coordination.
   Good at doing things rather than hearing or seeing.
   Good motor control, hand-eye, and muscle coordination.
   Possess an ability to create things and patterns with their hands.
   Excellent physical shape and strength.

These children just love evaluating how things work, and they do not like others telling them how they should perform. They follow their instincts and gut feelings. They cannot stay in one place for a long time, so they move around a lot. They also love outdoors and nature. In effect, they know their bodies and inner movements. Movements come naturally. The advantage of possessing this intelligence is the ability to display hand-eye coordination and skill to show dexterity.

Gardner believes that this intelligence has its origin in the body itself. I have observed this intelligence. Bodily-kinesthetic intelligence is a special ability that many children have and can be directed to encourage and support other intelligences; however, some may not be endowed with a studious and academic intelligence. I have used this strength to help children learn their math skills and their word recognition. "Jump to the beat and beat the multiplication tables." "Sing and dance to learn words." This intelligence is a super way to bring about multisensory teaching and learning. There are those who can create things and patterns with their hands. The direction of this intelligence is to encourage dance, sports, builders, actors, and the use of the body and movement of the mind. Movement! Use this for positive direction; however, it should be noted that movement can become harmful or useful to the child or adult.

These children can excel in sports, swimming, dancing, and other physical activities as they experience movement. They can be excellent architects and engineers considering they have a sense of movement within their bodies for mass, volume, shape, size, and pattern. In all, they could be super in those activities that demand action and movement. Spotting these children is easy since they are on the move. These adults are also easy to spot since they are on the move. These gifted individuals are getting on to the next thing! And sometimes at the expense of more important things, they do not put their priorities in logical order because of their need to physically express their gift of movement.

For clarification, it is important to note that processes of movement can occur within the mind, as well as within the body.

Development of strengths using other intelligences is paramount for the survival of a given lifestyle. Remembering my experience of teaching on an island where the kids had very high bodily-kinesthetic intelligences, they felt "no need" to use other avenues except their social, emotional, and physical gifts; it was very tough to energize the students to use their linguistic intelligence. Whole image thinking without details!

As I was driving in the snow today, with hazardous conditions, I realized that my Body-kinesthetic had been trained to react in an automatic way that was rewarding. I reflected on responses; several things came to mind. Things that are automatic after going through the training process: driving, dodging, dance steps, and sports. I will now look at the basketball player differently: automatic or "on the spot" determination of movements.

Motor or motorically viewed with the bodily-kinesthetic intelligence, I have observed subtle anatomical movements that are essential to the expression and communication of human thoughts and feelings. Smiles!

Visual-Spatial intelligence involves the recognizing and using of patterns. I see in my mind pictures or images that represent concepts. I learned to read by seeing words as pictures.

For me, as a teacher, visual-spatial intelligence is closely tied to some of the other intelligences. As I have observed my children and students, this intelligence is well exhibited through design as related to visual processing. Thus the movement of design expressed in a visualized way is how a son journeys through his dental practice and another son sculpts from a lump of clay. Another son designs computer programs by first seeing the process as a whole picture and then breaking it into the detail of parts. Detail after detail finally becomes the whole program. Another son's spatial thinking addresses what he does with what he sees in his head, seeing the whole and then the details. People skills! As we venture through life, we all have challenges and gifts.

Visualizing a three-dimensional structure both *in and out* of the head, one can recognize and apply dimensional concepts. Visualize what is obviously seen and how it can be extended to create a fullness of the concept. Visualize that which is unseen as a concept in your head.

Interpersonal intelligence is the capacity to understand other people and interact with them both individually and in groups. Understanding intentions, motivations, and desires of other people creates an avenue for working with them. It is easy to think of those who need to have or strengthen this intelligence: religious leaders, educators, salespeople, political leaders, customer service, and those who work in counseling positions. It is pertinent to know what others are thinking and feeling.

I believe there is a needed effort to extend our interpersonal gifts beyond the empathy that comes from walking in another's slippers. These expressed feelings should flow into the caring about others, even though their journey is unknown.

Intrapersonal intelligence is the understanding of one's self. Being alone is comfortable while finding one's self; one's self-pondering of life and reflecting on its meaning, finding answers, and having more questions would be satisfying. Being my own *me* and being alone is fine as I think my independent thoughts. Others may not understand my thoughts, but they are mine, and I know how they work. I know that I am just fine being me. Having the appreciation of one's feelings, and all that goes with understanding those feelings is rewarding and also challenging. As we understand ourselves, we can forward our energy for good or for ill. Our world needs the direction of being positive and good. Safe!

It has been enlightening to feel that I am in concert with myself and have unity with my creator. Today, I stood in nature as the snow fell. I felt that I was in concert with the world around me. As I understand my intrapersonal intelligence, I move toward my interpersonal intelligence. I think that I am moving toward a more harmonious *me*. Selflessness!

146

Dr. Gardner and his colleagues have looked at other possibilities:

Naturalist intelligence is the ability human beings have to understand the environment. With this knowledge comes the ability and sensitivity as to how to apply this understanding, i.e., how to care for the earth in all its dimensions. Some have said that this is "nature smart" and can be applied in an intelligent way to all aspects of our earth and how we choose to share its beauty and conserve natural resources. Start by lying down on the ground, looking up through the leaves of trees with all their beauty painted with varied colors and shapes.

Spiritual intelligence is far more complex. According to Gardner, there are problems with the 'content' of spiritual intelligence, viz., the beliefs that surround *truth* as to what it is and how we live it. For me, I am in touch with my spiritual intelligence when alone.

Existential intelligence is how we live our lives. Do we even give it a passing thought as to how and why things were like they were yesterday, today, or how they will be tomorrow? Gardner says, *"I find the phenomenon perplexing enough and the distance from the other intelligences vast enough to dictate prudence – at least for now."* These ponderings, coupled with thoughts about why people are born and why they die, are philosophical. And for many people, it seems that these passing thoughts are not considered deeply. The existential intelligence looks at more than the obvious. Why do we think what we believe and how does it fit into a broader picture of the world to purpose and meaning? Why does it matter?

Existentially intelligent individuals tend to mull over "deep" thoughts. While most people just shake these kinds of thoughts away, these existentially intelligent individuals are particularly keen about their existence and explore such questions. They also have the capacity and sensitivity to tackle thoughts about what lies beyond life and death. It has also been called spiritual or moral intelligence.

Mindy L. Kornhaber, a researcher involved with Project Zero, has identified some reasons why teachers and policymakers have responded positively to Howard Gardner's presentation of Multiple Intelligences:

"... the theory validates educators' everyday experience: students think and learn in many different ways. It also provides educators with a conceptual framework for organizing and reflecting on curriculum assessment and pedagogical practices. In turn, this reflection has led many educators to develop new approaches that might better meet the needs of the range of learners in their classrooms. "

This information will change how you look at yourself and others. It has been a giant step toward improving the human condition. Seeing is believing. Your gifts of intelligences are many! **Use them thoughtfully!** These intelligences are the cognitive processes of which I speak. Talents!

As I understand the nature of cognitive processing, it is critical to know how I think and what I do with that thinking. Pondering words I heard at an International Dyslexia Association meeting, they seem to describe the application of cognitive processing from the sensory input: acquisition, interpretation, organization, and recall. As I thought about this, I know that I can make choices with what I acquired at birth, and I can use energy in developing those gifts or talents. I can take the weaknesses with which I was born and through my strengths, I can compensate for those weaknesses. In every way, I have achieved success through pushing myself: focus, discipline, and hard work. I will try, try, and try again! So can you! Know and explore your Multiple Intelligences! From the days of childhood to the seasoned years of age, I have not yet experienced or perhaps even dreamed of treasures that could be harvested; treasures experienced that are ocean deep with reservoirs, unexplored.

My brother Charles Leslie Hoskins was bright and troubled by what he couldn't do. If only, he had celebrated that which he had done well. Hope!

148

21

Marital Relationship Nightmare:
Angry and Dumb

As I looked through my notes and my memories, I found a treasure of information. The school district sent me a new friend. Carol had asked the district for help with her daughter; I was asked to help with the situation, and I did. Well, she became a good friend as we shared the experiences of teaching her daughter. Carol opened up her heart about how life had been for her. Hard! She shared her feelings as written.

I Feel Dumb
By Carol

I feel like Inspector Jacques Clouseau in the Pink Panther shows. This show was never funny to me; I always felt sorry for him. The show was an enactment of my typical day, my week.

Here are six areas of life that presented major problems and challenges.

Memory: I cannot recall names of people and places, nor can I bring up events that others remember vividly.

Spelling: I cannot spell simple words like *flood, balance, pencil, necklace*. I have to look up everything.

Math: I can study my multiplication tables with my children and know them well one night, and they will be gone by morning.

Reading: I avoid reading everything like newspapers, instructions to a new gadget, a magazine, a book, etc. All reading seemed hard, until recently. I have a set of scriptures with large print that I can focus on and read much more easily.

Verbalizing: What I have learned in a lecture, I can understand and yet be all confused when I try to repeat it.

Organization: How I organize my time, my kitchen, my house, my desk, and my laundry, I find difficult.

I feel that if dyslexia causes a ton of problems, then the self-anger causes at least one or two more ton on top of the original problem. The anger is as destructive or more than the dyslexia itself. When I discovered that I was dyslexic, I was relieved! Happy to have a cause and relieved to have something to attack. (The reason has a label.) Something I could learn about and maybe do something to help. As I look at my life, I would not be surprised to learn that my dyslexia was a contributing factor in my divorce. I could call this story, *Relieved*.

Carol's story helps one to understand the brain and mental health. A therapist interviewed Carol, and the interview is revealing. At the conclusion, Carol was relieved to figure out that she was not crazy.

Carol is a fifty-year-old, divorced woman with dyslexia. Her problem was diagnosed one year ago as she sought help for her daughter who was struggling in school with reading, math, and English. The teacher that worked with Carol's daughter also has dyslexia and was able to detect Carol's dyslexia symptoms easily. Gently and tactfully, this teacher talked to Carol and informed her of the observations she had made.

When Carol discovered her problem was dyslexia and began to learn more about it, she related her feelings to the interviewer that she felt like "the doors of the prison, which held her in bondage—feeling dumb, burst open and for the first time since the 2nd grade; she felt free."

For nearly forty-five years she had "felt dumb, stupid, and at times worthless." She had felt so much anger and self-hatred that her self-concept had been deeply scarred. She then realized that she was not a bad person but that she had a problem, which made her life very difficult. As she learned more about dyslexia and the areas of life that are affected by it, she began to see why she and her husband had had so many problems. Approximately seven years ago her husband divorced her. She feels that her life with dyslexia influenced and in many ways caused her divorce.

Carol, like most with dyslexia, struggled in school. Her family was very loving and supportive but did not know about or understand dyslexia. While he was trying to help her read, Carol's father would at times be frustrated and impatiently say, "Come on, just read it for heaven's sake!" She was held back in 2nd grade and struggled from then on.

Math, spelling, reading, and writing were her most challenging subjects. She also had a difficult time communicating her thoughts and feelings. She felt that she had friends but was not accepted by her peers. After Carol finished high school, she went to a small college where she was forced to take freshman English three times before passing.

At about this time, Carol and her husband met and were married. Carol had been married just short of twenty years before her husband left her and filed for divorce.

In the interview, Carol described her husband as "a force mode person." She felt that his strong personality had been the cause of much pressure on her and stress in their marriage. She felt that he was demanding and expected her to accomplish his orders in a manner that was acceptable to him. His personality made him successful in his business, but his actions toward Carol caused her a lot of anxiety.

Carol's husband was elected mayor of their community until he was called to a high position in his church. He was later called to a position with a greater responsibility that took him away from home many evenings after work. He was very organized and had high expectations. He was very well respected in the community and became very wealthy.

Carol felt that she was not able to meet her husband's needs. Despite her honest efforts and intentions, she felt she just did not have the organizational capability to satisfy either his or her expectations. In social situations, Carol had trouble remembering names and communicating with people. She often could not comprehend the conversations or understand jokes. Her dyslexia affected her ability to organize herself, her home, and her affairs. She also had trouble sequencing. For example, when she started to clean the house, do the dishes, or any other task, it was necessary for her to stop and decide what she should do first. Often she started doing one thing and soon jumped to another. When her husband came home and found that she had cleaned part of the kitchen, leaving the dishes unfinished, it would drive him crazy. He felt that everything should be done in an organized and orderly fashion.

Carol also reported that time orientation was a problem for her; she was always late. She felt that to a well-organized businessman like her husband, this behavior was very unprofessional. She felt that her inability to be prompt caused her to be a constant embarrassment to her "on-time" husband.

Communication between Carol and her husband was "totally lousy." Part of the reason for this was Carol's belief that conflict was "evil." Whenever a conflict arose, she withdrew and "clammed up." From Carol's perspective, her husband believed his decisions were the ultimate source of authority in the home, which consequently minimized any input, she might have had in their discussions and decisions.

Since Carol was diagnosed with dyslexia, Carol has become aware of how this disability can negatively impair one's ability to express thoughts and feelings accurately. She is convinced that her dyslexia played a key role in confused communication. Since Carol was unable to express herself clearly, she felt that she was powerless to assert herself and reason with the domineering character of her husband. As a result, she felt that she was incapable of defending herself and her feelings.

As Carol discussed their marital discord, she began to realize how dyslexia had also influenced their sexual relationship. An emotionally satisfying sexual relationship requires the establishment of an intimate bond. Carol felt that she and her husband were unable to develop this bond partly due to Carol's inability to articulate the delicate feelings that enhance sexual intimacy. She felt that had she been a better communicator their sexual problems may not have been as severe.

152

It is obvious that in Carol's case more factors were leading up to the divorce than just dyslexia. It is also apparent that Carol's dyslexia did play a part in the marital unrest and conflicts. It would be extremely insightful to interview Carol's husband to gain information as to the frustrations and disappointments that he encountered as the spouse of a wife with dyslexia. The husband had his pathology which appeared to be high functioning in the community at large, while the spotlight stayed on Carol. Misunderstood marriage!

Had Carol's dyslexia been diagnosed earlier and had they been aware of the insights gained from this study, they might have been better able to identify and help manage the problems caused by this deficit.

Conclusions

Dyslexia is a lifelong disability that can cause innumerable problems when woven into the fabric of everyday marital life. Marriage is difficult, in and of itself, and when combined with the intricacies of dyslexia, it can produce situations, emotions, and behaviors that often are neither understood nor properly managed.

The literature on this subject is scarce. Conclusions drawn from Carol's story are rarely dealt with in the professional journals. Other reference sources may prove useful in the treatment of couples who are dealing with dyslexia.

Although many people are becoming more aware of dyslexia and its effects, there are still many who have never heard of the disability. Lesser known are the problems that frequently occur when a person having dyslexia marries a person who does not have dyslexia. As a result, couples tend to enter into marriage underestimating the impact dyslexia can have on their interpersonal relationships. They may be aware that the one spouse has a reading problem but do not realize the potential struggles in other areas with which they have to deal. If they do realize that the problem is severe; they may deny it and not seek professional help as would a couple, not in denial. It would be helpful to have a marital therapist who understands cognitive processing issues.

Dr. Gene Shumway reviewed the previous story, and his energetic response follows: "In my opinion, it is crucial, indeed imperative, that graduate schools of Social Work offer content that concentrates on cognitive processing differences. These differences in processing have a large impact on the development of personality, as well as influencing the behavior of children and adults. Knowing this information will determine how to respond to educate future clients. I hope that this material has been woven into the curriculum. I feel passionate about this subject, and the cocoon that surrounds me is beginning to crack open."

Dr. Shumway, with his over forty years of helping other people problem solve, stated emphatically, "It is clear to me that what is now known about learning differences could have been very helpful to many of the people for whom I have been a therapist. And with that, I am thankful for my field that has brought caring people together to serve the *'heavy hands that hang down.'"*

**The mix, of strengths from Multiple Intelligences, are gifts.
Find out about your cognitive gifts early in life to bring peace and hope without confusion. Precious!**

22

An Understanding Marital Therapist:
Dean Anderson, Clinical Social Worker

D ean F. Anderson is a Licensed Clinical Social Worker. He has been a practicing therapist since 1987. In 1991, he started a private practice now called "Lighthouse Counseling" and provides individual, marital and family therapy for adults and adolescents. In June 2006, Dean added Life Coaching to his repertoire of therapeutic techniques to assist individuals and couples in negotiating life and its challenges. Since 1988, Dean has also made a career at Wasatch Mental Health where he is currently the Director of the Adult Outpatient Clinic and the director of Mountain Peaks Counseling. Here he is administratively and clinically responsible for approximately thirty staff including therapists, secretaries, and Ph.D. and Masters level Graduate students. In addition to administrating the department and training therapists, he has had a career of providing thousands of hours of group, marital, and individual therapy and has developed a large number of therapeutic specialties. Dean has also been employed at LDS Family Services where he assisted the agency and LDS bishops by providing therapy and Life Coaching to individuals, couples, and families for a few hours per week. Dean also enjoys speaking and giving professional and motivational presentations. He has presented at numerous professional and religious conferences. He speaks on a variety of different topics including Trauma, Grief and Loss, Domestic Violence, Depression, Anxiety, Coping with Stress, Building and Maintaining

Emotionally Close Relationships, and Changing the Brain One Conversation at a Time.

Education and Training

After completing his Associates of Science Degree at Snow College, Dean received his Bachelors and Masters Degrees in 1985 and 1987 respectively from Brigham Young University in Social Work. He has received specialized training in Life Coaching and therapy for such issues as Life Adjustment Difficulties, Depression and Anxiety, Grief and Loss, Marital Difficulties, Post Traumatic Stress, Bipolar, Mental and Physical Disabilities, Personality Disorders, Sexual Dysfunctions, Physical, Emotional, and Sexual Abuse, and Domestic Violence.

Personal Information

Dean is blind as a result of an inherited eye disease called Retinitis Pigmentosa. This potentially debilitating eye condition has been a major catalyst for success in his life. With a tenacious work ethic, resilient attitude, and support from family and others, including personal and professional coaches, Dean is effectively negotiating life and its transitions. He is a successful businessman, Life Coach, Therapist, administrator, husband, father, and grandfather. He has been married for 31 years and has five children, two daughters-in-law, a son-in-law, and four grandchildren. His passions include traveling and spending time with his family, training, mentoring and encouraging his staff, and providing quality care for the individuals, families, and couples under his care.

Awards

In 1987, he was awarded the Joseph N. Symons Social Worker of Promise Award by the Brigham Young University Graduate School of Social Work.

In 2001, he received the Wasatch Mental Health Leadership Award.

In 2007, he was again honored by Brigham Young University School of

Social Work that presented him with the W. Eugene Gibbons Social Worker of the Year Award.

One of the threads woven into this book is what it takes for a person with dyslexia—specific language disorder to become successful in the larger and uncomprehending society within which the person with dyslexia lives. This person also has to find a way to communicate one's thoughts, needs, and feelings. It's like having an invisible broken leg that nobody can either see or understand. Its handicapping nature expects you to jump up or run like a normal person. "After all, you look normal to me, and I'm almost never wrong in my assessments."

I am grateful for Dean Anderson who shared his Publishable Paper written for the Graduate School of Social Work, *The Effects of Dyslexia on the Marital Relationship.*

The Effects of Dyslexia on the Marital Relationship
by Dean F. Anderson

Abstract

In the past several years there has been a considerable amount of research done on the subject of Dyslexia in children and how it affects them academically. In the area of adult Dyslexia, however, there appears to be little research available. Although adult dyslexics may no longer be in school, there are many areas of their lives that may be affected by this disability.

Dyslexia is a lifelong problem; dyslexics may continually struggle because of their learning disability. It appears that an association exists between the struggles a person experiences with Dyslexia in childhood and the social and interpersonal struggles the person with Dyslexia may experience as an adult.

The purpose of this paper is to develop from the related literature a list of Dyslexia-related symptoms, then to analyze the case study of a couple in which the husband is dyslexic in terms of this list. It will also be demonstrated that these symptoms negatively impacted the marital relationship. This couple experienced a period of marital dissatisfaction before the disability was diagnosed. After studied and correct diagnosis with appropriate intervention, a higher level of marital cohesiveness was developed.

Implications of this paper are given for aiding professionals in their understanding and treatment of Dyslexia and the complications it may present in marital relationships.

Introduction

In the past several years, much research has been done on Dyslexia and the impact of this disability on the way children learn. However, there has not been a great deal of focus placed on adult dyslexics and the struggles they encounter. Dyslexia not only impacts an individual's academic and scholastic functioning but also has life-long social and emotional implications.

This study will not go into detail as to what Dyslexia is neurologically or what areas of functioning it impairs in terms of the processes of academic learning. Rather it will focus on the impact of Dyslexia upon interpersonal relationships, particularly upon a single marital relationship. It will first attempt to develop a list of life-affecting Dyslexia-related symptoms. Next, it will draw up two propositions: first, that previously undiagnosed and untreated Dyslexia will contribute to marital tension and dissatisfaction, and secondly, it will show how proper diagnosis and treatment of Dyslexia may reduce marital unrest and increase marital satisfaction.

Definition of Dyslexia

Dyslexia is one of the more commonly recognized learning disabilities.
A learning disability refers to a biologically based cognitive deficit(s) that interferes with one or more of the following central nervous system processes: . . . perception, . . . cognitive and sensory processing, . . .

158

memory, . . . language or motor behavior. (Cohen 1984 page 23.)

"The word Dyslexia is made of: dys—poor or inadequate [learning or mastery of], and lexia—verbal language." Dyslexia is "a specific language difficulty." (The Orton Dyslexia Society, 1984.) Disabilities that interfere with reading, such as letter recognition, phonetic associations, perceptual discrimination, short and long-term memory, and left-right orientation, are often referred to as Dyslexia. Lenkowsky and Saposnek (1978) report that (with dyslexics) reading, spelling, and writing disabilities are not primarily caused by low intelligence, emotional disturbance, or organic deficits. It is obvious from the many other talents that dyslexics typically exhibit that the problem is not due to a lack of mental ability, nor is it due to a physical handicap except on a very subtle neurological level in the brain. *"The problem is not mental retardation. The learning-disabled youngster has average or better intelligence."* (Stevens 1984, page 15.)

A dyslexic's hearing, sight, and motor functioning develop much like other individuals'. However, the person may have trouble reading in class and may get letters mixed up, such as <u>b</u> for <u>d.</u> A person may not be able to think of the words they want to say or may get words mixed up like <u>saw</u> for <u>was</u> or <u>left</u> for <u>felt</u>.

Galaburda reports that there are neurological differences between the brains of people with and without Dyslexia. *"The left side of the brain is primarily dedicated to the areas of language, reading, writing, and arithmetic. The right side is important for certain aspects of spatial perception and for basic skills in art and music."* (Galaburda 1984) Concluded that when there is a slowing of development in the left side of the brain during fetal life, certain areas of the right side may become larger. When the development on the left side of the brain is sufficiently slow, the child can be born with Dyslexia.

This might explain why the person with Dyslexia may exhibit superior skills in the areas of art, architecture, engineering, photography, mechanics or athletics despite difficulties in learning languages and how to read or write. Psychological testing shows that dyslexic individuals are superior in the right hemisphere skills.

Dyslexia Impact: Self-Esteem, and Interpersonal Relationships

A child who has Dyslexia usually begins to feel its impact very early. As dyslexic children develop language skills, they often become frustrated with their inability to form and create sentences. When they begin to learn to read, they are further frustrated and discouraged at how difficult the task is for them while their classmates accomplish it with seeming ease.

Continuing through school, these children are often teased and put down by their peers. Their damaged self-esteem is further scarred when an insensitive teacher has them read aloud in class and calls them stupid or accuses them of being lazy because they don't know how to read.

In an effort to cope, the dyslexic person soon learns how to hide his or her dyslexia. Some children are good at hiding it, and they somehow get through high school and graduate without knowing how to read much beyond a 2nd grade level. Many students are so scarred by their failures and difficulties, as well as by the taunting and ridicule from their peers, that they drop out of school and never finish. By the time people with Dyslexia reach adulthood, the problems they face may not only be rooted in academics but also in the social, emotional, occupational, and interpersonal areas of their lives.

If dyslexics don't understand their problems, they often think they are stupid and not as good as their peers. Because of their chronic frustration and frequently poor self-concept resulting from their difficulties in communication and failure in school, many dyslexic children develop emotional and behavioral disorders. They tend to be slow, immature, emotionally unstable, aggressive, defensive and tend to act out in conflict situations. (Lenkowsky and Saposnek 1978, page 60)

The marital relationship, it is believed, offers a condition where serious problems can arise if the Dyslexia is not diagnosed and worked with properly. The problems described by Lenkowsky and Saposnek—low self-concept, frustration, behavioral disorders, slowness, immaturity, emotional instability, aggressiveness, and defensiveness—have serious implications for marital relationships.

In a case study (Lenkowsky and Saposnek 1978), it was found that the dyslexic husband struggled because of the impact that Dyslexia had on him and his family.

He continually felt inadequate, incompetent, not masculine, dependent, helpless, guilt-ridden, embarrassed, while the other family members felt imposed upon, burdened with unwanted responsibilities, and fearful of his impulsive temper. (Lenkowsky and Saposnek 1978, page 63)

On the basis of the above, the following propositions are derived.

Guiding Propositions

1. It is proposed that the presence of Dyslexia in a marital partner will contribute to an observable negative impact on the marital relationship.

2. It is proposed that the identification of Dyslexia in a marital partner followed by an educational remediation of the consequent learning disabilities will contribute to an observable positive impact on the marital relationship.

Methodology

This study will employ a case study approach to explore the impact of Dyslexia on a given marital relationship. The investigator conducted a series of interviews with a married couple who went through a period of marital dissatisfaction before it was discovered that the husband had Dyslexia. During the interview sessions, the investigator recorded the participant's backgrounds and the problems they encountered in their relationship. The sessions focused on what problems were occurring prior to the diagnosis of Dyslexia, what changes occurred in the dyslexic partner's self-concept in response to the diagnosis and treatment of Dyslexia, and whether or not there was an increase in perceived marital satisfaction for each of the partners.

The table below contains some of the primary characteristics that a person with Dyslexia exhibits; these will be the focus of this study (i.e., Lenkowsy and Saposnek 1978, Stevens 1984, Galaburda 1984, Cohen 1984)

Table 1. Potentially disabling elements in Dyslexia as manifested in interpersonal relationships. **Characterized in the dyslexic spouse.**

Primary Elements
1. Reading
2. Writing
3. Organizing
4. Sequencing
5. Mathematics
6. Mental Processing
7. Time Orientation
8. Memory
9. Language
10. Motor Skills
11. Articulating Feelings
12. Communicative Skills

Secondary Elements
1. Low Self-Esteem
2. Risk-Taking
3. Frustration and Anger
4. Denial
5. Slowness
6. Immaturity
7. Emotional Instability

8. Aggressiveness
9. Defensiveness
10. Inadequacy
11. Incompetency
12. Not masculine
13. Dependency
14. Helplessness
15. Guilt
16. Embarrassment

Table 2.   Potentially disabling elements in Dyslexia as manifested in interpersonal relationship. Characterized in the non-dyslexic spouse.
1. Imposed Upon
2. Burdened
3. Fearful of the Dyslexic Spouse's Impulsive Temper

Limitations

A single case study, particularly one limited to a few hours of interviewing, does not result in the convincing proof that may be obtained in a statistical analysis with a large number in the sample. This study is further limited by the fact that it is a *post hoc* analysis. The marital partners were asked to reach back in their memory to identify the way things were both before and after the diagnosis and treatment of Dyslexia. There were no objective data except for a measurement of reading ability at the beginning and end of the educational intervention.

Case Presentation

Stan is a thirty-nine-year-old male who was born in a small rural community. Just hours after his birth Stan's mother died of complications from diabetes and toxemia. Stan was his parents' third child. The first child died in infancy. The second child was raised by grandparents, and Stan was reared by an aunt and uncle in a family with six children. All six children were blond and fair-skinned while Stan had dark hair and a dark complexion. Despite the physical differences, Stan felt like he was well-accepted and felt a part of the family very much.

Stan and his new family lived on a farm for several years until they moved to work in a steel mill. After graduating from high school, he completed two years of vocational training in cabinet millwork. After finishing his vocational training, he began working in the steel mill where he was employed for eighteen years before being laid-off due to the mill's closure.

Stan's wife Jane is a thirty-eight-year-old female. She was born to a family of seven children. Her father was a county commissioner for several years before beginning a career in teaching. Upon her graduation from high school, she earned a B. S. degree in elementary education at a university near her home. She is currently attending another university part-time working on a master's degree in education.

Stan and Jane met at a dance while Jane was attending a university. They were engaged three months after they met and were married one year later. For nine months of their engagement, Jane taught school in another state. During the time Jane was away, the two communicated through letters. Jane noticed that Stan had difficulty with writing and spelling, but she did not think much about it. After their marriage, Jane quit her job teaching, and the two lived near the steel mill where Stan worked. They currently have three children: two boys and one girl.

In our interview, Jane proudly informed me that Stan had built the house they were living in by himself. It was obvious that Stan is a gifted carpenter and builder. In his backyard, Stan has a carpenter's shop where he says he likes to go to get away. He explained that his shop is his escape where he can go and feel he is in control. In it, he can be alone and get away from the pressure of social situations; the things he creates in his shop make him feel good about himself.

Elementary school was extremely difficult for Stan. He reported that he struggled with learning to read and was frustrated because it was so difficult. When his family moved to the larger community, he began junior high school. It was here he realized he "could not read or write." He knew reading in elementary school had been difficult, but it was not until junior high that it dawned on him that he really had a problem. Stan indicated that math was fairly easy for him; however, because of his reading difficulty in high school, he was continually placed in remedial reading programs and did not take the English classes offered by the school.

Reading in front of a class or just being asked to read out loud appeared to have been the hardest and most embarrassing thing for Stan. He reports that he would do everything he could to get away from having to read in front of people. The few times he did read aloud and was laughed at by the other students was enough to keep him from ever wanting to read aloud again. Once he took a Spanish class, but he lasted in it for two weeks.

Stan's family was supportive of him, but they were not aware of the seriousness of his problem. Stan reports that his family avoided discussing unpleasant things. Stan's parents felt that if you do not talk about a problem, it will not be a problem. Consequently, Stan learned to deal with his problems in much the same way.

Wood-shop was Stan's favorite subject, and he became very skilled. He also was successful in sports and athletic activities. Although he did not play ball for his high school, he did play on many city and church teams. It was through athletics that Stan developed a few good friends who provided strong support for him in school. He reports that he is still close to many of these friends. He also felt that he lived in a good neighborhood which provided him with some good friends. Because Stan was shy around girls, most of his friends were boys.

Jane reported that she did very well in school. She did so well in high school that she was able to graduate one year early. To do this, she had to take extra classes in languages, history, and science. Languages, such as

German, were her favorite subjects. She felt that the university was easy compared to how hard she worked in high school. She was admitted to the university on a scholarship which she kept for two years. She is currently in graduate school and feels that she is able to do the work with relative ease.

Jane, like Stan, was a little shy around the opposite sex. She always felt that she was a little overweight which made her feel uncomfortable. In talking about his wife, Stan was proud to say that she is very talented, especially in arts and crafts. Balancing the checkbook was the only thing that either of them could think of that she did poorly.

Although Stan and Jane have certain similarities, such as their creative abilities, they have more differences than similarities. Not only do they differ in their academic abilities, but their attitudes about travel are also very different from one another. Jane loves to travel and has traveled extensively in the United States and in many other parts of the world. Stan does not like to travel, and he usually stays at home to spend time in his shop or do something else for which he feels good. This situation has proven to be a source of stress in their marriage.

Another source of stress was the differences in their social preferences. Stan was not as fond of parties and social gatherings as Jane was. She really enjoyed getting out and mingling with others. Stan, on the other hand, felt very insecure about meeting and talking to people he did not know.

With each passing year, Stan and Jane grew further and further apart. The differences that they experienced began to work like a wedge that split and separated them. Stan spent most of his time either at work or in his shop building cabinets. Jane spent most of her time with the children, doing arts and crafts, studying, or traveling. Even though they were both good with their hands, they could not work together on projects. Stan felt there was only one way of doing things. Jane felt that projects could be done another way. Even simple projects, such as doing the dishes, had been an area of conflict for them. They each had different styles and techniques for getting the job done. *Stan saw the whole of a task while Jane saw the parts.* When they worked together on problems, their efforts were often counterproductive. It did not take them long to realize that they had conflicting ways of processing things in their minds.

These problems were further complicated by the frustrations they experienced because of Stan's reading problem. When they would go to restaurants, Jane would often have to read the menu to Stan. When Stan tried to read the newspaper, he usually asked for Jane's help in reading some words. Stan not only had a difficult time in reading, but he also had difficulty *sequencing* things. Looking things up in the dictionary or using the alphabet was a continual problem for him.

Stan belongs to a church, which has a lay ministry, wherein the members are expected to participate. This has created stress for Stan. He dreaded getting up in front of the congregation to speak. He learned to skirt around this problem by only going to church every other Sunday so as not to have an assignment for the next week. He avoided having to read scriptures in front of others by not taking his scriptures to church. When their first child was born, Stan was petrified to go up in front of the congregation and give the infant a blessing. He was also asked to be a Boy Scout leader that he enjoyed until he was asked to give a training presentation to other adult scout leaders. Having to read and write things on the chalkboard was terrifying for him. Stan's avoidance behavior was interpreted by his religious wife as a lack of religious commitment, which created further marital tension and dissatisfaction.

Although math was not a real problem for him, Stan often incorrectly wrote numbers. For example, in writing checks, he would write the check out for the wrong amount. This was very frustrating for him. Jane reported that she is not good at math and cannot balance the checkbook. As a result, Stan had to do it despite his occasional numerical misprinting.

Despite troubles in other areas of his life, Stan had been successful in his work at the steel mill and had always been a good worker and a dependable provider. However, about four years ago, Stan was laid off from his job because of the mill's closure. This presented another stressful situation for Jane and Stan. Although Stan was a good worker, he could not fill out job applications. He and Jane were both frustrated because of his inability to read the application, but also because there were many jobs that he could not be hired for because of his reading deficiency. Fortunately, Stan was called back to work before the unemployment benefits ran out.

As was stated earlier, Jane was aware that Stan had difficulties in reading and writing. In his letters to her during their engagement, she noticed that Stan had trouble spelling and would often use a word incorrectly. Stan, of course, knew that he had problems with reading and writing, but neither he nor Jane ever talked about it. Neither of them realized the seriousness of the problem and both went through a period of denial. When they had been married about four years, Jane began working with the adult reading program. It was here she realized that Stan's problem was more serious than she had previously thought. She tested Stan's reading and found that it was at about a 2nd grade level. When Jane realized the severity of Stan's problem, she tried to help him improve his reading. This turned out to be extremely difficult for both of them. Jane worked hard to help Stan, but he seemed to resist her efforts. He felt like he was revealing a deep and hidden secret that he did not want anyone to know. He was afraid and intimidated by his inferiority to Jane's academic superiority. He felt that she thought less of him and he did not know how to deal with that. Stan had a difficult time dealing with the discrepancy between his and Jane's reading levels. The experience of Jane teaching Stan to read was so stressful for both of them that they dropped the subject and did not face it again for many years. Once more, they denied the problem.

Time orientation has played a troublesome role in Stan and Jane's relationship. When they were dating Stan would always be a few minutes late. This bothered Jane. Even today when the two of them are late, it is usually a result of Stan not being ready. Jane also complained that Stan would go out to his shop to do some work or cleaning. Later, Jane would go out to find that he had accomplished only a small part of what she thought could have been done in that amount of time.

When Stan was laid off from the steel mill, he and Jane thought that he might have to be self-employed building cabinets. Jane knew that this was not a good option since he did not use his time efficiently. Jane was frustrated by the thought of her husband not being able to provide for their family. Jane was so upset by these concerns that she began to have physical symptoms of stress, such as asthma, indigestion, and diabetes.

In addition to problems with time, Stan also had great difficulty in taking messages over the phone. Often when someone would call and want to leave a message, he would not write it down and would then forget to tell Jane that someone had called. Stan and Jane then set up a system where Stan could write the message on a piece of paper. Since Stan has such poor spelling and writing skills, this method of taking messages was not much more effective.

Communication between Stan and Jane has been a problem as well. Stan can communicate quite well with most people on a superficial level; however, when he tries to express something at a deeper level or in any detail, his speech is cumbersome and vague. He knows what he is thinking and feeling and what he wants to communicate, but often the words just do not come out right. This has been very frustrating for Jane, who is a well-educated person and feels a need to talk about personal feelings and to have intellectual conversations.

Expressing himself has been very difficult for Stan. In interviewing them, questions were directed to Stan that Jane immediately answered. Jane's answering for Stan has apparently become a habit.

At times Jane feels burdened by the problems that she and Stan have encountered. She has even felt somewhat betrayed because Stan did not inform her of the seriousness of his problem. As her children grow up, she sees them, especially the boys, struggling with the same problems Stan faces.

Jane struggled with her inability to help either Stan or their children. In her words, "It is one thing to see your husband fighting to survive, but it is another to see your children struggle as well." She feels "trapped and extremely frustrated," realizing that this is a problem that will never go away—this is the way it will always be.

It seemed that every area of their marriage had problems, intimacy and sex were no exceptions. For years Jane felt inadequate as a sexual partner because she was not able to turn on sexually. She wanted to be able to turn on and enjoy sex, but she felt that she was incapable of it. As a result, she tended to avoid sex with Stan, felt guilty, and at times angry, that she could not satisfy either Stan or herself sexually. Stan also felt hurt and rejected.

After fourteen years of marriage, their many problems wedged deep into their relationship. The only thing that held the marriage together was the freedom that they gave each other and the bonds they shared as parents who had lived together for fourteen years.

In giving each other freedom, Stan allowed Jane to go on all the trips, to work on all the crafts, and to have all the educational stimulation that she wanted; Jane allowed Stan the freedom to spend as much time in his shop as he wanted and did not force him to go on vacations with her. Their relationship deteriorated to the point that it became two separate parents existing in the same house, seldom seeing each other and almost never spending any time together.

It was while on a twenty-five day trip to Europe that Jane stepped back and took a good look at their relationship. As she evaluated the past fourteen years, she realized more completely the extent of the pain and problems she had been experiencing. She felt this pain more intensely than ever before and knew that things had to change or she could not continue in the marriage.

Originally, Stan had planned to go to Europe with Jane. Shortly before they were to leave Stan decided not to go. Jane asked if she could go, even though he did not want to. Stan consented but resented it when she actually left. While Jane was gone, Stan's resentment increased. He had previously been willing to let her go on vacations, but he always had an unspoken feeling of resentment about her going without him.

When Jane returned from her trip to Europe, Stan told her that the next time she left either he was going with her, or he would not be home when she returned. They both realized that the marriage could not continue without something being done.

It was soon after this that they sought professional help from a marriage counselor. The counselor began working with them on communication. Through this, they realized that Jane needed to have not only someone that could communicate on an intellectual level but an intimate level as well. To this point, Stan had been incapable of fulfilling either of these.

Stan knew that if he didn't make some changes, he would lose everything he had—his wife, his children, and his home. At this point, he made a commitment to do all he could to turn things around.

In his efforts to improve his marriage, Stan determined to improve his reading skills and go on more vacations with Jane. By doing this, he hoped to be better able to fulfill Jane's intellectual needs. He also hoped to increase their mutual interests and give them more to talk about.

Committing to go on more vacations was very difficult for Stan. Traveling was extremely frightening to him. He did not like to go very far from home, or from the area with which he was familiar. His fear was almost phobic.

In talking with the counselor, Stan related his reading difficulties and asked if he knew of anyone who could assist him in learning to read better. The counselor sought help from the local school district. Stan was referred to a professional teacher who works primarily with adults to help them improve their reading skills. This was the step that began to turn things around for Stan, Jane, and their marriage.

It did not take this teacher very long to determine that Stan had Dyslexia. Stan wondered what Dyslexia was and what could be done about it. With the teacher's help, Stan and his family began to understand Dyslexia. They also attended a workshop on Dyslexia, which was given at a local university by Dr. Drake Duane and the Slingerland Institute. The workshop furthered their knowledge, not only about academic aspects of the disability but social and interpersonal aspects as well.

Stan was relieved by the new knowledge he had gained about his problem. There had been so many feelings that he had kept inside and had not expressed or dealt with that he could now face and confront. Previously, he had felt very inadequate and even helpless.

Stan and Jane's knowledge and understanding of Dyslexia increased; Jane became more empathetic toward Stan and his problem. For years, Stan had tried to hide the problem from his wife, family, friends, and colleagues. But now he did not have to hide the problem as much; he no longer felt that he was stupid. Now, he knew he was a smart person who, because of a learning disability over which he had no physical control, was kept from learning and developing in many areas. Now, he understood why his thoughts, which were clear in his mind, were poorly articulated. This new knowledge gave him a feeling of freedom, excitement, and hope. In addition to being more empathetic, Jane began to be more patient, supportive, loving, and helpful. With his new inner-strength and his wife's support, Stan began to feel more confident that he could make some changes that would help him feel better as a person, as a husband, and as a father.

Stan and Jane learned more about Dyslexia; it became apparent how Stan's disability had affected nearly all parts of his life and had played a major role in shaping his personality. For example, they recognized Stan's pattern of spending a lot of time in his shop as a defense mechanism. It was his escape from having to communicate with other people. They also saw that his resistance to attending parties and social events was not an anti-social behavior, but it was caused by his fear of being embarrassed by his poor speech.

Stan's hermit-like behavior concerning travel had an explanation. Stan dreaded going on trips with his wife, not because he did not like to be with her or because he disliked traveling, but because he was afraid of getting lost or finding himself out of control. Since he could not read signs or maps, he would often experience panic attacks when he found himself away from home and unable to find his way back.

It appeared that even their sexual problem was affected by Dyslexia. Where Jane had previously blamed herself for being an inadequate partner she now understood the problem was an outgrowth of their inability to communicate effectively on any level. It seems Jane felt alienated physically from her husband because in other aspects of their life together she was not receiving the emotional and intellectual nurturing she needed to make their relationship complete. Had Stan felt adequate in communicating with Jane on a similar intellectual plane, she might have felt an increase in overall closeness that would have contributed significantly to their sexual relationship.

Jane felt a solution to the problem might include increased intellectual stimulation between them, which would help improve their relationship and would consequently carry over into their sexual relationship as well.

The reading teacher working with Stan understood Dyslexia very well and helped Stan substantially improve his reading. In January she gave Stan a "SORT" test (a reading inventory). The results showed that he read at about a 4th grade, second-month level. The following September she gave him the same test and found he was reading at a 5th grade, 3rd month level. As his reading ability improved, his self-esteem also improved. He is excited to be able to read at a higher level than ever before.

Since the diagnosis of Stan's Dyslexia, he and Jane have been facing the problem. They no longer try to deny the disability. As a result, they are spending more time together, trying to find new ways of coping with the problem. Both spouses have suffered because of the problem and both need each other's support. Since they have been spending more time working, playing, traveling, and coping together, they have become closer as friends and as a couple. This is not to say that everything is solved and their marriage is perfect, but it has improved considerably.

Testing of the Propositions

Dyslexia is a lifelong disability that can cause innumerable problems when woven into the fabric of everyday marital life. Marriage is a difficult proposition in and of itself, and when combined with the intricacies of Dyslexia, can produce situations, emotions, and behaviors that often are neither understood nor properly treated.

Although the literature on this subject is very scarce, a list of Dyslexia related symptoms was compiled based on the few articles found in the literature and two tables were drawn.

Table 3.   Testing of guiding propositions # 1.
Testing of Table 2.

Manifested

1. Imposed Upon

2. Burdened

Not Manifested

3. Fearful of Dyslexic Spouse's Impulsive Temper

Although fear of the spouse's impulsive temper was not manifest in this couple, a guiding proposition # 1 was substantiated.

Table 4.   Testing of guiding proposition # 2.
New feelings Stan and Jane experienced as their knowledge of Dyslexia increased.

Stan

1. Freedom

2. Excitement

3. Hope

4. Confidence

Jane

1. Empathy

2. Patience

3. Support

4. Love

5. Helpfulness

After the diagnosis and remediation of Dyslexia, both Stan and Jane gained an understanding of why Stan was having his problems (i.e., spending time in his shop, resistance to going to parties, fear of travel, speaking in front of groups) as well as why Jane was experiencing her problems (i.e., lack of emotional and intellectual nurturing, sexual alienation). As a result, both are spending more time together and have expressed experiencing an increase in their marital satisfaction. Therefore, guiding proposition # 2 has been substantiated.

Findings

All primary and secondary elements found in Table 1 were substantiated with the following exceptions.

Table 5.   Primary and Secondary Elements Not Found in the Case study.

Primary Elements

1. Sequencing

2. Memory

3. Motor Skills

 Secondary Elements

1. Emotional Instability

2. Aggressiveness

3. Unmasculinity

Those primary elements in Table 5 may not have been manifested due to Stan's vocational training and skills. Those secondary elements in Table 5 may not have been manifested because they were not adequately defined in the literature. For example, is it possible that while some dyslexics vent their frustrations against others, some vent them against themselves? Thus, impulsive temper (Table 2) may tend to become depression.

Unmasculinity could be challenged on the basis of sexual and cultural bias. For example, does unmasculinity refer only to those who are effeminate or does being inadequate also imply unmasculinity?

In the case of aggression, the question can be raised, is it always aggressiveness that the wife fears or could it be the shifting of the various types of moods that the dyslexic experiences?

In addition to those findings already discussed, several potentially disabling elements were identified in both the dyslexic and no-dyslexic spouse. These elements are summarized in the following table.

Table 6.   Potentially disabling elements were found in the case but were not found in tables 1 and 2.

Dyslexic Spouse

1. Unassertive
2. Intimacy (Failure to become Intimate)

Non-dyslexic Spouse

1. Betrayed
2. Bitter
3. Trapped
4. Frustration
5. Cheated
6. Intimacy
7. Anger

The nature of these nine elements was found to contribute to marital dissatisfaction.

Conclusion

Conclusions drawn from this study, which are rarely dealt with in the professional journals and other reference sources and which may prove useful in the treatment of dyslexic couples, are summarized below. The elements found in Tables 1 and 2 will be used to measure the impact that Dyslexia had on the marital relationship in the case study, both on the dyslexic and the non-dyslexic spouse.

Reading: Where one spouse has a reading problem, the couple may not understand that it is Dyslexia and the potential struggles they may confront because of the disability. The inability to read affects every aspect of the dyslexic's life including vocation and leisure activities.

Writing: When there is a wide discrepancy between the academic levels of the spouses, conflicts may arise. This is especially true for a dyslexic couple since the spouse with Dyslexia is less able to improve his academic ability.

Organizing: As a result of the dyslexic's inability to organize their time, tasks, and thoughts they may not be seen to be as efficient as non-dyslexics.

Sequencing: As was shown in Table 5 sequencing was not found to be in this case.

Mathematics: Depending on the severity of the Dyslexia, a person may find himself unable to perform such tasks as balancing the family checkbook, reading bills, or other tasks involving mathematics.

Mental Processing: Dyslexics are generally right-brained people. Right brain or left brain theory suggests that the right-brained person sees the "whole" of a given situation whereas a left-brained person tends to see the parts which make up the whole (Stevens 1984). A right-brained dyslexic who marries a left-brained non-dyslexic may find the differences in lifestyle can lead to conflict and disagreements.

Time Orientation: The dyslexic's apparent lack of awareness of time can be very frustrating to a time-conscious spouse. Not only does the dyslexic have trouble being punctual but may also have an inability to use time efficiently.

Memory: As was shown in Table 5, memory problems were not found to be present in this case.

Language: Since the dyslexic has difficulty taking messages, the non-dyslexic spouse may become frustrated and angry when his or her companion fails to record and relay the information accurately.

Motor Skills: As was shown in Table 5, difficulties with motor skills were not found to be present in this case.

Articulating Feelings: In a marriage where one spouse is dyslexic, one of the most predominant problems that confront the couple is communication. Since the dyslexic has difficulty articulating thoughts and feelings, the couple is often unable to develop a close intimate relationship, which is an essential ingredient of a satisfying sexual and marital bond.

Communicative Skills: The non-dyslexic spouses may assert themselves to answer questions directed to the dyslexic. This pattern is established to save each of them from embarrassment due to the dyslexic's impaired communicative skills.

Low Self-Esteem: As a result of the dyslexic's continual frustration, discouragement, and failures during growing up years they suffer from low self-esteem. When a person has self-esteem problems, they will not have the inner strength to reach out and nurture the spouse. This, in turn, creates a further sense of isolation and alienation.

Risk-Taking: Those with Dyslexia have continuing embarrassment and frustration, he may try to avoid occupational, religious, or public positions that would require reading or speaking in front of people. This behavior is sometimes seen as a lack of motivation or extreme shyness to a spouse who feels that it is important to be a leader in these areas. As a result of inability to read signs and maps, the dyslexic may feel apprehensive about traveling for fear of becoming lost. If the spouse enjoys traveling, there may be disagreements on whether they should go or not.

Frustration and Anger: The chronic frustrations a dyslexic experiences may lead to taking these frustrations out on his wife and children in the form of verbal or physical abuse or to turn the anger inward, which is depression.

Denial: If the couple does realize that the problem of Dyslexia is severe, they may deny it and not seek professional help as would a couple where one of the spouses has a more obvious disability.

Slowness: Those with dyslexia have an inability to organize time and carry out tasks efficiently, they often accomplish work at a slow pace.

Immaturity: This concept can be inferred from many of the elements discussed, for example, denial.

Emotional Instability: As was shown in Table 5, emotional instability was not found to be present in this case.

Aggressiveness: As was shown in Table 5, aggressiveness was not found to be present in this case.

Defensiveness: When the spouses of dyslexics recognize that their companions have problems, they may want to assist them. The dyslexic spouse may become defensive and interpret the action as an act of superiority.

Inadequacy: If the dyslexic feels inferior, they will feel uncomfortable going to parties and other social activities. This behavior can be very frustrating to a spouse and may be a source of conflict.

Incompetency: Due to the disability of low self-esteem and frustration, this individual may feel inadequate and incompetent in fulfilling his or her perceived roles.

Unmasculinity: As was shown in Table 5, unmasculinity was not found to be present in this case.

Dependency: Considering that the dyslexic cannot read they may become dependent on other people. The person may have to rely on his wife to perform such tasks as balancing the checkbook, reading menus, writing letters, and so on. If his wife does not handle the situation with empathy, it can lead to further contention.

Helplessness: It would appear that in the case of some dyslexics, the fear of traveling is so intense they develop phobia-like characteristics. These characteristics may appear in the form of "panic attacks" when the dyslexic is helpless in unfamiliar surroundings and feels unable to find the way. Feelings of helplessness may also be compounded by inability to read, write, and communicate adequately.

Guilt: The dyslexic may feel guilt as a result of the inability to read, write, communicate, or fulfill perceived roles.

Embarrassment: Due to many disabling symptoms, the dyslexic may feel embarrassed to attend parties, deliver presentations before an audience, or even allow other to know about their impairment.

Recommendations for Clinicians

A couple can manage the problems that Dyslexia creates in marriage if each spouse will be creative and willing to try innovative techniques that can help them overcome their challenges. A few examples of these techniques are:

A. When a dyslexic must give a presentation to an audience, instead of writing on a chalkboard, someone can help prepare written posters in advance. These posters can be displayed instead of writing on the board. The person will then be free to concentrate on organizing and expressing thoughts. A tape recorder can be used to minimize the need for written notes. It may also be used to prompt and cue as to what will be covered in the next presentation.

B. Using a tape recorder can also help in taking messages. Recording the information immediately after receiving a phone call can be an effective way of taking accurate messages.

C. The fear of traveling can be mitigated if the couple will spend time together making vacation plans far in advance. By studying maps and other travel literature, the dyslexic can become familiar with the roads and areas where they will be traveling; this will help the person feel more comfortable and secure. The spouse can update as to where they were, where they are, and where they are going.

Since the study of Dyslexia in the marital relationship is a relatively unexplored area of Dyslexia research, the conclusions derived from this study are not all-inclusive. However, these observations were made from interviews with people who were experiencing the difficulties Dyslexia posed in their marriage. These findings warrant consideration from researchers, practitioners, and educators who work with and treat dyslexics.

Dyslexia is presently incurable; it does not pose insurmountable obstacles. Through the help of trained professionals and personal creativity, the barriers that Dyslexia produces in a marriage can be overcome.

Recommendations for Further Research

To increase the knowledge base concerning Dyslexia, professionals may find it beneficial to obtain a large number of couples having marital problems. After screening them for Dyslexia, empirical studies may be used in the form of pre-test and post-tests, to determine the statistical significance or insignificance of Dyslexia's impact on marital relationships. Further research may also include investigations into the feelings and attitudes of the non-dyslexic spouse.

Thank You, Dean Anderson!

If we desire to teach appropriate behaviors and get results, we must first apply appropriate behavior to our lives. I found this tearful piece of paper wadded in a grocery cart. Why was I crying in the store? This child needs help with academic skills, and his heart was emotionally crying for help. Where is this child? Who could help?

Dr. Shumway said he felt he never had a day long enough while practicing Social Work. He was rewarded for his *living the walk* to succor the weak, lift up the hands which hang down and strengthen the feeble knees.

I stepped off the plane from having been to an International Dyslexia Association conference and greeted my world, "It is real, it is real! The brain is unique with different patterns." Dr. Shumway replied, "I know, I live in a nest of them."

23

Gaps in Academic Knowledge:
Dr. E. Gene Shumway, Professor,
Clinical Social Worker

D r. Shumway maintained a personal vision for the School of Social Work at Brigham Young University and contributed in numerous ways to the program. He earned his Doctorate at Case Western Reserve University in Cleveland, Ohio. He chose Case Western because it had one of the oldest and most respected schools of social work in the country.

As I wrote this book, Dr. Shumway and I visited about labeling. He wrote his dissertation on this subject in a unique way. For example, if a person ever becomes a patient in a mental hospital, upon his or her discharge from the hospital, the label *mental patient* follows for what seems to be forever. Dr. Shumway's dissertation which is entitled *Mental Patients' Role Conceptions* can be found at the Case Western Reserve University Social Work Library. In our society, labeling is a problem that extends far beyond the province of education.

Dr. Shumway was specifically recruited in anticipation of a master's degree in social work at Brigham Young University. In collaboration with the program director Dr. Gene Gibbons, Dr. Barbara Wheeler, and Dr. Shumway worked smoothly together as they designed and built each aspect of the program. It subsequently became fully accredited by the Council on Social Work Education. Previously, Dr. Shumway had the responsibility of helping to design the doctoral program for the School of Social Work at the University of Utah where both Dr. Gibbons and

Dr. Wheeler received their doctorates.

I am grateful for the knowledge and wisdom that I have gained from Dr. Shumway. His insightful suggestions have been of value while writing this book.

A Piece of the Puzzle
By Gene Shumway

A major thesis of this book is that our educational system, from the ground up, has been designed to be congruent with the typical brain functioning of most people. This educational system leaves many of the brightest and most uniquely creative among us drifting ever more deeply into confusion about what is expected of them and how to respond to it. The emergence of such questions about how one fits into the larger society can open up feelings of inadequacy and self-doubt. This matrix of questions and feelings can, in turn, unleash corollary feelings of resentment, as well as aggressive behaviors.

For about forty years, spanning from 1953-91, I served society as a social worker and a social work educator. This experience also included at least three decades of part-time private practice.

Argie Ella has written, *Please Don't Call Me Dumb!* It has profound implications for service providers and educators on every level in every profession. During my years of service to individuals and of teaching graduate students, I was only tangentially aware of what is in this book about how people learn and the impact that cognitive processing challenges can have on personality development, as well as on how we learn. Indeed, a great deal of what is known at the time of this writing was not known by the time I formally retired in 1991. In the year 1951-1952, during my first year of graduate study in social work at the University of Utah, my fieldwork practicum included spending two and a half days per week in the Jordan School District. I was supervised and instructed by one of the three experienced school social workers.

Finishing my master's degree in Social Work in June of 1953, I then spent fourteen months as a child welfare worker in Missoula, Montana. At the end of my thirteenth month, I was surprised by a telephone call from Claude Pratt, Superintendent of the Utah State Industrial School in Ogden, offering me a full-time job in juvenile corrections. Having spent my second year of fieldwork training in the Second District Juvenile Court in Salt Lake City, I felt very amenable to this offer and accepted it. I believe that I was competent as a juvenile corrections social worker, but if I had known more about how the brain processes information, it would have been very helpful. The social study that I wrote about each student stuck to the usual information about home and family, the student's progress in school, and a report about the individual's behavior in the community. Hmmm! A vast amount was not known or even alluded to in the social work literature about how the brain is structured and how its unique functioning contributes to the overall development of personality. The Utah State Industrial School's Clinical Psychologist shared valuable psychological information and his astute observations about the students on my caseload. His name was John Cambarreri, and I recall that he had a keen interest in the human brain and its functioning, but I am amazed to see how much has been learned since the mid-1950s. I am wondering if this same gap still exists in our correctional institutions be they for children, youth or adults. I suspect that a great deal of valuable information and penetrating insights are still "locked up," so to speak, in the departments of Educational Psychology and Clinical Psychology, without filtering into the social justice system where "the rubber meets the road."

I am now amazed as I reflect upon the pieces of information which were not present in my head, or even talked about with my colleagues, as I wrote all those "social studies" and counseled with literally hundreds of children and adults. My heart was there, but much information was not present in my head.

During the many hours, I spent untold hours making arrangements with families, schools, and community resources for the return of these young "juvenile delinquents" to the community. It is not without regret that our team's thinking about the whole picture for success did not apparently take into account the complexity of the brain with its Multiple Intelligences.

The terms "juvenile delinquent," "criminal," and "mental patient" constitute labels that society firmly attaches to individuals. These labels tend to be exclusionary rather than inclusionary. Societal expectations for a person must be centered around the positive picture of whom they are and what they may become not the negative image of a label. It is important that we see the person entering the community with positive energy rooted in strengths. In short, we must focus on the whole person and not the label. My dissertation was entitled, *The Effects of Rehabilitation Program Structure on Mental Patients' Role Conceptions.* (Case Western Reserve University 1969)

The point is that we go through life, taking on certain social roles according to the work we do, the relationships we develop, and assignments given to us, as well as the positions we accept. If we choose to engage in antisocial behaviors, society attaches negative labels which may be difficult to dislodge.

In 1955, I was working with adolescents in a correctional setting that was an enriching experience. It began with the process of helping them adapt to living in an institution and benefiting from whatever that environment offered, at the same time reflecting on what residing in the community had been like for them. Examining the various streams of thinking, feeling, and behaving, which had brought them as a "troubled child" into an institutional living, needed a serious look. Their present experiences morphed into preparation for the return to their homes, family life, and the community. Home visits then became the focal point in preparing for discharge.

Understanding organizational skills around the cognitive processing of the brain would have been helpful. The question would have been: "Does this individual initially see the world in parts or the whole

186

picture?" Analyzing the organizational skills to be accomplished and how to approach the task, step-by-step to achieve the goal, is a salient point to consider. If the adolescents had been observed for challenges in their academic world and the appropriate interventions in place to compensate for their weaknesses, would life have been different?

Teaching with the brain's cognitive strengths to understand the whole task with its parts for organization skills is the needed objective.

During the first few years of my professional career, for some unknown reason, I carried an assumption in the back of my mind that someday I would become a teacher in a school of social work. This unexplored but seminal thought included a corollary assumption that it would be well for me to gather as much experience across the fields of social work practice as possible. After spending a year in the field of juvenile corrections, I worked for a year as a caseworker at the Family Service Society in Salt Lake City. The next surprise was a job offer from the Primary Children's Hospital in Salt Lake City. After a year as a medical social worker, I accepted a job as a School Social Worker in the Salt Lake City School District. By this time (1957) it occurred to me that it was time to quit job-hopping, so I settled in for three years.

It was in the late 1960s, in the middle of my active career, when I became somewhat aware that research was being done on brain damage and its impact on personality development and individual behavior. We've come a long way since then. Good!

In 1982, I married a teacher who was trained in Special Education, as well as in Regular Education. She also had personal challenges with brain processing. I became usefully familiar with the range of difficulties in cognitive processing and its impact on the larger society within which we live. These experiences ignited a whole new bulb in my brain. Grateful!

If what we know now about cognitive processing and its impact on human relationships and behavior had been common knowledge during the last half of the twentieth century, I am stunned by how much more effective I could have been. What is of even more interest to me is that this particular state of ignorance was still widespread among the various professions when I formally retired.

Across the span of many years, while serving the welfare of many from the elementary school age child to married couples, I know that my Social Work energy was rewarded with success. At the age of 92 years, I occasionally receive kind words from those I helped. My field has been challenging but never was a day long enough. However, I know that the interventions would have been more focused had I known to incorporate data from Neuroscience in the effort to understand cognitive processing and the gift of Multiple Intelligences. The door is slowly opening to more information from practice, research, and education giving us an awareness of how the brain develops and functions. This information lends itself to a better understanding of psychological and social processes and hence to more effective social work practice.

The point of this story is what I have discovered with Argie Ella's help that people learn in different ways. By and large, our educational system is structured and implemented by individuals who operate primarily out of the left hemisphere of the brain. That is to say that their thinking is very organized, very logical, and very detailed. Some students, including myself, come to this system also operating from the right hemisphere, which is to say that we prefer to look at things first from the perspective of the whole, i.e., intuitively and globally. Details and the logical progression of analysis can become very confusing. In my case, I have instinctively compensated by looking at details as though they were under a microscope, which leaves me vulnerable to getting lost in the details and never getting around to even covering the *whole,* much less putting it together in an integrated way.

These mechanisms, linked with personality variables that might be described as somewhat *compulsive* and an overarching kind of mild anxiety have made it difficult to acquire a formal education. It also means that when the formal elements of my education came to an end, the informal learning was carried on largely without books. I have had an intensely felt need to buy books and journals and have them around me. I have always known how valuable and desirable it is to learn by reading and studying. I also know how painful it has been to do this. I have spent thousands of dollars on books of all kinds and do read around *in* them some, but I rarely feel that I can justify the time it takes to read the entire book. The exceptions to this ragged reading are novels and biographies. I have read the biographies of many of the founding fathers of this country and loved them. I've also enjoyed reading a wide variety of other biographies and thoroughly enjoyed them. One consequence of my brain functioning business is that I read very slowly, laboriously, and rarely finish a book unless it is perceived to be of vital importance. I choose books to read that are important to me and those I finish.

The twenty-eight years preceding my retirement in 1990 were spent in teaching with three years away for doctoral studies. My learning has come primarily from observing, intensely listening, direct experience, and interlaced with reading. This experience has left me vulnerable to high anxiety while functioning within an educational environment. Some things are apprehended intuitively on a very deep level.

Thank You, Dr. Shumway!

Information about the brain should start early. Chris read before he started school; he read word by word and could understand. Intelligence along with natural curiosity compensates for deficits. Curiosity is powerful.

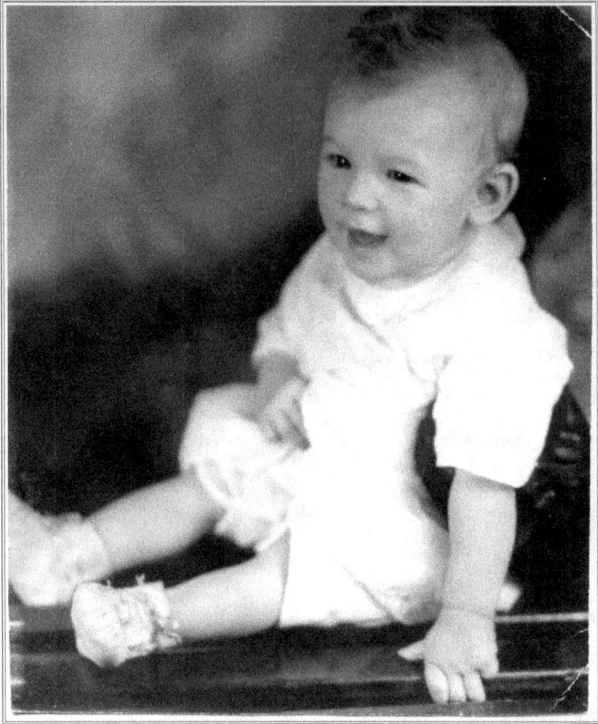

Brain dominance?

24

Hemispheric Dominance:
Weak Left with Strong Right

The study of hemispherical dominance is fascinating. As an individual, parent, and teacher, it is evident to me that some of us are more comfortable with one way of problem-solving over other ways of thinking. Reflecting back across my many years of teaching, I have observed this to be true. Through careful observation, we can see how we use given information to problem-solve. Continuing to be researched about how hemispherical dominance works, some say that the theory of brain dominance is a myth but others don't agree with the myth idea. The dominance theory continues to be accepted and popular. Hemispherical dominance is only part of the brain story.

Although there are researched differences of opinion when it comes to hemispherical brain dominance, it seems clear that some students are more comfortable with logic and reasoning than they are with creativity and intuition. There is uniqueness in both left and right hemispherical brain functioning.

Characteristics of Hemispheric Dominance

For this conversation, I use *left* hemisphere dominance words to explain auditory processing that is characterized by logic, reasoning, and details of the whole. I use *right* hemisphere words to explain visual processing that is characterized by creativity, intuition, and the whole without details.

In the literature, we find that people who spontaneously attend first to the details through logic and reasoning are referred to as having left hemisphere brain dominance. Those who first attend to the whole picture and then focus on the details are typically referred to as having right hemisphere dominance.

From my observations, I have found the following information about hemisphere dominance to be helpful. This insight is my observed, studied, and applied point of view. Having used this information in a way to create *learning style* lesson plans, I share.

I know from experience how my brain processes information. I know how my students' brains process information. Once a parent told me, "Argie, talking to you about my child's brain is like reading tea leaves." Well, knowing that I was not fortune-telling, I studied what she had said and realized the success of my knowing the child's brain came from taking the time to master some simple observations as to what was going on. We do not process alike because we have different configurations of intelligence and different life experiences coupled with the agency to choose our beliefs and behaviors; however, I know that for a given outcome the two hemispheres, to one degree or another, work together.

The person with left hemisphere dominance attends to the details while cognitively moving among the details, rather than beginning with a perception of the picture as a whole. Often the *details* of information are seen as the whole picture.

I had a large and colorful picture of a forest hanging in my classroom. I asked students to describe the picture. Some would describe a small *detail* and move on to another *detail* without looking at the whole picture. They would describe such details as specific color, design, or size. Rather than looking at the whole forest, the brain would look at just a particular tree. A student would occasionally see a *detail* as the whole. When the parents came for a meeting, I would do the same with them. Interestingly, it did not take long to find out where students got their DNA.

Then there were those who would look at the picture and see the *whole* picture and then the details. They would describe the whole picture in terms such as colorful, dark, feeling words, or just plain words, "I don't like it," or "Lovely, I love the forest."

What we have here is the brain looking for patterns that the brain understands. Some people see the details of the leaves and then the whole tree. Some people see the whole tree and then the details of the leaves. You got it! Details are left dominance, and the whole picture is right dominance. There are some individuals who *cannot* get beyond what they see. There are some who *cannot* get beyond what they hear.

Some people learn more effectively from their auditory input. As a teacher ties this to a left brain stimulus, the auditory learner will do well. Stimulus, as the dictionary defines, is something that causes a change or a reaction. This strategy is used well for learning. Left dominance.

My experience with auditory learners taught me a lot of things. They learn by hearing words, so they like to talk to hear themselves talk, like the visual learner who needs the auditory clarification. They learn and are good at anything auditory like remembering things they hear and by talking about what they have heard. They will often subvocalize while they are reading, as do visual learners, however, I have seen the visual learner subvocalize more than the auditory learner. My auditory learner students would tell stories in details. My visual learner students would tell stories without details.

When visual learners were having challenges with reading, I would put stories on tape so that they could orally read along with the recording. Given the instructions orally, they would sit in a quiet corner and read along with a book on their level. I had several recorders. The school would find me there very early, taping stories for my students on their reading level. After the reading, they had the opportunity to answer questions on the recorder, so I knew they were comprehending the content. When students were on the same level, I would group them. Auditory learners prefer not to draw pictures, but they could talk about the concepts, even record their stories. I appreciated my recorders.

Before continuing to move on with a discussion of right hemisphere dominance, it should be noted that for many, if not most people, the brain typically moves toward a functional integration of whatever is perceived by the dominant and sub-dominant sides of the brain.

From my life's journey, I will share my visual input experience with language processing. I have a brain dominance, and I will diagnose it as being very right hemisphere dominant with strong visual processing abilities. I look at my world with a holistic view void of details and organizational skills. My demand language skills are limited. Spontaneous language is strong. Just trigger my memory from the recall area of my brain, and I can talk all day. If you were to ask me a question about the same subject with detailed questions, I would wilt. My detail demand language is not high. And that is why tests are difficult for me. Ask me specific questions about the subject matter, I fail. Let me write an essay about the same subject matter, and there is no end to my thinking. My memory keeps triggering more recall as I write or talk. Remembering facts and names of things must be tied to the whole information load, not as a specific detail.

The rest of the story for understanding my brain is exciting. Even though I have a weakness in my left hemisphere and it struggles, I have learned to compensate. I know that I must consciously look at details as I organize my world, and I can do that.

My weaknesses can become strengths. When, with great relief, I figured out what my brain was doing, with excitement I desired to help others with their frustration over their brains. I studied and studied. With this came the invitation to give workshops to several schools and districts. I would be asked to visit with other teachers to write interventions for students.

My friend Dr. Steed, who was teaching at a university, came to one of my first workshops. Afterward, she reported, *"Argie, your presentation was coming off your right hemisphere with visual instructions, very informative but unorganized content. Start using your left hemisphere to organize your material, think about what you are saying and how you are saying it."* Sequence! What an assignment. Wow! Many workshops later, Dr. Steed said, *"Argie, you are organized with your*

194

presentation. If I did not know the truth of your right hemisphere dominance, I would say that you are left hemisphere dominant. You are using logical thinking, critical thinking, and outstandingly using your left hemisphere." My mind was smart enough to know what I needed to do. Wow! It worked. Grateful!

Later, Dr. Steed asked me to teach with her at the university. I am sorry that I did not accept the offer, however, I would have given up a good retirement if I had left my school district. Robin is gone, and as I sit near her grave, I thank her for changing my life; I made friends with my brain. I knew Robin Steed.

When the brain forms links or learns a new task, it encodes new information by enhancing connections between neurons. Neuroscientists from the Massachusetts Institute of Technology have discovered a novel mechanism that contributes to the strengthening of these connections, which are also called synapses. This information was not new to Robin! The brain has the capability to change. She talked of myelination, brain changing linkage.

I say it again! We shouldn't label people as left or right hemisphere dominant, but do need to discuss it. We need to be encouraging the integration of the whole brain just as Dr. Steed did with me. Seize the opportunity to design a plan to strengthen your weakness. I know my brain and how it prefers to be more dominant *here than there.*

No matter how analytical or creative we are, both sides of our brains are doing something all the time. When I do more analytical work, I get better at doing analytical work. If I spend my time writing stories and dedicated to better writing, I get better at writing. I have experienced a brain preference! Fabulous brains!

William Fox, a professor of history, and Willis M. Banks, a professor of chemistry at Brigham Young University, studied the quadrants of the brain. They found that 50 percent or more of the students were more right dominant and that the majority of the teachers in the school system teach in the left hemisphere mode. "When the two extremes clash, real learning rarely takes place," says Willis Banks.

195

Dr. Fox says, "By using holistic teaching techniques, you can help both right-brain and left-brain processors learn." "We actually think that any student can succeed if the student will use, or is allowed to use, natural processes to learn." Oh, my! Make your lessons full of attention to both hemispheres. I have seen this approach accomplish amazing results.

Banks said, "Research has found, that while it is extremely difficult for right-brain people to go into the left hemisphere, it is easier for left-brain learners to slide into the right hemisphere." (BYU Today, February 1986)

Researchers have studied the function of the brain for hundreds of years. One will recall that the French physician Pierre Broca researched the lateralization of the brain. Wernicke continued the study. Parts of the brain are named for them. And research continues on the subject.

Given my experience, I know that it takes a creative and academically secure teacher to orchestrate a class environment which attends to the learning styles of both the left—auditory, and right—visual hemispheres, along with the whole—integrated approaches to teaching and learning. It would be a bit uninteresting to not include the whole brain in daily planning. It takes planning and cutting through our natural brain preferences to arrive at a well-designed lesson plan with an open-end for spontaneity. Shifting from one side of the brain to the other throughout the day serves all in the classroom. As parents, it is important to do likewise. I found myself being involved in right hemisphere activities and did not engage enough in left hemisphere thinking for detailed training. I have experienced no absolutes. I started out processing with my visual right hemisphere, commiserated with the processing of my auditory left hemisphere, and determinedly designed integration of the whole brain.

While at the university, Dr. Fox assisted Chris with understanding his brain processor. He is using his right hemisphere as a dentist.

25

Appropriate Behaviors:
Better or Worse

I was teaching in one of the few Behavior Disordered Units in our district. As I taught troubled students, I found myself repeating, "I want to teach the parents how to deal with their children and for these children to be in this unit, it should be mandatory that the caretakers be an active support with their children." Since it was not mandatory, I took it upon myself to have meaningful and lengthy conversations with parents. I remember one evening when a parent and his son, my student, sat in my home problem-solving. These relationships changed lives. I share the following information to facilitate a change in behavior. Where does it start?

Suggested Ways to be an Effective Parent and Teacher

Always be at the crossroads for the child. You may be the most significant other in their life. You may be the only book they read.

Behavior Disability is what it is called within the classroom setting. As a team, we develop a plan to address the needs of acting out children and whatever challenges they may be having to cause the behavior. I prefer to call their sometimes intrusive behaviors a *call for help*. It is imperative that I address this *call for help* which faces parents in an ever-changing society. The question is how do we as parents, schools, and the community discipline and supervise our children to achieve the goals which will create a peaceful and productive society. Parents, you are the most important people in your children's lives, and *you must be in control*. Before we move on to the interventions which help with behavioral challenges, I will specifically address strategies for behavior management within the classroom.

1. Make daily lessons interesting and meaningful. Perhaps the student will desire to learn something new.

2. Reward with healthy food, computer time, appropriate music, free time, additional library time, create a story, a piece of art, or a time to "talk story" if appropriate. Student helps another student, if appropriate. This would validate the helping student. Train for internal reward rather than external reward.

3. Token economy: this buys so much of that.

4. Give time to complete an assignment.

5. Give back something when you take something away.

6. No profanity in classroom. Give student a substitute word or phrase to use instead.

7. Give assignment at an appropriate level for successful completion. Do not give student's a broken leg to overcome. If I have a broken leg, I can't run fast. Give me something that I can achieve.

8. Success builds success. Think how you feel about yourself when you succeed at something. Think how you feel about yourself when you fail at something. Pace the task for success. Step-by-step up the mountain with celebrations along the way.

9. Get to know people who are important to them.

Well, the list of how to change behaviors could go on and on!
The following are my observations which have been well studied and which I submit for your consideration.

Motivation is almost always the first pressing question that parents ask, "How do I motivate a change in behavior to better things at home?" This pressing question has been resounding with frustration for both teachers and parents. What should I give or not give to motivate? I have studied and studied this unhappy dilemma.

My experience has been to create a caring relationship with each student and not a paint by numbers relationship, but a relationship that is sincere and comfortable for both. A relationship of needed trust and friendship will be the foundation for building a student and teacher win-

win, environment. See the student as a person with whom you have shared interests. I remember time and time again when I would watch my students as they studied the moods of the ocean. When things were just right, they would take their surfboards and away they would go. My students knew I was there! The parades were made great by their appearances and participation, and they would be pleased that I cared enough to sit on the hard pavement and cheer as they marched by in uniform. My students knew I was there! Taking the opportunity to know students' families, showing graciousness in front of them, and giving praise when appropriate is of merit. My students knew I was there!

Positive reinforcements given for the completion of a task, such as praise and compliments with connecting sincerity, is validating and is as necessary as breath itself. I am convinced that motivation comes with the validating response of "I like the way you make me feel about me." My experience has been that relationships build success and students will continue to succeed. And that is what to give—relationships! Success builds success! Motivation!

The behavior you attend to first is the behavior you reinforce. For example, I walk into the class and ask a student to stop talking; I am reinforcing talking in my classroom; however, if at first, I recognize a student for working quietly and staying on task, then I am reinforcing the behavior of being quiet and staying on task. Be positive, not negative!

Positive and productive behavior should be recognized by showing approval through body language, words which come out of the mouth, a smile or a touch that says *job well done*. Yes, connecting with others when behavior is appropriate makes a powerful statement as to how we feel about that person. When behavior is inappropriate, we tend to respond with negative actions which we see as constructive but which can be damaging. No matter age or environment, it's far more *effective* to catch the person when they are doing or saying good things and reward the appropriate behavior or desired behavior. You know how you train your dog by rewarding the behavior which you are working to achieve. It is incredible how *good* will be *good*.

Speaking of positive and negative, listen to the sound of the voice, as well as the words spoken. Is the tone critical with a toxic intent? If so, change the negative to positive statements. "Please chew your food with your mouth closed," rather than, "Don't chew with your mouth open."

It is really difficult to change the habit of using negative words and criticisms. Changing negative words to affirmative words requires a clear and determined effort. This action isn't easy, but with determination, we can do it. It seems to be the nature of man to be negative. Redirect!

I have found that if I role-play, it helps. While I was traveling with grandchildren, I heard myself saying, "Please don't listen to that horrible music! Your taste is all in your mouth." The changed Grandma Argie Ella would say something like this, "My turn to listen to a different kind of music." Be creative and positive without sounding mean.

Avoid: "What did you do that for?" Try: "This is another way to do it."

Avoid: "Don't you know any better?" Try: "I can help you."

Avoid: "You've made a mistake." Try: "Mistakes are for learning."

Avoid: "I've told you and told you, but you still do it." Try: "Here is another way to think about it."

Avoid: "If only you would listen and pay attention." Try: "It is helpful to listen."

Avoid: "You have five words wrong." Try: "You have fifteen words right."

Avoid: "Just try a little harder, and you will get it right." Try: "Let's try it another way."

Task analyzing is important. That is to break the task into *parts* rather than stating the whole task which needs to be accomplished. General requests can be overwhelming. Be specific in requesting desired behavior as to how, when, where, and why. Engage the child in a dialogue addressing *why* the task is essential. It is convenient to make a general statement, such as "Clean your room," however, a better way to request, "Make your bed." After the bed is made, make another request, "Vacuum the floor." After *one* task is finished, outline the next task. *Teaching small steps* will in time teach the child to see the whole desired picture. Some children can see the whole picture and do it. Some need to see the part-by-part to get the whole picture. Short steps are easier to complete than walking the full mile. Remember, a *mountain climb* starts with one step. Deliberate step!

I remember Mother would say, "Take the garbage out" and before I had taken the garbage out, she would tell me to clean up my room. As I put my *toys* away, I was so frustrated—Mother was telling me to do something else, "Sister, please clean the dog poop up while you are taking the garbage out." I didn't know what I should do first and sometimes forgetting all that was asked. Saying to my brain, "When I have children, I will never tell them to do so many things at one time. I cannot remember all that stuff, and I don't know what to do first!" The message here is not only to give instructions step-by-step but think regarding sequencing and timing. And again, I say *sequencing and timing* are necessary for whatever you may be asking. This message applies to whatever you may be asking. It is difficult! I want things done *right now,* and I mean *right now.* Sometimes *now* is the right timing and sometimes *waiting* is more effective. One needs to have an awareness of what, when, and where. Much to ask of anyone!

Be hospitable with requests rather than demanding, demeaning, belittling, or being cold and unconnected. Please do not make a request that sounds like a scolding. "Please put the puppets in the box," rather than "Pick up that mess this instant." I like to respond to a capable person who is friendly rather than one who is a controlling dictator. Yesterday, an usher *smiled* and said, "Go that way." Yesterday, another usher *growled,* "Go that way." You got it! My heart was accepting of the *smile* while rejecting the *growl.*

We all are validated and feel a sense of contentment when we succeed. Help your child feel good by being able to succeed. I heard someone say that the way to teach a child to succeed is to work along with the child to finish a task. Celebrating the completed task with your child brings satisfaction to both of you. "The dolls need to be put away. It won't take long if we both help put them where they belong," rather than, "You shouldn't have taken all these dolls out at one time." Sometimes you can say, "After you put the things away, you will have the promised snack." Never say, "If you don't put the things away, you cannot have a snack." Create a positive picture in the child's head. If the child doesn't respond to your request, do not threaten! Consequences control behavior!

Let me be more explicit with a story about grandson Johnny and granddaughter Mary. After the movie, Mary would not put her coat on to go outside where it was snowing. "Mary, you stay here inside until you decide to put on your coat. It is cold outside." "I don't want my coat on to go home." "You can stay inside where it is warm. Staying warm is a good idea. I have my coat on so that I can go outside and wait for you. We must have our coats on to go outside. Here in Canada, you may get very cold and get sick unless you keep warm when you go outside. I will wait for you." After waiting patiently with no threats, Mary put her coat on and joined Johnny and me.

Now, if she had not complied, I knew what my next step would have been. Grandson Johnny and I would have gone back into the theater, ordered a bag of popcorn and sat down to eat. Of course, Mary would have wanted some popcorn. "Johnny and I have our coats on, so we are enjoying some corn before we go outside. After you put your coat on, we will share."

And still, Mary wouldn't put her coat on. "Grandpa, would you and Johnny go home and fix dinner? Mary and I will stay here until we put on our coats, and we are ready to go outside."

The tears and tantrums start. Ignore the tantrum. What is the tantrum saying? When misbehavior occurs, before you react, try to understand the child's reason and feelings. Think of the behavior as a language which is trying to communicate a message.

People nearby are thinking, "What a bad child, and her grandmother doesn't understand." By now you know that you have a troubled child who is in need of very serious parenting skills. A child who has gotten away with much too much. Tantrums and stubbornness have worked for her in the past. It is the parents who are in need of change! Start with the parent, not the child. The child's needed changes can come when the parent's behavior has changed. Tantrums can buy things, and tantrums can get bigger! Study what the tantrum is saying!

Time is an interesting and precious commodity for all of us. Help your child measure time. Rather than giving hurried commands, such as "Hurry up and put that stuff away. It's lunchtime right now." Give a warning, "In five minutes it will be time to clean up for lunch."

When talking with your child or anyone else do not shout across the room. Think of how you speak in the library and use their name to get their attention. Names are important identification. It is difficult to talk to someone across the room and feel that you have connected with them. Try to get close when talking and look the child in the eye.

I had a sad experience yesterday while sitting by the entrance to the security line at an unstressful and not busy airport. A mother carrying a baby and followed by a small and very young daughter was entering the line. An overwhelming person was seeing them off. He did not hug anyone with a goodbye. The small little girl didn't receive eye contact, one word of "see you later," or any contact at all. She reached up with her little arms extended but no response. Then trying harder to reach up, she stood on her toes and said something, but no response. The little girl's smile was gone. Such a cute little girl. My heart broke. Her mother encouraged her to follow her, and off they went. Missed opportunity!

An adult can look pretty threatening when towering like a giant, high over a child's head, especially when the parent is angry. It is important to physically and verbally get down on the child's level when talking with them and without anger.

As a young parent, I was threatening my children without knowing that I was threatening. I should have known. It is difficult to carry out inappropriate threats, and if they are carried out, the consequence is that both parent and child are unhappy. If a punishment given is too harsh and unjust, it only builds anger and resentment in the child rather than helping the child to take charge of their behavior in the future. For example, determinedly said, "Put those toys away and wash your hands for dinner this instant, or I will lock your bicycle up for a month." On the other hand, if unjust and obviously inappropriate threats are given and not carried out, the child soon learns that parental instructions can safely be ignored.

The lesson I learned and hopefully applied was the need to set up a positive framework for teaching. When a child has done something wrong, if we attack the child with anger and chastisement we are inviting resentment and rebellion as opposed to teaching out of love.

When misbehavior occurs, the child needs to have a conversation about *why* the behavior is unacceptable. Never are words like bad and evil associated with a child. And this conversation needs to be within the framework of love where they feel safe and secure. The child needs to know that it's the behavior you don't like, not the child who is exhibiting the behavior.

Consistency with boundaries will only work if they are always consistent. If there is a rule for taking shoes off in the house, this must be a rule for everyone. If a house rule is that you don't blow your nose in the kitchen, do not use situation ethics to break the rule. Set a few reasonable limits and be *consistent* in maintaining them. It can even be a fun activity to have a family get-together and brainstorm ideas for rules and the reasons for rules. Children sometimes like to role-play situations and learn to understand family rules. The game of reversing roles can be an interesting activity. In some situations, it may be appropriate for children to also participate in the identification of consequences for breaking the rules. At times, the parent may need to announce consequences without the child's input. The child needs to remember the truism that we can choose our behavior, but we can't choose the consequences. Sometimes it is best to ignore the behavior rather than bringing attention to advertise inappropriate behavior. T.V. coverage advertises inappropriate behaviors. Usually!

Sometimes the parent needs to react fast without conversation. The safety of the child and others are the top priority. Hold your child firmly but gently if their behavior is apt to harm. Of course, at the first opportunity, explain why you are determinedly holding the child. The choice to hurt or be hurt must be a consideration which momentarily takes agency away from the individual. One cannot take the time to wait! For example, when a child impulsively runs out into a busy street, we do not stop and flip a coin to see whether or not we will quickly and decisively intervene.

Model the kind of behavior you want to see in your children. I heard something outstanding, i.e., children learn by imitating. As my mother would always say, "Your actions speak louder than your words." We hear the saying, *Practice what you preach*. As adults, we can do things which are good or bad. As parents, we may be tempted to justify inappropriate behaviors by saying, "When you are older you can do this." If it is ethically or morally wrong for your child, it is also wrong for you. While I was teaching in an elementary school class, I had a student who started sharing what she had seen from her parent's bedroom movie. They had put it in the mailbox. She got it out of the mailbox, and she knew details that would curl your hair. Think about it. Moral decay is not positive in any society. The slope is slippery.

Something that worked both as a parent and as a teacher was to redirect a child into an activity that is acceptable when you feel the child is acting out-of-bounds. There is usually something that would be of interest and appealing which would quickly change an undesirable behavior; however, be consistent in not allowing an unacceptable behavior into becoming an acceptable behavior.

The lack of consistency creates a web of confusion. I feel the need to share one case history. A 2nd grader named Bessie kept challenging me for attention by writing off her paper. Writing did not stop at the end of the line but continued beyond the paper's edge, onto the desk and still writing. I grabbed a much larger piece of paper, and she was so intrigued that she focused on the paper. She liked large areas on which to write. She did not like to be confined, so I used the substitute paper to resolve the challenge. I then praised her good behavior of staying on the paper. I was hoping that she wouldn't use writing off the regular size paper to get the larger paper. Bessie didn't. The next time she stayed within the bounds of regular size piece of paper, I praised her and gave her an extra piece of paper to draw a picture.

Intelligent, colorful, and sensitive Bessie was conceived while her *flower child* parents were heavily involved in the use of drugs. In the 1960s, this was not uncommon among parents who took part in the uninhibited subculture of *love and peace*. How do I know? Her mother told me.

When given rewards or punishment, it appeared that Bessie did not learn from her experiences. It appeared that her protective filters were not in place. The following is an example. While Bessie was swinging very high in the air, she would jump off the swing with little regard for her pain or the pain of others as she landed on them. She was physically hurt, other children were injured, and the playground consequences were enforced. From the physical pain and the consequence of not being able to swing again until the next day, Bessie cried and cried, "It isn't fair!" This situation was an introduction to a tantrum of kicking, throwing and rolling into the fetal position. "Help!" and "Help!" was again the message sent by the classroom teacher as a student would run down the hall to summon me.

Throughout the years that I worked with Bessie, she was regularly medicated by a psychiatrist in the local Comprehensive Community Mental Health Center, but her highly dysfunctional and socially unacceptable behavior did not change.

This scenario was the story of Bessie's life as she grew into adulthood, "It isn't fair!" Even though the school and the community brought all their experience and resources to bear on the problem, Bessie did not change. For her, the world *was* "unfair." As an adult, Bessie shared that she did not *desire* to change. She saw her problem as being rooted in how her environment had shaped her, not as problems related to her accountability or her motivation to adapt, change, learn, and grow. Bessie's dysfunctional behavior persisted, even though she was regularly medicated with several kinds of psychotropic drugs, received continuous counseling from mental health resources, and caring suggestions.

As I visited the home to educationally counsel with her parents to assist Bessie with her behavior at school, it was obvious that the parents were undisciplined and chose not to be accountable for their behavior.

From personally knowing her parents and observing their parenting skills or efforts, Bessie was not taught the principle of accountability and personal responsibility for making behavioral changes. Bessie has not recovered from the consequences of her parents' behavior and her choices. One could ask, "Was she damaged neurologically by drugs used by her parents during Bessie's fetal development, and therefore, perhaps incapable of change?" A short leg is a short leg. With desire, one can learn to compensate. Yes, basic personality traits are not altered. I love little Bessie: intelligent, colorful, and sensitive. I taught and worked with many little *Bessie children*.

We can control the classroom environment. However, the real problem is that we cannot control the reality of the world in which we live. The informed, motivated, diligent and consistent application of correct principles by loving parents can make a difference. Society's institutions and services are not and never will be primary change agents.

Bessie and her parents could have made different choices. My opinion!

We need to help the child understand why sometimes things are okay and sometimes they are not okay. Rewarding that which is not safe is counter-productive. Most of the time this student acted as if she was *cute* and being freely creative. The parents' view of the behavior is often parallel to their child's view and vice versa. There is a truism that you never, ever reward negative behavior no matter how fun and creative it is. Bessie's parents were caring, loving, creative, and well-intentioned. My experiences in working with parents have been delightful and were rewarded by new friendships. It is difficult to be a parent!

Children will usually be consistent with what is expected at home. Social behaviors are learned at home, and ofttimes a child's behavior at school is an accurate "barometer" of what is going on at home. Parental consistency with expectations at home shows up in your child's social behavior at school; for that matter, wherever the child is living and breathing, it shows up.

If the child is allowed to be rude at home, that rudeness will be felt in other places. I heard some foul language come from a teenager and trusted that it was an isolated incident. It wasn't! What is, is! My question was, "Did he hear that from his father?" He hadn't; however, it was allowed by the father. This child's parents responded by giving in to the unreasonable requests of the child. Whatever tantrum the teenager could have thrown, it should have been ignored, not rewarded. Parents are sometimes afraid of the embarrassment that comes from out-of-control children, so they give in. Do not give in!

Teaching moments are given opportunities to highlight important things that a child needs to know. When a teaching moment exists, it doesn't mean to give a Sunday School lesson every time your child misbehaves. I have sometimes been guilty of this very thing. It would have been better if I had started off by understanding what the misbehaving was telling me before I started trying a lot of corrective words. The whys are always important to know and understand. Then we can better know what to say and how to say it. Another thing that is important to remember is that the situation needs to calm down before any reasonable solution can be implemented. You know, count to ten!

Managing or Solving problems makes a difference in how the child sees self, so let's talk about managing or solving problems. First and foremost, I strongly feel that the child needs to have an understanding of the *what* of the concern. Secondly, using the child's level of language, the child needs to understand the *why* of the concern. Thirdly, the child needs to understand *how* the concern will be addressed. These steps work toward a positive outcome to manage and solve the challenges. Finally, the child needs an opportunity to *express* his or her feelings about the total environment. The best way I can do that is to share experiences.

David, a 3rd grade boy with a visual and motor integration problem, doesn't visually spell correct; he spells phonetically and his handwriting is horrendous. Perhaps his handwriting looks like it does because he is overactive and doesn't slow down to focus on writing. He reads on a 5th grade level. He has excellent word attack skills with his auditory strengths and comprehends well with his reading ability.

David has a sensory weakness for being overstimulated while gathering information; a pencil scratching sound, by the student next to him, sends him into acting-out behaviors. He is labeled as a first-class behavior problem because of acting out inappropriately. It is time for the school talent show; he can't go since he has earned the discipline of staying in the media center to write sentences from the dictionary. He was not on task and didn't get his work done. The teacher kept him in at noon unsupervised, and he chased girls with a broom. Really!

David's mother and father are divorced. Mother works. His mother continues to blame David for much of her misery.

David is managed for his behavior. The reason for the misbehavior is not addressed, so the real problem is still there to surface again. What can we do to engage the problem?

Make sure that David understands the *why and how* of the situation. We need to look for the cause and not just respond to the negative behavior. Look at his test results and his brain processing. He has a visual processing weakness. We also observe how he responds to sound is a core problem in the classroom. The fact that David's parents are divorced certainly adds to the situation and should be considered by the school psychologist and a school social worker. Connecting with David and understanding how his cognitive processing works, and how his emotional health is relating to the situation, is utmost in finding answers. We are looking for buried feelings which are likely an important causal force in David's acting out behavior.

Another experience: Nate is in the 1st grade. He has a *receptive* language, as well as an *expressive* language problem. This problem means that both what he hears and what he says have processing challenges regarding both the accurate understanding and the expression of oral language. He also has both visual and auditory memory problems. He is struggling with reading, spelling, and certainly has a difficult time with understanding directions and can't express himself well with *demand* language. Nate learns by doing and has *spontaneous* language skills. *Demand* language is when someone asks you a question, and you have to go into your memory banks for the answer. Spontaneous language is when you are asked to speak on a subject, and you can just talk and talk without being questioned. His teacher says he is unmotivated, lazy, and inattentive. The teacher sent more work home to manage the lack of motivation! Doesn't work that *more means better*. His mother is upset! He has not done the work at school, so they stay up late while managing to get the work done. What can we do to solve the problem? Knowing the problem, we start to work.

Language processing is a fascinating mystery to me! It is how we communicate our thoughts and feelings. Frustration comes when we do not understand or cannot be understood.

To understand: Having a recorder in class to record lectures is also a good way to repeat a message. You can *start and stop* the recorder to have time to ponder the concepts.

If my students did not understand what was being said, I taught them to say, *Please tell me in another way.* They used this with their classroom teacher, as well as with their parents. It was always a reward when a classroom teacher reported that a student had used this statement to encourage a different way of saying or doing for clarification.

To be understood: One thing you can do is to have the other person repeat what you are saying, and each clarifies the meaning of the words. It may take longer for a conversation, but it will pay off in the long run. Another way is to practice organizing your thoughts. Sequence!

Another behavior: Angie is distracted from her work and she cannot sit still. She jabs Joan every chance she gets. Angie's inappropriate behavior earned the consequence of not getting to see the movie. What can we do to solve the problem?

Some say knowing that Angie will jab, it would have been better to isolate the problem before rather than after the problem. I agree. If you isolate before the problem is expressed, isolation is prevention. If you isolate after the expression of the problem, it is discipline.

Minimizing distractions is the best idea. Simplify the world around Angie. Joan needs to be seated someplace where she is safe from Angie.

There is not a panacea or simple answer to simple or complex problems. I am reminded of how a wise mother solved a problem. Cindy was talking to her father on the phone. Her little son Adam wanted to talk to Granddad. Cindy kept talking. Adam hit his mother. Now, we will see the difference between *managing* and *solving* a problem. Cindy could have *managed* the behavior by telling Adam to quit, could have spanked him, lectured, sent him to his room, threaten, etc. Cindy, his mother, chose to *solve* the problem. She excused herself from the telephone conversation and asked Adam, "What is your hit?" Adam responded, "I want to talk to Grandfather." Cindy acknowledged the request and said, "When I finish, you may talk if you wait quietly." She handled the feelings of a little boy with respect. Adam's request was a reasonable desire. Our hits, our bad behaviors, and our inappropriate behaviors are saying something. We need to start looking at *solving* rather than *managing* behavior.

Solving problems is a process. Managing problems may produce the desired product without solving the problem. We need to start looking at the process of growth, studying the whole picture, analyzing the parts, and asking if we are solving not managing the problem. Remember the saying, *winning a battle does not win the war.* Let's not glory in a battle won when the war is raging to destroy. Solve the problem!

Private things are things over which your child has control and in which your child is emotionally invested. Private things will help the child develop respect for the property and rights of others. Children, and for that matter adults, need to feel safe as they have private time with the ownership of things to respect and enjoy.

Uniqueness is being special in a special way. We have talked about this before, and here it is again and with good reason. All of us are unique. No two of us are alike and how do we know? Ponder your fingerprint and your brainprint. As parents, we cannot use our template to view our children. It is a truism that we cannot orchestrate our children's experiences for the same development, at the same place, and in the same way, as we developed. Our levels of Multiple Intelligences exist in how we think, feel, and our personality development. These elements make each child a special individual with a need for understanding from the caring of unique parents.

Unexpected events are to be capitalized with creative understanding. Use them as learning experiences and avoid hysterical and emotional responses to sudden changes. Have you been frustrated, disappointed, and wanting to cry because you haven't started or accomplished your goals for the day? That's me! Thinking of those who have tried to keep a strict schedule, but failed, I have learned to accommodate the unexpected events. Life is not a strict schedule.

Wherever reasonable, our children should be allowed the freedom to control some of their activities. Why? This freedom of choice enables them to learn to accommodate through success and failure, and they will be less likely to panic if there is a sudden break in the routine. It also helps to develop independence, initiative, and self-worth.

I know a family, a very smart family. You know, the CEO type. The children are a mess; they are *robot* children. They break because they are not flexible. Unexpected events will happen, so to be flexible is a survival skill. It needs to be lived by parents so that the child can respect their anchor as to how they solve the unexpected and how to be flexible. High functioning parents seem to feel they know *it all* and the children were trained never to make a mistake and recover on their own. I visited with one of their daughters, and she said, "Just let me make a mistake!" She rebelled. As parents, we need to look at ourselves and ask the hard question which needs to be pondered, "Am I the kind of parent that I want my child to become?" And be honest, not full of pride and selfishness, as you look at your strengths and weaknesses.

Caring for yourself is important. Speaking of ourselves, are we filling our emotional cups so that we can continue to assist? I might say and ask, without an emotional break! Remember the instructions given when you were on your last commercial flight? First oxygen to you and then to your child. This instruction also models the sequence for filling your child's emotional cup. There is wisdom in this sequence. This caring does not mean abandoning our children. It means that while they are away being productive, you are at the library or wherever. You are happy relaxing from the pressures of your sometimes very hard-driven and complex world of demands. Recognize your value as a *real* person, one worthy of respect, and self-worth. Do something positive for you.

Caring for others is kindness and love. Children will learn by seeing how individuals relate to each other. Demonstrate the depth of the interpersonal relationships that you have with others. Do you know how to connect with people in a caring way? Are you willing to serve others without a reward for yourself? Does pleasure come from knowing that you can be yourself while problem-solving with others? If not, ponder the why and actively mow someone's lawn or shovel their sidewalks without being asked. How does it feel when you see the look of gratitude?

I learned a treasured lesson when I was flying as a stewardess with American Airlines in the 50s. While I was offering services to passengers, services were shared with a kind and connecting heart. If the passenger had to ask for items, we were not caring but obliging. Our training and expected behaviors were to have a pillow, blanket, or magazine in hand, with a caring heart while extending an offer. We were taught how to give! Don't have children ask for your love. Give them love with a connecting mind and heart. The world would be a different place if we cared for each other, and the world did not need to legislate giving and caring. It is interpersonally uplifting to care. As a song goes, "Because I have been given much, I too shall give."

Boss, who is the boss here? Parents must be in charge. I address this issue which faces parents in an ever-changing society. Our communities have populations that are out of control. Parents are often out of control regarding their behavior, while at the same time failing to control their children's behavior. A strong statement is needed. Who is in charge It must not be the children controlling the parents. Children do not have the maturity or wisdom to organize a society with the order which keeps things working.

When I started thinking about the environment in which we rear children, the concept of what it means to belong to a society bounced around in my head. What is a society? It is an association of people who get together to accomplish goals with common interests and needs. This unit, whether it be small or very large, has activities of common interest.

Now, change the name *unit* to the name *family*. We look at the family as a place to nurture the well-being of all involved. For the family to survive and meet its goals, there must be order that is clearly defined with desired outcomes and working as a unit with standards of living or conduct. You can chew on that for a while. It appears that our larger society is evolving toward a weakened condition where the rules are less clear and less well enforced. This condition, in turn, weakens families, and the emerging children are less prepared to assume responsibility and teach it to the following generation.

The question is, "How do we as parents, schools, and the community train our children and instill the internalized drive to be self-disciplined and to have a personal desire for success? Parents, you are the most important people in the lives of your children. Parents with training, emotional support, and understanding how to discipline and supervise children are the keys to changing behaviors in children. Placing priority means looking at your daily schedule and placing first things first. **Do not let the least important be more important than the most important.** The government cannot do a better job than you. Find classes that will teach you to be an effective parent. Some principles will guide you into the best skills for your stewardship.

I recently heard a story which is too familiar. We could call this story, "Who is in charge here?" Opening the door to the home, one hears yells of arguing with the TV blasting in the background, and one sees food and cereal in bowls, scattered here and there. Little wonder why the mother was in the bedroom, discouraged, and embarrassed to come out. The children were in charge with no skills to be in charge, and the order of this home society was in complete confusion and disorder; a society not controlled by anything. Well, the children were barking commands at each other with no results. And the question remains, who is the boss?

Cooperation in our society takes more than one person. One day in the hot Arizona sun, I sat on a rock watching ants as they were living their lives. They were picking up and dropping off bits of wood and again, the same with bits that looked like crumbs. An ant carried something for about ten minutes, dropped it, and stayed with it as if waiting for another ant. And sure enough, here came another ant, picked the bit of something and continued to carry it to what appeared to be a known destination. Oh, and there went the helper ant into a tiny hole with that something that seemed to be larger than the hole. I watched ants, after ants, carrying bits of something into that same hole. Who on earth had told them to do the task of carrying? They were organized as a team to do it. It amazed me! They were sharing the labor and getting a job done. I understand that they build interesting and layered structures. Fascinating!

From watching the ants, I know that there was an interaction between those little creatures with effective communication. That is how it must be in a family for it to accomplish goals for peaceful living. If you are not "together" in the exercise of limits and discipline, children can become experts at "splitting" parents, thereby creating chaos which children can utilize to their advantage. This lack of cooperation is appalling for everyone.

Once, I visited the home of a student where the older child had taken on the role of the parent. She appeared to have parental control without the parent's input and suggestions. I have no idea from where her organizational skills came; however, she did have an excellent teacher who had taught her how to organize within the classroom setting. Teachers can teach wisdom which can't be measured by a test but can, nevertheless, change lives. My sister-in-law told me something worth repeating. She had a dear little niece as a guest. The niece shared something her teacher had taught about social skills, "You get what you get, and you don't pitch a fit." Teachers can teach contestable skills.

Discipline is not necessarily punishment. When a rule is broken, the discipline should fit the violation. Communication is of utmost importance in making it clear why consequences are being given. "This is happening to you because it will help you recognize or learn that we can't accept that behavior." Discipline should be consistent and given as soon as possible after the incident.

If discipline is too weak, children learn that breaking a rule is well worth the cost. If discipline is too strong, it can create anger, resentment, and rebellion, which the child feels is warranted.

After we impose a consequence, show forth an increase of love toward the child so that the child will not feel that you are an enemy. It is so important to keep the behavior separate from the child. "I love you but not the behavior. The behavior is inappropriate." Learning to tolerate testing of the limits by your children does not mean that you do nothing. They will test the limits but have your plan outlined to serve up the consequences and be consistent. The child must understand how behavior creates unhappiness. If the child doesn't care about the hurt, then the consequences must tell the child that it is wrong and not allowed. The discipline must match the offense. Hearts can break over the behavior of an offending child. Families can be torn apart, and other children in the family suffer when abused by another in the family. Privileges must be taken away from the abuser. These consequences need to be applied in a caring way to protect everyone in the family. If the abuser continues to abuse, then the parents need help in reconfiguring the consequences. What happens in these cases? The abuse will grow and perpetuate. The abuser may even abuse self, and things go from bad to worse. I know of several such very serious situations. While the abuser is using drugs and terrorizing the world around him or her, the society in which they live is in trauma. Someone needs to do something! Is that someone you?

Respect is a consideration for the dignity of others and appropriately treating them. Children need to learn what it means to respect others in their world. They learn this from those with whom they associate. It is necessary to teach children just who is making authoritative decisions. All this is accomplished through support and respecting parental authority. Actions speak louder than words. Words can diminish the role of parental authority and create a disrespect. Teach children about moral grounding. It is important that they see the most significant others in their world as examples in their lives. Therefore, I must live what I teach.

Do not allow yourself to punish the other parent by making him or her the bad guy. Hear yourself saying, "I agree with your mother. You should not do that," rather than, "You'd better watch out, or your mother will punish you for that." Respect is the caring for others in a real way.

Independence can be frightening. Figuring out how to encourage the road to independence in our children is a worthy goal, as well as the responsibility of every parent. I have experienced some success stories and some not so successful stories. So have you, as you live life. Having the skills to be independent doesn't necessarily come when the student graduates. It begins like the flower in the spring blooming after a gradual opening. Our children are growing and should slowly become independent of us so that as they mature and leave they have the skills, resources, self-discipline, and self-confidence needed to solve problems and cope with the world. As children grow older and demand independence, they may at times be unwilling or unprepared to accept the responsibility.

With every freedom comes the responsibility of stewardship. The child who is overly nurtured by a caring parent can become paralyzed within a co-dependent relationship. The parent who is unnecessarily taking care of the needs of the child may be doing so because of the unrealistic expectations of the parent. When appropriate, let the child fail; however, help if necessary. Orchestrate lessons for growth and independence. Be kind, for it is a stressful time for both the parent and the child. There will

218

be times when the child will slip into an earlier level of development, even though this seems like a regression. It is normal and can be full of pain for all in the environment. Let the child make friends with the pain of maturing.

Often we think of ourselves and what we want. I am here to tell you that our dear children need regular times available, just for them with you, and with no interruptions; you two together, talking with each other about whatever is important to the child. Talk to each other and plan together. Frequently ask yourself the question, "When was the last time I hugged this child and gave a heartfelt expression of my love?" Some children and adults are uncomfortable with hugs, and others do not want to be hugged. Figure out ways of touching the heart with a hug. "I know of your interests, and this book is one which I think you will like. I would like to take you to your favorite place in the park to enjoy the birds. I know you have been waiting for their return. I saw a Robin today. I am ready. When would you like to go? Lying on the grass, we will look up through the leaves while enjoying a moment to remember." Memories are made!

Thinking about behavior is what we could talk and write about for hours and hours. I will say that it would be well worth the time invested to explore the subject. I had a teacher say, "Do not put a piece of plastic over the brain and if it is there, take it off." Children who experience emotional abuse, physical abuse, or both bring a particular challenge to the learning process. The fears and disturbed feelings created by abuse are indeed like putting a piece of plastic over the brain.

When a child is sick or injured, is not the time to train for independence. Emotional support is what is needed at these particular moments in life. Teach while both parent and child are experiencing emotional strengths. Do not complicate a hurting child with unrealistic expectations. Building step-by-step to secure a healthy and caring relationship is beautiful. We need each other and caring comes in many colors. Today, a great-grandchild gave me a flower. Abby!

Given my experience, I have found that changing any behavior is challenging. Think about the behavior and intervene only to promote growth. Focus on the behavior, not on the person. Start by stating the job to be done, the expected behavior. Be consistent with the rules of the game as to where, when, why, and how to accomplish it. Rules are rules, and there is no choice but to obey. Role-play the desired outcome by showing and telling. Work along with the child until the child feels confident that the task is obtainable. Moving step-by-step to accomplish the behavior brings success to the whole task. Success builds success. By walking away from the task before it is completed, you make a statement that you do not have the same commitment which you expect of the child. So, when teaching, do not walk away until the child has built confidence that they can do the job or accomplish the behavior. Time and time again, I have seen the importance of having parents present both physically and emotionally as needed. The value of being together and without being angry bonds the child with the parents. Anger cannot bond togetherness! I will repeat it! Caring parents will be at the Crossroads for their children and know where, when, why, and with whom they are associating and what they are doing.

Brothers Randy, Chris, Brad, and baby Daniel.

26

Attention Deficit Hyperactivity Disorder:
Is It?

What are these things: **A**ttention **D**eficit **D**isorder—ADD, and **A**ttention **D**eficit **H**yperactivity **D**isorder—ADHD? They can be confusing. With my experience and studied opinion, I have found some information upon which to reflect.

There are three types of Attention Deficit Hyperactivity Disorder

1.   Predominantly hyperactive and impulsive is with hyperactivity and impulsivity. Those with these behaviors are energetically acting out, and the word which I think describes them is restlessness, on the move. They may have a difficult time with their bodies from top to bottom. Every part! With this, the behaviors can create either a positive or negative environment. It can look ambitious or criminal depending on the application of energy toward being appropriate or inappropriate.

2.   Inattentive is a neurological disorder that can cause a range of behavior challenges such as having a difficult time attending to directions, focusing to complete tasks, and attending to the needs of social interaction. These people are not disruptive with their behavior; however they appear not to be listening, off task, and disorganized with scattered thinking. The critical word—*appear* is a real situation; they are listening.

To continue to clarify, there are those who state that ADD is an outdated term, but the term ADD has continued to have some value because it describes a condition which parents and teachers have used in the past and with which they are comfortable. The term ADD now takes on another name, because it includes the same challenges as the term

inattentive ADHD. The correct educational and medical term that is used today is **inattentive** ADHD and has replaced the term ADD. These inattentive challenges are coupled without *impulsivity* and *hyperactivity*. Those referred with this condition are identified as having ADHD and are pre dominantly inattentive.

3. Combined hyperactive, impulsive and inattentive is still another view of the ADHD world. Take both the **inattentive** and **the hyperactive, impulsive** ADHD, and now we have this one. It seems to be the common one for most of those said to have ADHD. This ADHD will sweep a lot of other conditions into the conversation. Careful!

It is my opinion that these conditions are controllable. Observing behaviors and seeing what triggers them is the first step. Trying different treatments and knowing the condition can be figured out is another step.

You see and experience ADHD every day. Go to the store and there it is: distractibility or difficult time focusing on one thing, impulsivity or thinking quickly and making quick decisions with little information. These individuals have a difficult time waiting since it is a *now not later* response to almost everything in their world. And with that comes over-activity and emotionally hurried thinking and response. Help! Just force yourself to sit and focus, think and reach for a calm moment! Real as this condition is, ADHD must be attended to and not ignored.

You know what I mean by *overactive:* the overly active, little and big "guys and dolls" who are thus labeled by the parents, teachers, and the medical world. At one time the teachers would have asked, "Does the student have **A**ttention **D**eficit **D**isorder with or without hyperactivity, or should it be hyperactivity with or without **A**ttention **D**eficit **D**isorder?" Little wonder why the term **A**ttention **D**eficit **D**isorder is still debated!

For a professional medical definition, study the Diagnostic and Statistical Manual of Mental Disorders, DSM-6. This book is not without debate.

Given my experience, I believe that based on case study after case study, hyperactivity without an attention disorder is rare, and an attention disorder without either inward or outward hyperactivity is rare. Is this true or not? My overactive brain and body have learned to compensate by mustering a lot of energy toward sitting on my hands and thinking "Focus, focus, focus!" I don't appear to be hyperactive, and some even say that I seem calm. Are you kidding? It is hard, just ask me! However, it can be done and without drugs. Well, yes, it could be at the expense of the most significant others in my world. I need to concentrate on one thing at a time and bring all the powers of heaven toward that end since my mind is always spinning, spinning this way and that. It has been a difficult struggle even to have a personality; a personality that is acceptable to society. Society demands you think fast, answer intelligently, look people in the eye, and oh, yes, spit it out with wittiness, not to mention catch on to dumb jokes. Well, it could be worse, so they say. Yes, these are ideas of interest to me. However, not without thought.

When all else fails in behavioral management, I ask the question, "Does medication change the personality?" Well, what personality? I have worked with many children who have been medicated. Being medicated by well-trained doctors and wise practitioners was not the issue. While the effects of the medication may temporarily change a child's behavior, disposition, or temperament, I have observed that the basic personality traits are not altered. Furthermore, *habits* created either by an environment or *genetic disposition* typically do not change enough through medication to facilitate the changes in behavior which can optimize learning. I've seen it! Changes are drug dependent. Temporary!

Indeed, medication may make your child more able to learn by helping the nervous system compensate. It also does not change the results of poor parenting any more than do the "cure all" interventions of patterning, diet, behavioral modification, structuring, supplements, and special schools. Any and all of the many methods, some are very good, may have a place and can be helpful; however, they are not a panacea for the lack of an informed, committed, connected, and loving home life.

ADHD seems to be everywhere in our society these days. Have you noticed you could find it with anxiety, depression and substance abuse, as well as with the face of creativity? I have taught students who have ADHD, and many have had the diagnostic labels of learning disorders. When studying the conditions, there is a continuum from mild to severe.

I think I have both, but I have a little or a lot of everything. Keep reading! My hands are never still, and my mind is forever running from one side to the other side of my head. Some say I am a calm person.

ADHD was first brought to my attention with hyperactivity; however, there is such a thing as ADHD without hyperactivity. Same thing but less energy. My dog has the *with,* and my cat has the *without* challenges. Who has it? Both children and adults may have it.

Some smart people find ADHD is a challenge. They want to act now and not think about the details. They can reflect on the details but why bother. I have said to my sons, "Slow down and be patient with yourselves and your world." Stop, Look, and Listen takes a lot of directed energy and perseverance. *Focused control can happen!* It works for them.

The question remains: Learned Behavior or Biological?

Marilyn Wedge, Ph.D. wrote *Why French Kids Don't Have ADHD.*

"French children don't need medications to control their behavior." Continuing with Dr. Wedge's words, *"Is ADHD a biological, neurological disorder? Surprisingly, the answer to this question depends on whether you live in France or the US."* I suggest reading Wedge's writing. It has been of utmost importance for those dealing with ADHD.

Here in the United States, it is a known fact that we generally consider ADHD, which stands for Attention Deficit Hyperactivity Disorder, to be a medical disorder defined with inattention, impulsivity, and sometimes with or without hyperactivity that affects the child's functioning and development. Its causes are considered to be primarily biological rather than psychological and social. Therefore, in the USA, it is treated mostly with medication.

In France, ADHD is also considered a medical condition, but its causes are viewed as psycho-social and situational. Again from Dr. Wedge, *"Instead of treating children's focusing and behavioral problems with drugs, French doctors prefer to look for the underlying issue that is causing the child distress—not in the child's brain but the child's social context. They then choose to treat the child's problem with psychotherapy or family counseling. All this is a very different way of seeing things from the American tendency to attribute all symptoms to a biological dysfunction, such as a chemical imbalance in the child's brain."* I agree with Dr. Wedge.

As a parent and teacher, I can tell you that *what we eat* is indeed one of the essential elements in *what we are*. I have worked with many parents whose children's behavior changed when their diet changed. I discovered that a simple sugar-laden snack seemed to contribute significantly to elevating a given child's hyperactivity. Therefore, I have suggested to parents of my ADHD students that they consider eliminating foods from their children's diets which have sugar. In some cases, the changes were dramatic. A look at adding dyes to food is also a possible culprit.

A physician who was serving many families in my school's area heard about me through the parents and came to the school to visit. As we talked about the significant behavioral changes, I noted that this was the result of dietary changes; he decided to support this idea. When the diet changed consistently, the behavior changed. I cannot emphasize this enough. Also, there are certain preservatives and additives which some of us cannot handle. The medical doctor mentioned above was willing to work with parents on these issues, and I referred many parents to him. He reported back to me that he could not believe that our conversation about these things had made a difference. My question remains, "Why does this not seem to be common knowledge?" I must say that it is more known than it used to be. However, even if it were common knowledge, it has become apparent to me that being *consistent* with changing behavior is very challenging even when the results are positive. What we ingest should be studied alongside the results of what happens after we ingest. Could it be that what we eat is who we are?

Looking at ADHD through another lens, I have experienced what it means to understand how a given consequence for a particular action will contribute to a change in behavior. I have seen parents put their children on drugs to change behavior rather than take a look at their parental behavior patterns which may be feeding the negative behavior. They think they are good parents, but they support inappropriate behavior with their behavior. And onto the drugs, the kids go!

Where on earth did the word *structure* go? It seems that laissez-faire parenting is the standard and I am here to tell you, "It does not work!" This philosophy of parenting typically means too much *freedom of expression*. When is a parent too permissive, or to put it another way, when does permissiveness become neglect? I believe that neglect can sometimes amount to child abuse. Children need a given standard of behavior and to learn to live that standard with consequences which reward appropriate behavior. Turning the other cheek to inappropriate actions can be very counterproductive. And yes! Giving drugs to try to change that behavior is not principled. What I am saying is that medication will not cure learning disabilities, but perhaps it will help your child be more free to learn. And that is a perhaps. A learned behavior cannot be changed with medication. Children must learn self-control early in their lives. If they don't, they will learn it or not learn it from the larger society.

Consistently enforced limits can make children feel safe and secure. Clear limits make a child feel happier and more secure than fuzzy or inappropriate boundaries. At one time when speaking with a social worker who supervised the therapists in the children's unit at the Utah State Hospital, he told me that a young person said how he wished his parents knew how to say *no*. The earlier, the better and then perhaps the hyperactive child won't need medication!

226

One day during a 4th grade class, James Alfred III, one of my students, was sitting on floor pillows in a reading group. He was actively engaged in the learning process when he started to fidget, got up, would not sit down, and began to disrupt the reading group. As I sat there observing the whole situation, I heard a lawn mower cutting grass outside my window. The machine was large and very noisy. After documenting several observations of James Alfred's response to the noise, we were able to pinpoint what caused him to go *off* and what changed his behavior suddenly from being appropriate to inappropriate. He had a low tolerance for sounds which included music, voices, and indeed the lunchroom. I wish we could lower the noise in lunchrooms, but that is like telling the rain to stop. His mother bought earplugs. We taught James Alfred to monitor his sound environment, stop and think, and to make decisions about finding a more quiet place. After I had a conversation with an unwilling librarian, who did not desire to have behavior problem children in her library, she said she was willing to try to accommodate, but she doubted what I was asking her to do. It turned out that she was impressed with the results and willing to have my student. She was grateful that she had found a place for him to take tests, read, and calm down. Wow! No medication, just a quiet place.

Then I had other students wanting to go to the library to do their work. So again, the librarian carved out a place in the library for my students who didn't at times appreciate my creative and less quiet classroom. I learned that as a teacher, it was essential to know how the students select and process behavior. Students should have the freedom to be creative as long as they do not interfere with the learning of others. Consideration.

Here is another story about a very "off the wall" student during my first year of teaching as a regular classroom teacher. Having a dual major in both special education and regular education, I was always reading and keeping my ear to the ground. I read in one of my special education journals that someone had done a little research about fluorescent lights

227

and how they have a buzz which can annoy some students and create an undesired increase in activity. I had Tom, a distraught student, who would not calm down. I had tried behavior modification, and you name it, all my well-planned strategies did not work. I called his parents in for a conversation. I did not know what to do. They had the same challenges with him. I told them about the article which I had read about the fluorescent lights. We agreed that I would turn the classroom fluorescent lights off and bring lamps from home. They matched my plan with their plan to have no fluorescent lights in the house. They were so relieved and pleased to report that for the first time at home, Tom would sit on his father's lap and enjoy the reading of a book. After I changed the lights in my room, I had a *changed* student. I firmly feel that this idea should be studied. Try it! It might work for you.

I have heard there are two elements to human behavior; they are the ability to select a behavior and the capacity to process the action.

When a student has the habit of getting upset and then has a difficult time getting back in the "swing" of things, I try to look at what happened just before the explosion. I recently had a conversation with Ron, one of my past students. He said that with me he was calm and would get his class assignments done only to return to the anxiety of the classroom and again would act out like an unruly student. Also, he said his home was not calm. The difference was my calmness and expectations.

The next year I moved to another school. A misintended decision was made during the summer. That following year found Ron in a self-contained Behavior Classroom. After a year, the school system knew he had been placed in the wrong unit and changed the placement.

As I thought about that story, I was reminded of how you train an animal. My dog can read your calmness and your anxiety. A child, especially a sensitive child, can read the barometer of your emotions. This particular student said he felt comfortable in my class. Ron is now a successful business person with people skills; you would not ever know that he had a difficult time in school. Why didn't someone just ask him what was going on in his world which helped or hindered? He was identified with ADHD and a learning disorder which prevented him from learning. It was a *lack of focus* that kept him from learning.

There are those who believe that ADHD is neurophysiological rather than environmental in origin. How does the individual live through life with the energy which finds itself either positively or negatively expressed? Some suggest medication for management. I believe that medication should be the last option.

I have heard some say, "Bridle your passions." That makes sense! I lived on a ranch that had horses, and I learned what it meant to bridle your horse for control. I know the pain of an unbridled horse who never learned to be in control and what that horse can do to its world. I have seen it. Out on the ranch, I admired a wild horse and tried to make unbridled contact . . . . Also, my brother was on the professional rodeo circuit. "Bridle!"

Daniel Webster stated: *"Educate your children to self-control, to the habit of holding passion and prejudice and evil tendencies to an upright and reasoning will, and you have done much to abolish misery from their future lives and crimes to society."*

Our prisons are full of people with adverse behaviors as viewed from the mind of Daniel Webster. I have visited the prisons. I have a former student who is currently in prison. I have experienced having friends and family members who have not *bridled* their passions and have found their lives torn and tears shed. These memories are my experiences. I have opened the box of possibilities and invited you to look inside.

From the time I was able to get on a horse, I understood what is meant to be bridled. Control! What can I do this day to be in concert with what I know? How will I bridle my behavior? Make the decision to be disciplined so that control will have the face of ambition. Effectiveness is a given result!

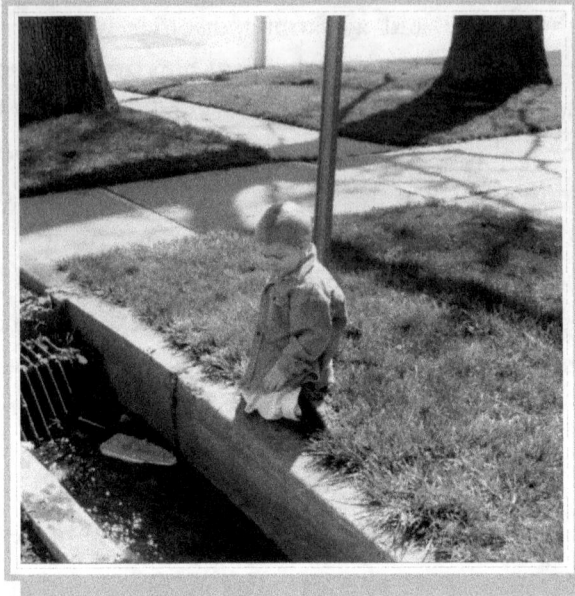

One hot summer day, I carried Brigham on my back across a weeded
and dry field: music and dance concert. He said, "I love you, Mama
Argie." Touch is a gem which writes on the Hearts of Heaven. The world
is better because Brigham was here. Silence speaks. I wish I could build
a bridge from Brigham to me without the sharks of time and space.
Listen to what our sensory input is saying.

27

Sensory Processing Disorder:
Brain Challenges

It is a widespread belief that people cannot be both gifted and still struggling in school. They can. It seems that we are still in the dark ages of understanding the cognitive functioning of our brains.

Asperger's, Autism, Gifted, and those labeled with ADHD are frequently diagnosed with a Sensory Processing Disorder. I would like to add myself to this list. Interestingly, individuals with no apparent neurological or physical challenges can also have sensory sensitivities. Statement of fact!

For years I have said, "I have a high pain tolerance," or "I have a sense of smell like a dog," or "I can hear the scratch of the pencil." Another awareness is grains of sand on the beach with their snowflake-like artistic beauty. I did not realize that these could be *Sensory Superpowers*. I do not know who coined the words *Sensory Superpowers*, but they are right, and I wholeheartedly agree with the statement. I want to say that I am grateful for the expression. I know that it is true. Being unusually sensitive or not sensitive can cause a lot of challenges in and of themselves but it doesn't mean it is wrong; it just is! However, this condition can be misleading and needs to be studied down several roads.

Giftedness, as I have observed, has sometimes been erroneously labeled as a learning problem or mental health disorder; along with times that a learning challenge has masked as giftedness. It is paramount that we look at what is and what is not. Whenever receiving a referral that a student was struggling, for whatever reason, my question would be, "Tell me how the student is also gifted." So, while some among the gifted are erroneously labeled and medicated for learning disabilities and sometimes for mental health disorders that they do not have, others are not recognized for disorders they do have.

There are many neurological disorders which can prevent the brain from correctly processing information. A Sensory Processing Disorder is not any different from other cognitive processing challenges—the brain is not interpreting sensory information which can be presented in various ways; it is information that is not organized and processed efficiently in our brains. I have an understanding that there has been stated categorization with systematical responses: sensory modulation disorder, sensory motor disorder, and sensory discrimination disorder.

If the person is overly sensitive to stimulation, limit overstimulation in the environment. Some individuals hear confused sounds. Many people with a Sensory Processing Disorder do not process *sound* the way they need to for a correct response: too loud, too soft, or delayed.

Along with the sound challenge, a part of all this involvement is with the field of vision. Again, an incorrect response is due to the brain not processing the information correctly.

Another sensory disorder is the lack of ability to have a proper response to what is happening to the body concerning movement and body balance. Where is the body and what is it doing? It seems to be an orientation as to space, and this will create confusion which is overwhelming. Although causes may be unknown, the problems are real. The brain must be reprogrammed to correct this situation. Can you go down an escalator? Just thinking!

Once, I had a student who had almost lost her life while drowning. Saved, but her brain starved because of the lack of oxygen. Mary Jane experienced responses similar to what seemed to be a Sensory Processing Disorder. As I taught her, she seemed to thrive on her relationships with the team who supported her progress. It takes an aware and skillful teacher to help the learner create compensatory mechanisms.

Mary Jane was always in a hyperactive state and excited to come to my room but quickly calmed down for the teaching moments. I believe the expectation of calmness in the classroom was essential for her being calm. Her disorder appeared to be multisensory, and it was disabling. As I worked with her using multisensory materials, she started to learn in spite of her body balance and movement. I was not able to help with the balance. Her handwriting improved with a determined desire on her part but was limited to the flow of continual movement from letter to letter. One letter at a time, she improved. Her parents were thrilled.

Although Mary Jane was oversensitive to touch, she learned well through touch. Some days, I must note that she was overly sensitive but was less so on other days. The behaviors with her sensory challenges seemed to have an *up and down* cycle. I was not the only one helping this student. She also had an occupational therapist and speech therapist. Great team! Without us knowing, I believe that her brain was correcting the overly sensitive frequencies because of her determined attitude, her focus, and parental support. I wish I could find her for an update. I was rewarded with needed experiences as I observed this student. She taught me how *touch* is a powerful sense to understand and use for positive energy.

Given my experience, I have observed that Sensory Processing Disorder, which was at one time called Sensory Integration Dysfunction, can be seen throughout our population with various labels or no labels. The symptoms are shared by other disorders and present a different picture, case by case, as they range from mild to severe. Therefore, not all experts agree with a particular diagnosis.

The following are some of the hyposensitive and hypersensitive symptoms: My observation with some students has been that being hypersensitive can be a way of compensating for being hyposensitive. Our brains survive by becoming selective and not processing on the overload or underload of sensory input. Consider the following for sensory selection:

1.   Touch, audible noises, smells and for me, even the noises of too

much visual is a problem because I see everything and try to process too much visual information at the same time, same with auditory processing.

2.   Making friends can be a challenge because of processing too many things at one time.

3.   It is reported that some have a difficult time sleeping because the brain won't turn off.

4.   Others have shared that eating and other daily tasks are difficult.

5.   Motor skill can be involved: clumsy and weak.

6.   Difficulty in staying focused in meetings, in conversation, and doing a task; so, therefore, not completing tasks. Too many stimuli that I call stimulus overload brings *distractibility* to the table.

7.   I am not like many other people who can stay on task because I'm afraid of failing at new tasks and with that comes poor self-esteem.

I conclude that these symptoms are not unique to Sensory Processing Disorders but are found and explained in many places. There is a continuum of hyposensitivity or hypersensitivity which can make life very difficult and frustrating, if not downright hellish. That which can be a virtue, taken to the extreme, can also become a vice: fits with sensory input. If individuals experience the extreme, perhaps the brain must be reprogrammed.

Along with the information on a sensory response, researchers have found that touch can ease the pain, lift depression, and touch is needed for the brain to develop human connections. Babies can die without being hugged enough. They may have the required nutrition, but without touch, they wither. Touch can be either positive or negative.

Touch can be the gem which writes on the Hearts of Heaven.

28

Autism or What?

Started wanting to learn more about autism because I had two kindergarten students, one identified as having traumatic brain injury and the other having autism. Study again! What is the brain doing? I was grateful that I had studied as I started to see more children with differing behaviors which seemed to point to the workings of the brain and not the workings of learned behaviors. In the next two chapters, I will address autism and Asperger's. It often appears to me that more research and education are needed for the adult populations.

Current labeling includes the syndrome Asperger's, as a part of the autism spectrum. I have another opinion. Well-published and highly respected individuals, as well as relevant professional groups, have both supported and challenged the current DSM-5 diagnostic criteria. From my personal experience, I stand by the opinion that Asperger's should not be included with autism anymore than it should be included with other diagnoses. This conversation, which is very energetic, leaves me convinced that we should not place a label on everything. I have observed, tested, and designed interventions for these populations. I have taught and had social interaction with many individuals who fit well within each of these categories. I am convinced that both autism and Asperger's do indeed have much in common, as do other diagnoses have in common with them. I have seen students who were labeled Asperger's to be more like the students who have been labeled Gifted than those who have been labeled with autism. Labels of having autism or Asperger's are confusing. Each diagnostic category is unique enough that they should remain separated and individualized. We are more alike than different. Why label? Why not label? In any case, let's move forward.

Is it because human intelligence desires to know all *things* about all *things* that we start categorizing everything? There is an exhausting overlap which says that this *thing—situation* fits here and there, and it fits with this and that. Well, are you confused yet? After we categorize things, we name and then start changing things again so that they will work better toward reaching some goal or developing a skill. Also, it seems to me that sometimes we name and then categorize. Both skills are necessary, but they can be misplaced. The order is critical. Depends?

We have a need to categorize, classify, name, and find an educational intervention and sometimes a medical treatment for each thing that we might have identified as a "problem" thing, and then the fun begins.

No, that is not all! The several disciplines will look through their respective lenses and find many subcategories. I can't end here. As we talk about problems that people have, *I find that most of us have a little of everything to one degree or another.* Since we are all unique, our brainprint is a mixture of lots of things that the world tries to organize into something called something: a spectrum. Dictionary meaning of spectrum: *a broad range of varied but related ideas or objects, the individual features of which tend to overlap so as to form a continuous series or sequence.* Oh, incidentally, everyone fits somewhere on the continuum from mild to severe of everything which I have written. Others not related to me have privately confided that they also have a bit of everything. I know why; we are all a unique mixture. Yes, we do share a range of problems and human foibles to one degree or another, as well as in the spectra of human strengths.

Now, I will address something called *Sensory differences.* It is not specifically related to autism, but certainly those with autism display such resultant behaviors. I have observed the situation with those diagnosed with autism in both students and others. Some people have difficulty processing sensory information from mild to severe. Sensory differences can cause people to react in protective ways. Sensory information can be read as either oversensitive, under sensitive, or both at the same time. Just as our sugar intake can be read as hyperglycemic or hypoglycemic, many things can be either hyper or hypo: sounds or hearing, sight, smell, touch, taste, balance, and body awareness. We need to be aware of the exertion of sensory information that is caused by hypersensitivity or hyposensitivity. The question is how does this affect the person experiencing these differences. Sensory stimuli can influence behavior in many ways, and the person's life can be a living hell.

I need to share this story again. One time, I saw it right before my eyes. One of my students seemed just fine to me, but his parents kept telling me that something was wrong. Their child would suddenly scream, and his behavior would change. Why? My Resource class was relatively quiet and ordered. Alfred was just fine. Where was the problem? I had not seen it. As we sat reading, a lawn mower started and was making the rounds outside my window. The student exploded with inappropriate behaviors. He was running and screaming, "Stop!" I watched and tried to calm the student. Evaluated what was happening—nothing different in my room. All the students were trying to stay on task in the middle of Alfred's running and yelling. As the lawn mower made its way from my window, Alfred came back and sat down. When it stopped, he was again on task. After class I called his mother, she had never considered the problem of sensory overload to be the challenge in Alfred's life. I quickly redesigned my intervention objectives in the Individualized Education Program. The mother sent earplugs to school, and we had a conversation with Alfred about his being sensitive to sounds. This child could not sleep when there was too much sound in his bedroom. Finding out Alfred was overstimulated by sounds changed his life. I couldn't believe what we had found. Seemed simple! This everyday sensory information overload can cause a person to struggle with life's experiences. It can cause stress, anxiety, and sometimes physical pain. It can cause discouragement which can be labeled as depression.

I have taught students labeled with autism and was not sure that the diagnosis was correct. I studied the picture of functioning and designed or redesigned interventions and accommodations to remediate the skills without getting hung-up on the label. Alfred did not have autism. Careful what we call behaviors; we may either oversimplify or unnecessarily complicate words of concern.

As I have questioned and have studied observations and opinions about intelligence, those with autism present a picture of complication when being tested. Nonverbal IQ tests, please!

The symptoms were there but so were other symptoms. That is to say, as I taught these students or did not teach these students, I studied their behaviors. They were all different behaviorally but had been diagnosed as having autism. Many of the responses should have been linked to Sensory Processing Disorder only. On the other hand, many students had been labeled as Attention Deficit Hyperactivity Disorder, however, as I observed them, they also had the same sensory overload challenges as those identified as with autism. I am not saying all students, just that some of my students, were helped when this became a consideration. Observe the whole picture, not just details.

Tom was in my 4th grade regular classroom and hyper as hyper could be until I had my fluorescent lights turned off and an incandescent light bulb installed. When his parents did the same at home, his father said that Tom sat on his lap for the first time without squirming. This student was not labeled with autism but could have been. He did not have autism. He just could not tolerate particular sounds from electromagnetic sources. Amazing what a difference a light bulb will make. Yes, and light also just went on in my brain. Thankful!

I taught with a teacher at a high school in Hawaii which found us both serving students with behavioral problems. She didn't have a fluorescent light in her room. Through the years she had experimented with the same and found that it was indeed a stimulus that some children could not tolerate.

I found something in an article from The National Autistic Society of the UK which has been interesting. *"If I get sensory overload then I just shut down; this is known as fragmentation . . . it's weird, like being tuned into 40 TV channels."* Persons will withdraw or meltdown. For the person with autism, fragmentation occurs when too much information needs to be simultaneously processed. And not just autism!

Very often those with autism, as well as others, are not able to "break" the whole picture into details as parts of the whole. They see the *details*, and that is what gets their attention. This detail is the whole picture of their thinking. They may see only the bits of sand and not the entire beach. This fragmented perception can affect all the senses.

Although fragmented perception is one of the challenges for the person with autism, I know that fragmented perception can also be how those without autism might process information; sometimes first seeing the whole and sometimes seeing the details alone does not necessarily spell autism. Careful as we label! I am glad that I did not label children as autistic when they were just naturally seeing their world in details.

Synaesthesia is a fascinating condition. It is a concept that is associated and experienced with autism. *"In its simplest form, it is best described as a "union of the senses" whereby two or more of the five senses that are normally experienced separately are involuntarily and automatically joined. Some synaesthetes experience color when they hear sounds or read words. Others experience tastes, smells, shapes, or touches in almost any combination. These sensations are automatic and cannot be turned on or off. Synaesthesia isn't a disease or illness and is not at all harmful. In fact, the vast majority of synaesthetes couldn't imagine life without it."* (Wannerton, James. President of the UK Synaesthesia Association)

Careful again, do not be fast to say that someone who has this condition, should be automatically classified as autistic. Why do I say that? Well, I have read that this "union of senses" has been experienced by those identified as having Asperger's and also dyslexia. I read this to a friend who has no label; she has experienced the same. Again, why label?

Given my experience, I know there is something in the brain that ties color to things in an unexpected way. I had students who could see letters and words in color inside their heads, and students who could not do that inside the head imagery. Yes, seeing the real objects is all they could muster. I don't know where or why the "union of senses" happens. However, when I bring up a memory, it sometimes triggers many senses. I will share examples, and I ask the question, "Can you turn the condition on or off?" If you can turn a condition on or off then what is it called? I ponder this because I can turn the "union of senses" on and off, but some say that it is automatic and cannot be turned on and off. When I experience it, I can turn it off, however when I concentrate on not seeing color, color keeps returning. I need to study this in depth!

I will share examples. Have you ever sat in the kitchen while your mother was baking bread? I remember the times when Mother was baking, and I was ironing. Waiting for a warm slice of bread with honey and heaps of butter, I can still smell the baking of bread.

Every time, I walk into the smell of baking bread, the memories jump right back into my heart. My memory plugs in the experience of being in the kitchen of my childhood; yes, I can *see* the color—green in the linoleum floor, *smell* the bread and *feel* the warmth of the kitchen. Memories flash! Grateful feelings flow as I again smell and taste Mother's loaves of bread. She made them with loving dedication in her role as mother. No bread *tastes* like Mother's bread! I believe that it is because I naturally create *a union of senses* and store the memory which is not forgotten. I don't just remember the smell but the taste, the look, and the words spoken. I can feel the *movement* of dancing with my brother in that kitchen. Oh, so many years ago! Rewarding!

As an infant, I can remember as I turned this way and that in the bassinet while seeing Mother swinging her spatula; I can smell the bacon as I see the woven patterns of the bassinet and hear Mother talking to someone. The more senses we use, the more secure the memory.

I don't know where my "union of senses" comes from in the brain, but I know it is there; I have tied a memory to experiences of emotion while simultaneously experiencing the senses of smell, seeing, touching, and the movement of dancing. Recalling and thereby again experiencing this "union of the senses" moves me to tears. With the western music in the background and feeling the rhythm of Pug Scott's fiddle, my brother and I danced in the smoke-filled room, feeling how proud Daddy and Mother were as they watched through the dim lights the movement of happy feet. I experience it with one click of a button. No label, please!

I have mentioned that I could not learn by sounds but by seeing the whole word in my head. I learned that a picture was a particular word. With the new word, I have used color in my head to learn. The colors which I can quickly turn on and off are red and black. I can see the whole word in black and then insert a colored letter. Since learning about the word *Synaesthesia,* I wonder if that word means what my head is doing. Sometimes, my dreams are in color. This color sense is tied to my visual in a real way. It sometimes can be tied to an auditory input: western and jazz music. As I have become older, the color in my head is not as real. I wonder if the color comes from the right hemisphere. Last night, the only part of my dream that was colored was a bush, red in various shades. I also could hear my mother saying, "Sister . . . ," and so forth. Questions!

When I heard from one of my high school students that he saw things in color, I reasoned that he was on drugs. No! It was real and not imagined and not tied to drugs. I worked closely with his therapist.

The subject of autism can become controversial; what it is and what it is not? Since 2009, I have followed the brilliant mind of a scientist Dr. Simon Baron-Cohen who was a professor of developmental psychopathology at Cambridge University and director of its Autism Research Centre. Baron-Cohen earned degrees in Human Sciences from New College, Oxford, a Ph.D. in Psychology from University College London, and a Master of Philosophy in Clinical Psychology at the Institute of Psychiatry, King's College London.

I know of none other than Dr. Simon Baron-Cohen, who has helped me understand the minds of autism and Asperger's than those with these conditions. I recommend a study of his books and writings.

Baron-Cohen has argued that while people on the autism spectrum are strong *systematizers*—showing a strong attraction to systems . . . so are their parents. His most recent idea is that autism may be the result of the assortative mating of two strong systemizing parents. Evidence for this includes the finding that both mothers and fathers of children on the autism spectrum have excellent attention to and memory for detail—as measured on the Embedded Figures Test. The grandfathers of children with autism, on both sides of the family, are more likely to have worked in the field of engineering, which demands good systemizing skills. Information from (Synapse Inc.)

Those who are professionals looking at autism agree that it is somewhat defined by poor social skills, communication difficulties, limited interests, repetitive behaviors, inappropriate laughing, no fear of dangers, insensitivity to pain, may not want cuddling, eye contact, and spins objects or self.

A critical view has changed; you either have it or you don't, to the idea advanced by Baron-Cohen that *everyone* **has it**. He explained this by the analogy of measuring height. All of us fall on the spectrum of height as we do on the spectrum of autism. As he sees it, *we are all a little bit Autistic,* some more than others: preferring to be alone, disliking lack of routine, understanding patterns, along with systemizing and giving attention to detail. Careful what we label!

Dr. Baron-Cohen continues to share information that the same genes that make a person good in an occupation of systemizing like math, physics, engineering, and I believe in many other fields, may be the same genes that contribute to autism. I recently watched a video clip where he shared that Albert Einstein said, "I do not socialize because [it] would distract me from my work." He was more interested in how things work.

Why do we hear these terms more and more? Baron-Cohen said, *"I don't think it's the right way to think about Autism as an epidemic."*

29

Asperger's or What?

A special education teacher shared experiences which I have also encountered. We have by definition had students with autism, as well as those labeled as Asperger's. Subsequently, I have interacted with them socially. This awareness has given me a longer view of their social interactions. I stand by the opinion that Asperger's should not be included with autism anymore than it should be included with dyslexia.

From *my* point of view, and some hold this idea to be controversial, I feel that autism and Asperger's are uniquely different. My concern is to note precisely how Asperger's and autism are frequently lumped closely together, probably considering they have symptoms in common.

Living in a society that has concerns along with its efforts to help children learn, it has categorically created labels and designed what it deems to be the most effective educational interventions for students having these conditions.

More than once, I have taught students who have been diagnosed as having autism and others having Asperger's. There is an overlap of symptoms that are *alike* between autism and Asperger's. However, there is also an overlap of symptoms with other declared but more general diagnoses, such as Behavior Disorders, Emotionally Disturbed, Dyslexia or Learning Disabilities, along with being Gifted.

The same goes for students who have been labeled with dyslexia. They all might have difficulties in getting along with other people. Even with the challenges of communication skills in both cases, individuals with dyslexia, as well as those with Asperger's, tend to show language and cognitive development closer to that of the typically developing child. My sampling is limited to my experiences. It is easier for my mind to wrap around an ocean of *differences* between those said to have autism and those with Asperger's. The following characteristics have been displayed with individuals said to have Asperger's.

Difficulty with Social Relationships

Unlike people with classic autism, who often appear withdrawn and uninterested in the world around them, many people with Asperger's Syndrome *try very hard to be sociable and enjoy human contact*. However, they do find it hard to understand some of the subtle implications of social interactions. They often have a difficult time with understanding—following conversations with others; however, others may have a difficult time understanding them. This lack of understanding and interest level can generate a given response which can leave all without satisfaction. This situation could occur with either an adult or a child. Is it a deficit? Who has the deficit?

Difficulty with Communications

People with Asperger's Syndrome *may sometimes speak very fluently, but they may not take much notice of the reaction of people listening to them*. They may talk on and on even if the person with whom they are speaking is not connecting with them. Despite having excellent language skills, they may sound more concrete in their thinking; it is like following a pattern. Their intellectual capacity is often more involved and in-depth than those with whom they are conversing which can cause an emotional gap. I ask, "Who has the deficit?"

Special Interests

People with Asperger's often develop an interest in something with an obsession and hence with an absorption of time and energy while blocking out other benefits in their environment. Usually, their interest involves arranging an interest in patterns. And again, we find that researchers have some of this obsession, I ask, "Who has the deficit?"

244

Routines

For people with Asperger's any *unexpected change in a routine can be upsetting*. In other words, changes in the details of behavior can be very upsetting regardless of whether it is a change for self or others. The observed details are driving the engine. "Who has the deficit?"

Poor Concentration and Easily Distracted

These are very common for those with Asperger's Syndrome as they often *appear off task and may be easily distracted*. Are they *off* task or so focused *on* a task? I have seen my students who seem to be off task, but were not! Concentrating! And then some outside stimulus rack their brains? And then the fact that something else was going on broke their concentration. Distracted! They are extra sensitive to *touch, sound, smell, sight, and what others are feeling*.

A researcher and designer for teaching interventions, Ron Davis shared his opinion that since *"Autism has only been recognized since the 1940s, there is speculation about deceased individuals as to diagnoses about brain function. Their post diagnoses are based on reported behaviors, rather than on psychological assessments."* Ron Davis not only includes himself in the list of having the characteristics of autism, but he includes other known and historical persons on the list. This list consists of those who could have had dyslexia, autism, or Asperger's. You can find information about famous individuals from the internet, libraries, and personal experiences.

I recall a student who I would like to share with you. Let's call my student Anthony, who has Asperger's. He wanted to come to my room because there was order, routine, and no noise. He didn't seem to know how to organize things like his books and papers. He only focused on one detail at a time. I remember showing him the whole picture which included the folders we made for each subject and where to place the papers in different folders. He just wanted to put all the papers in one folder. He saw that one folder as his whole world and perseverated on

245

that detail without seeing a need to categorize into separate folders. Also, his regular classroom was filled with an attitude of exploration and *noise*. Anthony had a very low tolerance for noise.

Anthony did enjoy going to university football games. We realized that he enjoyed the rules of the game with an understanding of *why* things changed and enjoyed watching the game unfold. But, when other fans got excited and stood and yelled, he would swear and yell at them because he didn't have the words to tell his parents he couldn't deal with the noise. Not yet understanding this, they would punish him by withholding food and treats at the game. That didn't work, so they tried rewarding him with treats if he would just sit still and not use such bad language. That didn't work either. Nothing worked until they realized that it was the *noise*. So our next move was to try earplugs, and it worked.

Anthony would bring his assignments to my relatively quiet room where he was able to accomplish things after he took a run around the track. This activity seemed to ground him and distract him from his messed-up day in the regular classroom. After the run, it was back to my room for getting the job done, and Anthony excelled. Because of his keen interest in books about how things in this world work, I rewarded him for a job well done with such books to read. It was not food that I used, but it was his interest in books that opened his world.

Anthony was a bright student for whom the following statement works well."How to think smarter about who thinks differently, sometimes or always." Who has the problem? I know and Hallelujah!

Again, I have doubted the value of placing students in a particular pattern of classifying and labeling. No matter what the label, my success was based on my *relationship* with students and the specific intervention plan that addressed many problems. I did not discount the testing and observation, but I viewed them as *part*, not the *whole*, of understanding the student. Having an open mind and thinking outside the box was my path to getting a job done. I never let a label influence and predetermine an outcome.

In 2013, there was a study which interested me and that I feel I must share. This study was by Frank H. Duffy, Aditi Shankardass, Gloria B. McAnulty, and Heidelise Als entitled *The relationship of Asperger's syndrome to Autism: a preliminary EEG coherence study.* The debate was centered on the subject as to whether Asperger's Syndrome should be considered as part of the Autism Spectrum Disorders or whether it should be a unique entity. By now you know where I sit in judgment with my limited experience and with limited case studies. The Duffy *et al.* study uses EEG coherence to measure brain connectivity and to explore possible differences between autism and Asperger's. The discussion continues.

The Duffy study concludes that when the autism and Asperger's populations are compared directly, they are distinctly separate. The Asperger's population appears to constitute a neurophysiologically identifiable and normally distributed entity within the higher functioning tail of the autism population. Asperger's function at a higher intellectual level. As I understand the issues from my experience, I believe there is an overlapping of symptoms; however, not unlike other syndromes.

Given my experience, I have observed while teaching students who struggle with each of these two conditions that it is more helpful to emphasize the uniqueness of these two conditions than it is to conceptualize and emphasize their commonalities. However, I remain with my opinion that there is a difference between the two entities; they are different. And does it matter? It shouldn't; we should be addressing the stumbling blocks to functioning in society and figuring how to help. Again, I find that labels are just that, labels. Do we know with precision *what to call what?* However, I find them sometimes helpful and sometimes limiting. How do we have the power to understand?

As I have observed and taught students with these diagnoses, I have seen how living in the world is for them; they are overwhelmed, and I am overwhelmed just knowing what the issues are for them. The behavior of these individuals is frequently misunderstood by the adults in their world.

This misunderstanding also applies to adults with the same brain design. As I have learned from my experiences, I have searched for others who have the same opinions on the subject. Is it or is it not? Overwhelming!

In my searching, I have found a knowledgeable person, Lori Pedro, who has a handle on what I believe to be true. She shares the following insight for all of us to ponder and apply. Lori is aware that she has this brain gift which has been called Asperger's. Look for Lori on the internet. Lori does an excellent job of summarizing salient points about what should be considered in understanding the world of Asperger's. Lori says, *"It is a hypersensitivity to stimuli and not a lack of engagement or recognition that causes Spies* [Asperger's] *to strongly react or shut down."* As a teacher I have seen this to be true!

Lori also shares what I have studied, and many others have reported true that these individuals can be oversensitive to sound, touch, smell, taste, and what they see. Sensory input! I know that they love deeply and sincerely. With this love, they can be hurt and have a difficult time with articulating a response. Also, they are unable to refute negative messages that they hear about themselves as they hold the belief that the message is *true,* and they hold a very deep hurt. They do not just listen; they apply the information they hear and live up to the labels they are given. I agree with empathy for everything mentioned and have observed these behaviors many times. And again! I do not like labels. Those with this brainprint are intuitive and can read the feelings of others with accuracy.

Have you ever felt like *nothing* as the monster called, *"You're not good enough,"* takes over your soul? Through this lens of looking at a small, inadequate detail of the person rather than the whole person, the reality of life can be viewed as a distortion of the truth.

Now, how on earth did this thinking surface? Yesterday, with ease, I opened the kitchen door, just living life as usual. I closed the door and then opened it; fine it was. Tried to close it and it would not close. Tried again, and it would not close. It seemed to be broken, and it only took seconds to break. I could not get it closed!

Grandpa came to check out my screams for help! I could not seem to do the fixing of the door. He tried, and it still would not close. After I studied the situation, a small bit of virtually invisible wood was found hiding in the corner, which was keeping the door from shutting.

As I problem-solved around the situation with the door, it became symbolic of life's story. In my relationships, a small but impinging something can keep a relationship from moving forward. It is difficult to not look at the whole relationship as a failure rather than moving the *small bit of wood* out of the way, and I often need help in moving that small bit of wood out of the way in a relationship. Relationships, yes, need the bits of wood out of the way! As I have interacted with my Asperger's students, it has been a joy to look beyond the details of differences to see the whole of a very talented and gifted person. I must move the bits of wood, not them.

Dr. Asperger said, *"For success in science a dash of Autism is essential."* And I add that for success in life a dash of Asperger's is essential. I am an aware teacher because I can identify that which I see in myself. Dr. Hans Asperger, who came up with this syndrome, also had the conditions he observed and described. That is often the case; who we are, we recognize in others. *"We discover in ourselves what others hide from us, and we recognize in others what we hide from ourselves."* (Vauvenargues, 1715 – 1747)

There is a bit of Aspergers in all of us. Well at least in some of us.

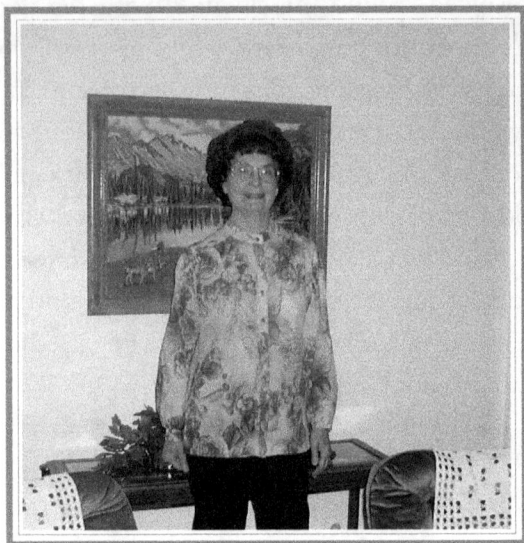

Dr. Betty Harrison and I took the opportunity to visit for hours as we renewed our treasured friendship. As a Special Education educator, she shared her mind and heart for her profession. With an inspired attitude, Betty encouraged me to share her message of wisdom to teach needed skills. I will share.

30

Learning Disabilities:
Dr. Betty Harrison, University Professor

I was retiring from my exhausting but rewarding teaching job in the Alpine School District. For years, I had a postcard tucked away in my file cabinet announcing with enthusiasm the opportunity for a special education teacher to come and enjoy the Hawaiian spirit. My adventurous heart said, "Let's go!" For this, I must prepare, so I went to visit my friend Dr. Betty Harrison to tell her that Hawaii was calling.

This day, I spent over three hours with Betty. She taught at BYU where she was a noted professor in the Department of Educational Psychology and Special Education.

In 1982, I remembered first walking into the office of Dr. Harrison. I was as scared as a fearful rabbit and as uncomfortable as if walking on hot coals. I didn't want to be there. However, I had come to Utah from Arizona, and I had to see Dr. Betty Harrison to get information from her so that I could continue with some classwork and start teaching in Utah. She was the "big wheel" in the Special Education department, and I was scared of her. Scared! She knew so much about my field that left me feeling like a shadow of what I wanted to know and didn't. She had the *shoulders of a giant* on which I desired to stand. I gratefully took some classes from her and stood amazed at the information she expected her students to wrap themselves around.

By the time I had finished some classes, Betty knew me. I did a class project that she said was equal to a master's thesis. Betty would have known. I was relieved that she was impressed. Our relationship unfolded until she was recommending that I become active in the C.E.C. (Council for Exceptional Children). She suggested that I run for a state office. Subsequently, I became the state of Utah vice president working with Steve Kuchic.

Steve Kuchic was an excellent example of what the President of the Council for Exceptional Children should epitomize. His mantra was *Mainstreaming is an attitude, not a place.* I liked that mantra, and it became part of my educational philosophy. The best practice for teaching is not *a* place but *all* places. For me, this has meant without diagnostic labels.

Through the years, Betty and I have had many educational talks, sharing philosophies, and visiting about more personal situations. Betty became my friend with a friendship that I have valued without fear or being scared. When my plans began to materialize for teaching in Hawaii, I needed Betty's inspiration. This writing summarizes the visit.

Betty went to Hawaii for the teaching year of 1967-1968. She took leave from BYU. Her assignment was to teach half-time at the University of Hawaii and half-time doing research at the Linapuni School K-3. This school is on Oahu in Kalihi, and it had an alternate Kindergarten. The school was a challenging environment; however, it didn't take Betty long to appreciate her experience and to love the children.

In 1967, Betty's work included introducing her expertise at the Varsity School for Learning Disabilities in Honolulu. This school was the first pre-school for Learning Disabilities in the state. The Apgar test was used for placement.

Betty wrote the draft on Learning Disabilities Education for the state of Hawaii and presented it to Hatsuko Kawahara, an educator on the faculty at the University of Hawaii at Manoa. Hatsuko was involved with the Center for Oral History. She was a teacher, an administrator, and also served on the Board of Education. Betty respected Hatsuko Kawahara.

Betty handed me a tiny piece of newsprint with information that she had kept with fond regards.
Star Bulletin news: *"Hatsuko Furuhashi Kawahara died Aug 1, 2004.*

252

She was 93, of Honolulu, a retired educator. She was born in Honolulu. She is survived by daughters Billie Ikeda and Carri Kawahara, sister Betsy Furuhashi, two grandchildren, and two great-grandchildren. Private services."

In 1970, Betty went back to Hawaii to give a workshop on Learning Disabilities.

She said she feels that three things are necessary.

- Structure
- Security
- Understanding the brain

Structure, security and understanding the brain: As she sat with the student or students, she said, "I have a secret. I know something about you that you know about you. When you learn something new, how do you learn it?" As she followed their comments, she learned about them as they were learning about themselves. She heard them saying, "Learn by doing, singing, jumping, eyes closed, no students talking, drawing pictures, small bits at a time, notes on the board, pictures of the subject, talking about the subject, and by hearing stories to associate meaning to remember." These are some of the ways they said would help them learn. Kids came up with their own strategies! And we thought we knew the know-how.

What a great idea Betty! As she guided their *learning about learning*, she was learning the answer to her secret. How did the students learn?

The students became secure in their ability to figure out how they could remember what needed to be learned. Through this information, Betty created the structure with which she taught given information. This structure, in turn, created a foundation of security which let them know that they were not *dumb* but could learn with certain tools. As their understanding of the brain unfolded, the students had a tool for achieving success. I call this approach *Learning to Learn*.

From the time the child is born, the *sponge* called the brain is seeking

253

information and soaking it up. Our brain is like the animal called Sponge. They are diverse and come in a large variety of structural complexities. Sponges are known for their exceptional ability to absorb water. The current artificial household sponges are designed after a natural creature of the sea. At one time the skeletons of these animals were used to mop water away. I remember my mother telling me about how this sea creature soaked up water. Artificial sponges are made because they are less expensive. Our brains will do the same *soaking* with sensory information. And with that comes the responsibility we have as caretakers to carefully *shovel* the appropriate information into the mind since it will come out at some point. What goes in usually comes out!

Betty's Classification Story

Betty Dodge was born in Wyoming and had a somewhat unusual educational start. As a teacher, when we are making educational decisions, this following experience that she had was one through which we can glean wisdom.

When Betty was eleven years old, her mother moved the family to Provo, Utah. The first day of school found Betty with other new arrivals to be placed in appropriate classes.

The principal asked the children, "Where are you from?"

The first child stated, "Herriman."

The second child stated, "Herriman."

The third child stated, "Herriman."

Betty didn't know where she had lived. When the principal asked, "Where are you from?" Betty quickly replied, "Herriman." Seemed to Betty to be an understandable response.

When the school found out she was from Wyoming, not Herriman, Utah, they figured she was mentally retarded and placed her in a special unit.

Later, Betty was declassified and did well in her new class. Of course, the moral of this story is that we have a responsibility to review gathered information, set an intervention in place, and apply the intervention to the *best practices* to assure the success of the student. Again, I say we should not label and classify. However, we should know the skill level and place an intervention designed for achievement.

On that day, as my time with Betty came to an end, I knew that Hawaii was calling me. I wanted to go where Betty had been, and I desired to continue her journey with my shorter footprints, never to fill her shoes, but inspired by her wisdom. I knew that Waianae High was where I longed to be. I love and appreciate Betty Harrison, my mentor, and friend.

Thank you, Dr. Harrison, for understanding the phenomenon called Learning Disabilities—disabilities are when a deficit interferes with normal functioning. We know that everyone has a deficit.

As Betty and I visited, she shared that which she felt to be just good teaching; good teaching is good teaching, no matter what, with or without labels or classification. It has been my experience that the following suggestions of "best practices" should be considered in every classroom. Some of the suggestions can also be considered by parents who are seeking answers as to what to do when their child is not learning as expected.

For the national government to be involved with education, they felt the need to call certain deficits a disability to create guidelines for control and thus forward support to remedy the situation. My belief is like unto Betty's studied outlook: a deficit does not always need to be *fixed,* only when it interferes with normal functioning.

Written by Dr. Betty D. Harrison as Shared with Argie

Definition: *Students with special learning disabilities exhibit a disorder in one or more of the basic psychological processes involved in understanding or in using spoken or written languages. These may be manifested as disorders in listening, thinking, talking, reading, writing, spelling, or arithmetic. They include conditions which have been referred to as perceptual handicaps, brain injury, minimal brain* *dysfunction, Dyslexia, not due primarily visual, hearing, or motor handicaps to mental retardation, emotional disturbance, or to environmental disadvantage."* First annual report – National Advisory Committee of Handicapped Children, January 31, 1969, p. 34, US Department of Health, Education and Welfare, Office of Education.

Characteristics of Learning Disabilities

1. Appears to be bright but doesn't learn.
2. Appears insatiably driven or hyperactive.
3. Excels in one subject, fails another, and may fluctuate.
4. Appears to follow other students rather than directions.
5. Appears to be listening for auditory clues instead of watching visual clues.
6. Appears forgetful of repetitive physical—environmental situations. Student can't find the desk in the classroom, bus, office, cafeteria, pencils, books, or yesterday's assignment.
7. Reverses letters, parts of words, or whole words when writing.
8. Has short attention span and is easily distracted.
9. Appears not to hear or mistakes what is heard.
10. Clumsy: drops books, pencils, bumps into others, and has general coordination problems, can't catch ball without using whole body, falls easily.
11. Appears to forget what was learned yesterday or even a few minutes ago.
12. Appears unpredictable emotionally, and angers easily, tires easily, impulsive in behavior, inappropriate emotional responses.

Identification Procedures

A. Learning disabilities occur on a continuum ranging from mild to severe, depending on the number of characteristics manifested and the intensity with which the symptoms occur. There is a tendency for learning disabilities to become more severe with age due to emotional overlay which may develop as a result of repeated exposure to the experiences of failure in the classroom, as well as in the home situation.

B. Although it is desirable that as much medical, psychological, academic, and social information be obtained on the person with a suspected learning disability, treatment should not be delayed until this information is gathered in its entirety.

C. Students with learning disabilities are usually identified first by the discrepancy between actual performance in the classroom and the expected level of functioning. The expected level of functioning should be based on some normative combinations of mental age, chronological age, and achievement tests. *"When a significant discrepancy is found between expected and actual performance (e.g., in reading, a discrepancy between CA and individual or MA [chronological age and mental age] and the level of difficulty of the misarticulated words), a disability exists."* (Bateman 1967) Attention should be paid to the variability of performance on subtests rather than on global scores due to the expected erratic performance of persons with learning disabilities.

D. A detailed, comprehensive, and behavioral description of the disability should be obtained, usually through the use of checklists of potential deficit areas.

Types of Programs

Placement in a program setting should be determined by the severity of the learning disability, the intensity of treatment needed, the amount of emotional overlay which has been built up in connection with the learning deficits, and an analysis of the ways in which the person both differs and approximates the characteristics of others in given age or social group. Emphasis should be placed upon keeping the student in as normal a school situation as possible while receiving treatment.

Programming

A student's need for assistance in overcoming his learning disability may vary from placement on a full-day basis in a special class, part-time placement with a resource teacher, or minor adaptations made by the regular classroom teacher so that student may remain with his regular class. The following suggestions are made for helping the student to remain in the regular classroom setting.

1. Hyperactivity: Shorten the length of tasks, cut seat work papers into sections for greater variety and varying degrees of difficulty.

2. Problems of memory: Teach with available information rather than depend on a faulty memory: multiplication tables, abacus, dictionary, writing work on board for quick check, testing for number of syllables by "chin drop," mnemonic reasoning for recall. "Remember to tie a string around your finger."

3. Discoordination in writing: Have student use graph paper, give paper guides for arrangement on page, have student fold paper for arithmetic, spelling, and whenever a guide is needed.

4. Distractibility: Let student move to a quiet corner of the room away from the auditory—sounds or away from the visual—windows, bulletin boards, etc., less decorative corner of the room.

5. Reversals: Have student finger trace the shape of the first letter in a word, if possible, or encourage student to learn to typewrite and then type assignments.

6. Dependence on auditory or visual clues: Present information by both approaches by writing on the chalkboard and also verbalize instructions to the class.

7. Sequencing: Arrange papers in proper order with written and oral instructions, step-by-step instructions, sequenced pictures to compensate and trigger taught information. Tape instruction for accessibility. Teach categorization to learn the skill of ordering objects. Teach with an organized and sequenced lesson plan.

8. Emotional lability: Recognize inappropriate emotional responses as being symptoms of the student's inability to organize

appropriate responses and not as personally directed attacks.

9. Basic coordination: Give experiences with body movement activities—Simon says, dancing, walking lines, hopping, skipping, using chalkboard.

10. Perception: Analyze tasks for figure-ground, form constancy, spatial relations, and directionality problems before presenting lesson to class, and give students hints for dealing with task before class starts.

11. Conceptualization: Help student to use all the sensory information received and to approach learning systematically. For the student with a *leaky bucket* or one not able to hold the given information which has been taught and apparently learned, design opportunities with experiences to learn the concept. For students with a *sticky bucket* help them tie concepts to other information.

12. Receiving sensory information: Give individual basic training in different ways that we receive information: listening exercises, visual practice, tactile-kinesthetic experiences.

13. Focusing: Teach student to listen or watch for specifics and sort out what is important.

14. Associating with past experiences: Help student to see relationships with present information on an inter-related basis.

15. Organizing a response: Give adequate time for student to think about making a response. Give credit for response pattern, as well as the end answer.

16. Making a response: Help student choose the most appropriate response and to learn techniques of transmitting information on spoken, written, or gestural bases.

17. Monitoring the response: Teach students how to check their work, and check other's work when appropriate.

Summary

This information may be recognized as nothing more than just good teaching. By sharing the teacher's specific and recently learned knowledge of the person's learning challenge and by encouraging mutual observation of that learning behavior, both the teacher and person may discover things which can be helpful in modifying the teaching and learning approach. If this results in an improvement, talk about what the process was and move on to the next step in the remedial plan. Task by task, the goal is achieved.

Thank you, Dr. Harrison!

Given my experience, I know that the term "learning disability" is vague, and anyone who fails to learn what society wants or expects is labeled. I have recently heard someone say, "I have a disability since I don't feel close to the Christmas Spirit." We have become ridiculous about the meaning of disability and are trying to label everything. Deficits are not disabilities unless they create a dysfunction. I will also say that attitudes and moral decay are not cognitive deficits but moral deficits, poor judgment or both.

One may ask the question, "Why are you writing to share ideas?" My answer is simple: *I too must give.* As a successful teacher, I have learned much from my peers, and we have shared. I desire to continue to provide ideas which have worked for me and others. Sharing!

My message will extend this information to the broader community: a community which has a desire to understand better how to reduce the barriers to learning while improving the quality of learning and applying those interventions for a better life. As a result, successful teachers employ strategies that lead to improved student outcomes. Successful students, parents, teachers, and community service caretakers can be distinguished by the number and types of successful strategies that they employ daily to address situations that arise in homes, classrooms, and working environments. For those of you who are dumbfounded and yelling for help, keep up the energy.

Strategies will be extended throughout this book. It may sound like I am saying the same things over and over again. I am! Trying to say it in another way will hopefully tie into your mind a way that will not be forgotten and will work for you in varied situations. As you read, you will probably say, "Argie Ella is saying that again." I am intentionally repeating so that you will know it is very important. Keeping an open mind and knowing there is not *one answer for all situations and all children* is the pathway to being creative and forever learning. Don't give up!

Betty Harrison instilled hope in the world of Special Education and in those whom she knew. Her attitude was to paint a picture in the minds of others that there is a way through the tunnel of darkness. Find it!

I wish my children had experienced teacher's who had known the strategies that Dr. Betty Harrison has outlined so well for us. As I wrote this book and visited with family members, my son Brad shared his feelings about how it was difficult for him in the world of cognitive differences. He expressed his pain in being bullied because of his processing uniqueness. I feel that because we are all unique with differences in our brainprints, we all can question how others are viewing us and our competencies. This message could be your story. Brad will share his story of living with his unique brain. Brad Reneer is a computer programmer for a university. He is a successful father and community member. Not *dumb*!

Bullies
By Bradley Reneer

We all want to be good at something, and we don't enjoy failure. We usually think of bullies as physical aggressors; however, those who excel in any area can become bullies, and those who don't excel at anything can also become bullies. For example, a professional investor and expert at managing portfolios may look at a client as a dimwit, even though this client might excel in other areas.

I've seen the same thing among computer experts because they are skilled with computers, they may look down on those who don't know computers. Computers are the center of their expertise, and they judge others based on their own interests. Several times, I have heard computer programmers say things like, "You have to remember that all of our users are idiots" or "Why are they so stupid?" This sad story has even happened more than once in an academic setting where users hold doctorates in psychology, history, physics, and other fields. It was obvious to me that these were not idiots, but the idiots may have been those of us who couldn't write a computer program that was intuitive enough and clear enough for people to use without needing to become experts in computers themselves. We may have programmers and computer programs that are basically technology bullies.

When we have an area of expertise, we may be tempted to treat that area of expertise as the most important, and we value others based only on their skill or lack of skill in that area. Thus, we become bullies.

Another example refers to people who are very good with interpersonal skills and how they choose to use such skills. They can use that power to manipulate those who are less able in personal and verbal skills. One reason that lawyers have a negative reputation, despite there being many good lawyers, is that their knowledge and skills give them great power. Too many lawyers use this advantage unfairly and arrogantly. Such misuse of power makes them bullies.

Growing up, I experienced being bullied physically, as well as emotionally and academically. I think everyone has probably been bullied at one time or another. Some may not have recognized it as bullying because we tend to use that term in our society for physical bullying. Although we have begun recognizing cyberbullying and other forms of emotional bullying, I think other forms of bullying are much more common than we realize. We may even experience a form of bullying from a salesperson who uses knowledge of the product to manipulate us into buying.

When one grows up with a learning disability, it is easy for those who don't struggle in the same way to be at least perceived as bullies. They can unintentionally make someone who has a learning disability feel *dumb*. Instead of recognizing that a person's talents may lie in other areas, such as being physically talented, musically talented, having a special rapport with animals, interpersonal skills, empathy, or artistic skills, they can feel stupid because they are not as skilled in one narrow area of ability.

It is difficult for someone who is not good at numbers, or who is not good at reading, or not good at writing, to not feel stupid. Despite how the public educational system portrays itself, it has lots of intellectual bullies. They could excel in reading, writing, mathematics, or some other specialty. If a person does not have strength in the same area as that professor or top of the class student, the student with the low grade may leave school feeling inferior, flawed, rejected, and even worthless.

Some will get validation in sports, music, or some other "approved" alternative. But even then, the athlete may go through life feeling inferior because of not succeeding academically. Some bookworms may feel uncomfortable in other areas. All are left feeling inferior because of their *lack,* instead of feeling validated in the area where they excel. And those that fall outside the high-status areas will especially feel inferior.

I think it is unfortunate that programs like wood-shop and auto mechanics have been cut from the curriculum. Students who could excel in those areas may be left with the awareness that they aren't good at college-bound skills.

The academic system emphasizes the supremacy of those who have succeeded inside the academic system. Often accomplishments outside academia are either dismissed, minimized, or openly mocked. A student who may struggle with reading should be helped with reading while also being recognized for abilities in other areas, such as skills in mechanics, with animals, or for being friendly. If they don't excel in academia which includes areas that are admittedly important in modern society, they are

263

made to feel less than important. Someone who has incredible mechanical ability, who would make a great auto mechanic, who would even be great at designing or inventing, may never reach the point where they can do that kind of design if they don't make it through this filter in our educational system that requires great reading and math abilities. Such students will often take on anti-social roles in a system that puts them down. Someone who is struggling in important academic areas should be helped in those areas, while simultaneously being recognized for their other intelligences and abilities.

While I don't remember my early education clearly, I am confident that my mother and excellent teachers were persistent and patient with my slowness. As they were persistent, I compensated for some minor learning deficits.

In 1st grade, I was sent to the reading area of our classroom. I sat there with a friend as we both read copies of the same book. I began reading quietly to myself, but my friend was reading aloud. It was very difficult for me to concentrate on my reading while he read aloud. I was reading faster than he was reading aloud. It was slowing me down to hear him. Finally, I asked him if he would mind reading quietly. He was fine with that and read silently. I was surprised a few minutes later when he finished his book, first. Apparently, reading silently, he read much quicker than when he read the words aloud. For me, there wasn't much difference in my reading speed. I didn't understand that some people could read faster silently than aloud.

Math and reading are critical in our society. We must have those skills to compete and survive. For example, being mathematically ignorant opens one to all sorts of foolish decisions, everything from buying lottery tickets to making bad loans. Poor money decisions are rampant in a society where basic math skills are lacking. I, myself, am not a great reader. I am a very slow reader. As a child, I found a great deal of joy in books and reading, even though I read slowly.

It appears that our educational system values writing skills and publishing over any other ability. The pinnacle of learning seems to be, in the educator's mind, the full professorship. As in every other area, it is natural, a result of our pride, our egotism, that we want the area we succeed in to be the most important area. As institutionalized in the structure of our educational system, it makes those whose greatest talents are in other areas feel diminished. I'm grateful for teachers who, despite the structure of our system, reach out and make students feel valued and help them overcome learning challenges.

My mom remembers when I was in the 3rd grade. In the middle of the school year, the teachers decided to advance me to the next grade considering that I was doing well in all subjects and was bored. However, I remained a slow reader which concerned the teachers. Mom said one reason I was a slow reader was that I would sit and study the pictures on the pages until I had memorized them. She said that I liked the dictionary because of the pictures. Mom would watch me as I studied and said that I was using my visual processing more than my auditory processing. And she would know!

Deficits are not disabilities.

The first pine tree on the island of Lanai was a Norfolk Pine. I sat looking up through the needles and I was fascinated that here in Hawaii I was enjoying the magic of pine trees. All over the island! Reflections are like looking up through the needles.

31

Reflections:
Leaving Hawaii for the Mainland

Dear Little Journal,

You are my second journal this year. Here at Eagle Valley, our principal has asked us to reflect historically to summarize our feelings about our experiences as teachers. He also challenged us to share our minds about this school year of 2004-2005. The end goal is to engage in forward thinking about "Building a Professional Community in Schools" where students and teachers will benefit from *empowerment* when a professional community commits to fundamental changes in teaching practices. There must be support within the school for teachers who want to take risks and try new techniques and ideas. Otherwise, lasting change cannot be sustained. There should be daily opportunities for discussion among small groups with common interests, such as academic departments or grade levels, as well as regular meetings with the entire faculty. Look at the past to improve the future. Great ideas!

As I sit here thinking where to begin, it is with tearful pondering and sometimes frustration that I write. The precious moments of satisfaction and reward will also be written. So much I want to say, words and more words.

After teaching in a high school on Oahu in Hawaii for the school years of 2002-2003 and 2003-2004, my old district here in Utah hired me back and celebrated my return for 2004-2005. However, I am returning to Hawaii next year 2005-2006. Hawaii will hire me to teach another year which will be my third year there. Excited!

Reflecting back to the year 2004, I decided to return to the Mainland. The reality of the decision started on the peaceful and quiet island of Lanai. Lanai had a high school opening for the year of 2004-2005. We had flown over to explore the possibility of accepting a position. The love energy that flows from the Polynesian people says "hello" to my heart.

I did not pursue that opportunity. I felt a pulling at my heartstrings to go home to Utah. However, I had desired to explore the possibility as to the desirability and opportunity of such a placement in the future. Yes, I would have very much enjoyed teaching on this timeless island so far removed from what I perceived as a rough sea of change.

Lanai is the smallest of the Hawaiian islands. There wasn't even a security check at the airport. Only one town of modest size and its charm grabbed me like none other. Few people lived on Lanai—about 3,000 people. I could have had a lasting and treasured relationship with this island.

Lanai! It is a study of harmony in contrast. It is a place with the hot sun, cool mist, desert flowers, and rain forests. Its sheer cliffs, sparkling beaches, unpolluted air and water along with other faces which brought me to a place of softness and the lack of confusion. I loved the imported pine trees, the incredible history, no stoplights, and few people. Peace came to my soul as I fell in love with this precious island. Its face is real and without pretense. My dream is for the family to live in this place of peace and simplicity. I have touched an eternal feeling of contentment, light without confusion, and a picture of an honest relationship with the world and self; the harmony in my little oasis felt real.

The decision, which pulled at my heart, was the need to go home to the Mainland. I had missed opportunities for my family to be part of my dream. Longingly!

Knowing that I was returning to Utah for the next school year, I called my old school district in Utah and told them that I was returning. A few days later while I was wrapped in the comfort and joy of isolation in the surreal world of Lanai, the phone started to ring. Startled back into reality from my *dream come true*, I committed myself to teaching on the Mainland with two very competent principals, one at Pony Express Elementary and the other at Eagle Valley Elementary, west of Lehi, Utah. The road between the two schools was the setting of the old Pony Express route back in the history of the "mail by horse" pioneer days. Unique settings!

While sitting on the porch of the rustic Lanai Hotel, the whole of me was enjoying the sweet morning air with the freshness of another stressless day, eating a breakfast of fruit, yogurt, herbal tea, and muffins, I accepted a job to teach at two elementary schools for another year back in Utah.

Then I was surprised by another phone call from a friend and principal with whom I had taught for many years. Kim called a few hours after the first principals had called. He offered me a job. This call was a difficult moment in time for me to contemplate the desires of my heart. My heart was on Lanai, and another heart was in Utah, two hearts. Oh, if Kim had only called earlier. I had just committed to other schools in the district, but I would have jumped at a chance to return to Kim's school. I had been a successful teacher with Kim as the principal. I desired to repeat that experience. What a dilemma having committed to an unknown situation and here is Kim with a highly desirable offer to return to his school. What a difficult bind. What a difference a few hours can make. Awkward!

I am clear about the concept of "your word is your bond" and my parents would have been disappointed in the values of their daughter had I changed my direction due to my self-serving preference. I would have been disappointed in myself since I had just said "yes" to the two principals. To this day, I wonder how it would have been, had I said "yes" to my friend and principal who called me after the fact.

I had just finished teaching for two years on Oahu, this change in placement from the beautiful islands of Hawaii back to Utah came because of my love, concern, and commitment to being a mother and grandmother. I felt I needed to be closer to the family. I wish they would move to *my* dream.

I have been in education for many years, about thirty years, more or less. It all started as a way to survive hard times with a husband who was sick and four little children who needed care by parents who were not functioning well financially. I never desired to be a career person; however, my world forced me into that position. My dream and desire on this earth was and is to be a mother and a grandmother without complications. I have made some abysmal choices that turned a peaceful tide into a dangerous wave; sometimes too difficult to successfully ride safely to the shore. On occasion, the lack of faith and the control of fear have weakened me into poor decisions. On the other hand, my faith has been a great comforter, a friend, and companion to carry me through some trials. Growth has come with insights and lessons which I have learned and remembered as needed.

As I continued my journey with the desire to "amount to something" to fulfill my Daddy's dream for me, I furthered my education. What I have learned from that adventure and how I have used it has been a reward for my family, friends, and students.

Back on the Mainland, this year with Pony Express Elementary and Eagle Valley Elementary has brought the challenge of driving for forty minutes to Pony and continuing to Eagle for another twelve minutes making it about an hour's drive from my home. As I calculate this math problem, it means I had to spend about two hours a day on the road, and this is not the Road to Hana. However, the reward for all this driving was to daily feed on the beauty of the vast semi-arid desert of Eagle Valley. Loved it at seventy years young.

I found myself going to school as early as 5:00 a.m. and staying as late as 11:00 p.m. in the evening. The reason is that I was managing the Special Education program in two schools.

At Eagle Valley Elementary, I did not have a room of my own at first, so I moved from "here to there" and finally ended up with "there" being a very small room off the gym, the coach's room. It housed the smells of the day: food, bathroom, etc. The students were packed into the room side-by-side and lacked the needed space to separate their energies. I have an organizational situation in my brain with difficulty sequencing details. Hard! Along with this cognitive malady, I am a perfectionist, so I always seem to find myself in the throes of its energies. The whiteboard was over a cabinet, difficult for the small children to write on, and it was challenging for me as a teaching tool. The pleasure was that it was a room only for us. The other resource teacher was a delightful young man who was a warm Polynesian. Even though he was sick, he continued to teach but soon resigned.

Pony Express had about sixteen students to serve, along with an excellent aide when she was there and not helping somewhere else in the school. She helped with my load of five self-contained students.

I was at Pony from 8:00 a.m. until 12:00 noon. I traveled to Eagle arriving around 12:15 p.m. I never suggested a change.

My students at Pony did better academically than the ones at Eagle. For some reason, I had better control of the situation at Pony. However, I had challenges at both schools, and I cannot say which school presented the most challenges, considering they were very different. I believe it was Eagle that gave me the biggest challenge, due to the room situation. I taught with limited supplies, but only because it is hard to bring "stuff" from Pony. My problem!

The principal at Pony was grooved into his job. The one at Eagle had the challenge of being new to the school district, in a new community, and having the personal energy of a locomotive. He seemed to be a perfectionist and determined to have his school excel without exception. The faculty and staff which he chose were without a doubt outstanding. His energy was well rewarded.

I have been in education one way or another for many years. I started on this adventure in Nogales, Arizona as a manager of a private school, the International School of Language. I ordered supplies, interviewed teachers, signed up students, and taught classes when teachers did not show up for class. My world then took me to Gilbert, Arizona as a 4th grade teacher and on to Utah as an aide in a unit serving intellectually handicapped students. Next came teaching for many years as a resource teacher in the elementary school setting.

My school district here in Utah has been very good to me. After earning my reputation, I had the opportunity to teach workshops on learning styles, brain processing, multisensory intervention, and helped teachers design interventions, and accommodations that kept students out of special education. However, with good intent, I have also assisted many students in the resource setting. At one point, I was involved with the Department of Educational Psychology at BYU where I gave workshops on interventions. These were gratifying experiences. I had to pray for humility because at one point I felt *pride* in my heart. I humbled myself. I had parents, teachers, district people, and the like calling on me for suggestions. Serving was rewarding.

My friend Dr. Robin Steed encouraged me to continue speaking, presenting, and looking toward a university setting. I appreciated her trust in my ability. She validated my brain.

I looked at my life and said "no" to expanding my workshop involvement and becoming more active in the university setting. I decided that I wanted to be in the classroom and not sacrifice my time with my family for the rewards of success outside of the home. I have done my best no matter how limited. It was hard to back out of the role of the "mover and shaker," relax, and listen to the spirit as to what was best for my world.

One of my strengths has been working with parents and contributing to problem-solving in complicated situations. I remember the district calling on me to go to a high school for a doctor's son who was in special education and the doctor was threatening to sue. After solving the problem, the student enrolled in my summer school.

Oh yes, another thing I had going in the summer was a program for children with reading and problems with mathematics. BYU teachers referred parents to me, and it was a very successful summer adventure. My philosophy has been clear to my heart and mind; *we change a child, we change the world.*

I feel that the first thing to accomplish is to establish a community of close relationships within the school. Every child should be included. I believe in compassion without a political or self-serving agenda. The student's needs should be addressed before the stated or unstated, selfish or unselfish desires of the system. There are objectives, which are not and never will be countable, such as showing progress in the hearts and minds of children with their "ever telling" eyes with love. This feeling has been warm and rewarding.

Years later, I have had parents thank me for saving their children from the resource setting. Thanks are appreciated. However, the given fact that their lives have made it without resource is exciting. Only yesterday, I was shopping when I felt an arm around me; sixteen years ago, I had her son in a special program. She was grateful! My reward!

The frustration of this year has been that there has not been time to use the energy of my strengths to make a difference with which I could have made a difference. Time is a valued resource.

During my first month of school at Pony, I offered to share the possibility of a presentation, which I had put together for the benefit of the teachers. A presentation which I was privileged to give to teachers and administrators on the islands of Hawaii, Maui, and Oahu. It contains a wealth of information for new teachers and an excellent reminder for seasoned teachers. The presentation is for all classroom teachers. Didn't happen!

I did my best with the students, and I felt well rewarded for that contribution. That is what being a teacher is all about. Children are precious. Sometimes, I wish that adults were children.

The special education teams at Pony and Eagle have been a source of great comfort and inspiration. Working as a team member with other teachers leaves me in awe of their skills. I appreciated a school psychologist and three of the teachers in particular. We had some laughs together, as well as problem-solving some severe situations. Such relationships enhance the view of what should be done to get a job well done. Great people!

Our school psychologist has been tender and knowledgeable, an example of being both firm and friendly. I loved her "tuned-in spirit" and ability to set boundaries with kindness. She is organized and "right-on" with her personal and professional world of understanding. Inspired by another teacher, Pauli, a teacher with an Aloha heart spread warmth through his class. Students loved his mild-mannered and caring attitude. Wow!

As I reflect back on my first year of teaching in Special Education, Richard Ellison holds my appreciation as an outstanding school psychologist. I have been privileged to have worked with many competent school psychologists.

Talking about school psychologists, I have a story. At about age forty, needing to return to school, I poured over the Arizona State University catalog. My eyes spotted the Educational Psychology department. Now, that is what I wanted to be, a school psychologist. I bounced into the office of an advisor and signed up for classes. During the middle of the first semester, I realized that I was signed up for special education. Yes, to become a resource teacher! I had not asked the right questions. Assuming that Educational Psychology was to become a school psychologist, I had inadvertently set myself on an unexpected course . . . *Please Don't Call Me Dumb!*

During this year, I must include our school psychologist as one of the finest without a doubt. She knows her boundaries and professionally keeps them. She is well trained. It has been a joy to know and to have worked with her.

I hurt my back the last of January while breaking up bricks with a ten-pound double jack or as some call it, a sledgehammer. At the same time, I found that I had a dangerous parasite. I have exerted dedicated contemplation to get well. I have missed school, day after day and week after week. I have observed and felt the reaction to my injury from different people in different ways. At first, I felt a caring concern with support for a fast recovery. When the recovery was not fast, the following response was to tolerate, and the next reaction was one of disbelief and puzzled inquiry. I understand all the faces of reactions.

The reasons are without knowing who I am and my work ethic, dedication, and the powerful desire to do my best. And best for my body is to let it heal itself with its energy and time. No schedule.

I am so sorry about the school world of 2004-2005. I have done my best with a difficult opportunity for growth. My injury has caused some reflecting. Sometimes, my husband has come to school with me so that I could make the trip with my ice bag. His understanding heart allowed me to go to school when he felt I should stay home. I wish I had been more wise—*hammering on the bricks.* Oh yes, I ruptured two disks. A determined physical therapist has been encouraging.

School year, you will soon end and become another chapter of history to be judged as good, bad, or indifferent. I have learned to depend on others to do what I know that I could do better. They needed to experience the lessons that I have learned. I know that first the blossoms and then the fruit. I was teaching teachers.

I have had silent rewards come to the heart. The Golden Apple Award was a generous award I received years ago from the district, but the lasting award is how life has been lived. It has been my trial and my blessing to know my heart, and this is probably the same for all of us. Thank you for this year as part of my adventure.

I do not believe in the practice of segregation. In college, I became convinced that Inclusion is a place in the heart not a designated place in society. For Inclusion to work well, there needs to be educational reconstruction on every front. It will not be easy. The One Room School concept will be refreshing and rewarding. The concerns of the *special needs* students must be addressed by educated professionals, both in and out of the classroom. Proper interventions and accommodations are the overarching goals. A special class is necessary for remediation of the skills that are lacking. This class could be after school or the consideration of twenty-minute sessions of one-on-one—teacher and student, during the school day.

Johns Hopkins University has a model of educational reform. This model is an idea which implements proven reading programs which match the skill level needs of students. This skill level reform model, created by the Center for Data Drive Reform in Education, provides for consultation with district leaders on the strategic use of data in the selection of proven reading programs that will meet needs of students. This application of data, "Data-driven" means carefully examining specific unique needs and matching them with specific proven programs. This match is the overarching value of the model. It's the teacher's job to create interventions which meet individualized needs to build skills. This concept is not a new idea, but one which gets lost in the mix of a lot of conversation and supposedly new and better programs. Real solutions!

To be forward-looking in exploring opportunities to change education, I know that to be successful we need to look at each person's brainprint and respect the differences. This study needs to be well intended with an open mind, penetrating with dedicated time to integrate, and thus apply a message of hope.

Post-note: Hawaii calls, my heart says,"Yes." After another year on Oahu—third year and back to the Mainland for yet another year, and again back to Hawaii for the fourth year, I finished up at the age of seventy-three on the Big Island. I did not want to quit my experiences as an adventurous dreamer. I started writing and writing.

32

Deficit or Disability:
We All have Deficits

I found another piece of the puzzle. A piece I knew was there, but it was as if I was the only one who knew it existed. Did I have a deficit —impairment or barrier to mental processes, or a disability; what did all that mean to me as a person, a parent, and as a teacher? Well, as I studied the word *deficit,* it became evident that we are all born with deficits. It matters not who we are or where we happen to be in life's journey from the little embryonic person to an older person. We are a mixed bag of a lot of different elements or aspects of intelligence. With that in mind, I continued to puzzle over the brain with its magic of why and why not.

As my life's journey has taken me through chapter after chapter, I have been puzzled by my brain functioning. *Some* would call my brain functioning a disability: cognitively challenged or beautifully gifted. At one time, I believed the *some* who would call my brain a disability. They were only confused. As I heard the other *some,* I realized that I am both cognitively challenged and beautifully gifted. I have found that I can figure out or problem-solve on a higher level than most. Yes, I have been confused by the meaning of the words. What is my deficit? Only when a deficit has a negative impact on one's ability to enjoy life, problem-solve, or be productive does it become a disability. I know that at times my deficits have been *disabling,* but I also know how important it has become to identify them, understand them, and compensate for them when they do intrude upon my personal and professional behavior. It is also comforting to realize that by their very nature, these same deficits bring with them special *abilities* which bring satisfaction, competencies, and understanding.

A past president of the International Dyslexia Association, Emerson Dickson, shared the following pertinent information in an article entitled *Perspectives on Language and Literacy*, published Summer 2007, by the International Dyslexia Association, which I applaud because a deficit without negative consequence is not a disability. *"For example, a sense of direction and the ability to track and shoot game to feed our families which were essential skills 400 years ago are no longer critical to our survival. The ability to dance, sing, or play a musical instrument were never critical. Thank goodness! However, to survive in the world of today, among other skills, we must know how to read."*

It is true in our society that the need to read is paramount. However, I have known a few people who have survived comfortably without knowing how to read. Deficit or disability?

Although, while I was teaching in Hawaii, I met former prisoners who didn't read. They were involved in the drug traffic and felt no need to read. I told them that I could teach them. They told me they didn't need to read to survive. I told them that they were smart and didn't need to do drugs. Their replies, "Like to do drugs. No need for change." Their drug culture had kept them uninformed and trapped. Oh, my! This awareness was painful for me to behold. They were disabled!

Analogous to this attitude was what I heard the day I took a meal to a group of homeless people on the beach. My heart said, "I have been given much, and I too must give." These homeless promptly informed me that they had the fish of the ocean and the wild pigs up on the mountain to feed their families, and they quickly dismissed me. As a teacher, there were times, while teaching students to read, when I was dismissed with that same energy. "No need!"

It is painful in the world of today for those who can't read, and it presents a handicapping situation. If the deficit is not interfering with a lifestyle, is it a disability? Yes, it can be, and some do not know it! Rejoice in knowing how to compensate so that they don't become disabilities.

33

Einstein's Brain:
Dr. Dean Falk, Anthropologist

Dr. Dean Falk is an impressive evolutionary anthropologist who splits her time between Santa Fe, New Mexico where she is a Senior Scholar at the School for Advanced Research, and Tallahassee, Florida where she is a Distinguished Research Professor and the Hale G. Smith Professor of Anthropology at Florida State University.

For further reading about the evolutionary patterns of the brain, one could read the following article by Dr. Falk, *Interpreting sulci on hominin endocasts: old hypotheses and new findings.*

In May 2014, Dr. Falk discussed new evidence as she addressed the evolution of sulcal patterns associated with cortical reorganization in three parts of the hominin brain: (1) the parietotemporo-occipital association cortex, (2) Broca's speech area, and (3) dorsolateral prefrontal association cortex.

It is my very shallow understanding of the Broca's area that it is one of the main areas of the cerebral cortex responsible for producing language. Broca's area is located in the lower portion of the left frontal lobe. It is in the area that can have communication difficulties which are language centered. I learned this from my association with researchers who have dug into the complexities of the brain. Sometimes, I can't get my Broca to wake up!

There is another area called the Wernicke area which is also associated with the processing and understanding of language. Complex!

Dr. Falk's article about Einstein's brain is especially interesting to me. "As *an adult, Einstein famously observed that 'the words or the language, as they are written or spoken, do not seem to play any role in my mechanism of thought. The psychical entities which seem to serve as elements in thought are certain signs and more or less clear images which can be 'voluntarily' reproduced and combined' (Hadamard 1945). Einstein laughed when informed that many people always think in words (Wertheimer 1959), and emphasized that concepts became meaningful for him 'only through their connection with sense-experiences' (Einstein 1970). He was a synthetic thinker. Family members and friends have documented that, when stuck on a physics problem, Einstein would play the violin until, suddenly, he would announce excitedly, 'I've got it!'"* (Bucky 1992)

"It is interesting to contemplate that such synthesizing may have contributed to Einstein's insights and that his extraordinary abilities may, to some degree, have been associated with the unusual gross anatomy of his cerebral cortex in and around the primary somatosensory and motor cortices. Although these views are speculative, the identifications of previously unrecognized cortical morphology on Einstein's brain will, hopefully, be of use to future scholars who have access to new information and methodologies."
(Dean Falk 2009)

This information is interesting to me. I have experienced, with a few students and myself, the phenomenon of thinking in concepts without language. How does that work? It is like this; I can understand the concept in my mind's eye without hearing or seeing words. Sometimes, I can see the word, understand the word, and not be able to recall the sounds that make word. One day as I sat in a classroom in Hawaii teaching reading to a student who spoke Hawaiian Pidgin in everyday casual conversation and did not read well, it happened again. I had one of those *aha* moments when suddenly I experienced something that I had seen in myself. Wow! It has happened again! There was an insight or

280

realization that a human could understand the printed words, but their memory could not orally recall the words. Their brain had an understanding of the concept wrapped around the unspoken word that had no name. This student then took the concept—idea and told me what the sentence meant with his Hawaiian Pidgin. He had not said one word in standard English; when tested, he could not bring the words up to say them, but he understood the concept! Incidentally, he is artistic.

I immediately remembered my experience as a 3rd grade student. I stood there that day in the class trying to read the word AWFUL. I could not bring to memory how to say the word; however, I knew what it meant. And, ironically, that is how I was feeling at the moment, AWFUL. Yes, Albert Einstein, thank you for helping us understand that a person can understand a concept without being able to remember how to say the word! Yes, many people do think in words, but my brain and my student's brain took a long road around the word or words, to understand the concept of a word.

Word, whatever is a word? I believe the profound and awesome mystery of the brain is in the beauty of something conceived: an idea, impression, understanding of a concept and how it works, not necessarily with words. Without words is how my brain walks me through life, and I am grateful that I understand how my brain is unique. Knowing this gives understanding with hope.

Dr. Falk explains, *"It is also well known that dramatic changes may occur in sensory and motor cortices during a human's lifetime as revealed by medical imaging studies of Braille readers and upper limb amputees, which show that the cerebral cortex can exhibit long-term adaptations, including enlargement or relocation of specific representations, such as those for hands (Amunts et al., 1997).*

Further, gross cortical features entailing sulcal depths or patterns have been identified in people with exceptional abilities, such as highly trained musicians (Amunts et al., 1997; Bangert and Schlaug, 2006; Schlaug, 2001) and the world-renowned physicist who is the subject of this report, Albert Einstein (Witelson et al., 1999 a,b)." For those of you who would like to study this information in depth, go to the writing entitled *New Information about Albert Einstein's Brain.* (c. 2009 Dr. Falk).

I have been fascinated with the brain and what it does and does not do. Even as a child living in Santa Rita, New Mexico, I was very aware of different brainprints. I knew that they were not the same. I did not look at them as being less than or more than.

As I study the trees, I revere them as having different patterns and beautifully different. Same with people! I enjoy the beauty of differences. Patterns are both different and the same. Also, I enjoy the beauty of sameness.

When I was an airline stewardess, I had Helen Keller on one of my flights. What an experience! I do not have words to share the feelings that I have for her. Speechless! Can't imagine what her brain was like as it processed information. How little we know!

Also, Van Cliburn, an American pianist who achieved worldwide recognition in 1958 was one of my many famous passengers. As we visited, he asked me where I was from, and I told him Animas Valley, New Mexico. While I was serving a meal, we were flying north and very close to Animas Valley. He said, "Miss Hoskins, we are flying near your home. It is right over there." This event happened before the internet and all the current technology. I had not told him the location, but he had it in his head. Where and why was it stored? Genius!

Passenger after passenger shared their thinking in unique ways. I was astonished by the information that people would spit out of their heads. Danny Kaye with his quick humor and dancing feet had me amazed that the body has so many parts that can work together.

I think of the brain as the Mission Control Center. Who is pushing the controls? Ponder! Dr. Falk shared the uniqueness of this Mission Control Center.

Thank You, Dr. Falk!

34

Mainstreaming:
Step by Step

The terms Mainstreaming and Inclusion, two educational models, are often used interchangeably in education; however, they differ from each other. These terms have been confusing as to what they mean to both the regular education and special education teachers. This confusion has undoubtedly been felt by me in the mix of conversation and educational philosophy.

The Mainstreaming model *returns* the special education student to the regular classroom. When a special education student has been removed or pulled out of the general education classroom for remediation and has achieved the desired objectives in a particular subject, the student will return to the regular classroom for that specific subject. Mainstreaming requires the child to deal with and adjust to the regular class, depending on the teacher.

Mainstreaming has meant the same thing for years as mandated by the federal government for students with *special needs* who have a deficit which has become a disability. These students have been pulled out of the regular classroom into smaller classes which constitute the Least Restrictive Environment for skill level remediation determined according to the professional team's observations and test scores along with a parental representative. This remediation means to pull a student out of the regular class for the appropriate time needed for remediation, and this is determined by the needed amount of skill development. After the student acquires the skill level in a subject, the student will be placed back into the regular classroom with their peers who have not been diagnosed with disabilities; however, sometimes the skill level has been achieved in one subject but not in another. Therefore, the student will remain in the small class for only needed skill remediation. This achievement is a needed step toward taking the student back into the regular class for more regular education time. All students have the considered right to be educated with the general population of students wherever feasible. This Mainstreaming is done without putting the goal of education at risk. The extended time to be in the regular classroom setting is a studied response to the needs of the student.

Inclusion is a newer term used to describe the placement of students in the regular classroom for all or nearly all of the school day. Although in some Inclusion models, students are there for only part of the day, students in Full Inclusion remain in the general education classroom for the entire day. Inclusion classrooms have a team of specialists supporting the teacher and the child in the regular classroom.

For me, the concept of inclusion has existed since the first days of Mainstreaming. Inclusion model means that the student needs more time in the regular classroom than the Mainstreaming model provides.

The *balance of time* as to where the student most appropriately fits to learn skills and for a healthy return to the regular classroom is an important observation and application. There are advantages for students spending time in programs for one-on-one instruction, following an individualized plan for remediation; however, studies have shown that children profit from spending time in a regular classroom for activities that are experienced only in that setting.

Given my experience, I believe sometimes Mainstreaming is the answer and sometimes Inclusion is the answer. How we decide the path to travel is not to be discounted as an easy decision. You always have a team of connected and well-meaning educators and parents along with student input to develop a well-designed plan. It has been my experience that student involvement is essential for the plan to work out well. After students have an understanding of place, time, the amount of energy to do the job, and willingness to give a positive commitment, the more successful the plan has been. The parent representative needs to hear *it* —commitment from the **student**. This student commitment was not an easy idea, but it worked for me in Hawaii when students, parents, or grandparents were involved. Everyone on the same page with an energy which could not be defeated was the key to success.

The special education teacher needs to be an educational *support* to the regular education teacher. To expand and develop an understanding of the needs of the *special needs* student within the regular classroom has always been a goal for the student's success. The view must be clothed with realistic expectations of what can be accomplished; then the attitude of Inclusion can be achieved. Yes, Steve Kuchic, *Mainstreaming is an attitude, not a place.*

For the mildly handicapped student and those with learning problems, the special educator needs to have the skills to help the regular education teacher deal with the student's problems directly. For the student to be self-reliant and self-sufficient, within the regular classroom setting, I found myself doing the needed training for teachers, parents, and administrators. Is it the special educator who needs to train the regular education teachers?

I know that teacher training programs in colleges and universities should be doing a better job of training the regular classroom teachers for including a diverse population of children. Another very important piece of this educational puzzle is for the schools to have smaller classes and support teams in place to accommodate that diverse population. For the child who falls in the marginal areas of achievement with cognitive processing, physical or emotional challenges, and it is uncertain that the regular classroom is the best place, then another placement should be studied. The competencies of the classroom teacher are needed to help make these decisions. The point is that if a new breed of special educators appear, it is also necessary that a new breed of regular classroom teachers also appear. Keeping the student in the regular classroom setting is ideal but not always best for the student who needs one-on-one skill remediation. Placement is a tough call which requires serious consideration.

I chose to be a teacher with a dual major in both regular education and special education. I have felt very strongly about this direction. I was educated in impoverished school districts with a shortage of funds. In some of the classes, the regular classroom teachers did a lot of things that I see being done in the resource room. And the same thing today, I know teachers who are *teachers*.

I firmly believe that if we can keep from classifying students, everyone is better off.

Every brain is unique, which makes every child born or unborn, a gift of beauty.

All included with the voice of "It is all right to be you, and you are included in the fabric of love."

35

Inclusion:
Kathy Cheney Caballero, Special Education Teacher

I had the opportunity of teaching with a seasoned special education teacher while I was teaching in Hawaii. Kathy's story is inspirational as we ponder how to bring hope to challenged students. Her experience with Inclusion will share a piece of what Inclusion means to her.

How Do We Make It Work

The following are suggestions to operationalize—how to manage a system with an attitude of Inclusion for all students. An awareness of our own and others' feelings are the backdrop for a conversation about the subject of Inclusion. Along with this, we seek information about our own and others' brain processing. An Inclusion plan cannot work without you pondering how you think and feel about *feeling dumb*. And if you have ever felt *dumb*, how did someone help you compensate? Compensate by creating a support team with parents, regular education teachers, *special needs* teachers, and the administration. Before starting, please be confident the student will succeed. For those who say it *won't work*, it is so important to stretch the vision into *it will work*.

No matter how you slice it, bringing *special needs* students into the regular education classroom generates virtually insurmountable problems. On the one hand, we are trying to protect the *special needs* student from self-image damage while on the other hand not overloading the regular education teacher. Such overloading far transcends the numbers game. The regular education teacher must acquire the additional knowledge and

287

skills needed for teaching reading, writing, and arithmetic to *special needs* —special education students whose education necessitates the skills for highly individualized educational techniques and processes. On the other hand, 100 percent of the teacher's time is needed for assuring educational progress on the part of the regular education students in the room.

In an ideal world, a portion of the classroom teacher's time should be devoted one-on-one with each *special needs* student. If more than one such student is placed in this regular class, it seems quite probable that the demands on teacher time could rise exponentially.

If there is more than one student with a unique challenge, the regular teacher needs and must have help. We discovered the need to hire additional professional personnel. If the regular education teacher-pupil load is reduced commensurate with the number of special education students coming, the demands on the teacher's time far exceed those in a room without special education needs.

We have just created a perfect formula for educational failure, as well as highly elevated stress upon the teacher. Chaos may well turn out to be the reward for our good intentions.

Kathy's Story
By Kathy

I attended both public and private schools. I didn't read until the 7th grade, but I learned to read; I became a voracious reader. After high school was completed, I worked as a telephone operator and as a secretary for an insurance company. Realizing that I wouldn't ever get anywhere or where I would like to get, I needed more education. I returned to school and was the first in my family to earn a college degree. After college was finished, I volunteered for the Peace Corps and spent four years teaching in Paraguay. For the next two decades, I was a special education teacher at the high school level.

So you will understand why I became so passionate about Full

Inclusion, you will need to know just a little about me. I was born in San Francisco, California, a third-generation Franciscan. My great-grandparents arrived in 1852 to seek their fortune. My family moved to a farm when I was four where I learned to ride horses and raise chickens. Later we moved to Redwood City and then to Pittsburg, California.

I was a normal little girl who was unfortunate enough to go from kindergarten through 3rd grade in a school that was taken over by the state for being fifty years behind the times in their teaching methods and textbooks. The reading program didn't teach phonics; in fact, they taught very little. At the end of the 3rd grade, my family moved. After we had moved, the school was taken over, and I missed out on all the help the students who were still there received, which brought them up to speed.

I could not read, write, or do the math, but since I was a good little girl and no problem for the teachers in my new school, I was forgotten. No-one knew I came from *that* school. So there I was with no schooling and didn't understand most of what they were trying to teach me. Thanks to Heavenly Father for an excellent memory. If I heard it, I could usually answer questions orally, but it was another story when it came to written work or tests. When I failed most of the time, teachers would blame it on nerves or failure to study. Many just passed me on to someone to correct the problems which did me no good at all.

I remember that in the 6th grade we took a test, and I passed at the post-graduate college level in English literature. I answered all the questions correctly about Shakespeare and Greek plays. My teacher called me to his desk and asked if my parents were college graduates. Of course, they weren't. Mom had graduated high school, and my father had a 3rd grade education. My mother explained that every Thursday, she and I watched Channel 13 at 4:00 p.m. when they showed classical movies and plays. I loved them. We discussed each program, and with my very developed memory, I had no trouble remembering who wrote what, when it was written, and the plot; I didn't know who Hansel and Gretel were, which bothered my teacher for some reason.

My teacher never kept me after school on Thursdays. After that event was over, he would question me about what I had seen. Years later, he told me how he and other teachers had tried to figure out how I could have such a deep understanding of the play's subject and yet be failing in school.

I got fortunate in the 7th grade because one of the teachers was completing his Ph.D. and researching why students who seemed to be *normal* could not read, write, or do the math. He chose eleven students who couldn't read at grade level for no apparent reason. My sister and I were two of the lucky ones. It took him one semester to teach all of us to read better. My reading level went from 2nd grade to 7th grade during that time. Even though I could read, I was years behind in grammar and math. I failed my first year of college simply because I had no idea how to study or write at the college level. I finally graduated with a 2.45 GPA. Everyone said it was a shame considering I had such a good brain. My IQ tested at 159. They said I was just a lazy girl who was just looking for a husband. Yes, they did! Maybe they should test me again. Unfortunately, I bought into all this, except the husband part. I truly felt stupid, even though I knew I could function academically under the right circumstances.

Later in life, I found that I have learning disabilities which prevented me from accomplishing everything I wanted to accomplish. It wasn't until I realized that I was very intelligent that I was able to return to school and do very well.

I graduated from California State, East Bay Area, University in Hayward in 1972. I did nothing much with my degree except go into the Peace Corps. When I returned, I used it to get a government job. I went back to school twenty years later for my teaching credential. Chapman University's Concord campus accepted me. I received my credential in 1993 and my Master of Arts in Education in 1995. By then I had figured out how to study, learn, and graduated with better than a 3.0 GPA, something I had never been able to do in grammar or high school. Even so, every time I got an A or B I was surprised and lived in fear that I wouldn't be able to do it again with my next class.

After I received my credential, I taught a 3rd grade bilingual special class, but I was not rehired. Not being hired was a blow to my self-esteem, but with three small children to support, I persevered and got another job as a special education 4th and 5th grade bilingual special education teacher.

I hate to admit that after two years with satisfactory evaluations, I was not rehired. This time I was mad. I knew I was not a bad teacher and did not deserve to be let go. However, the situation turned out to be lucky for me. I took an interview for the position in high school just to get the practice and liked what I heard. When I was offered a position, I accepted. I have said, "I died and went to Heaven." I loved teaching this level and excelled at it.

As for my personal history, I was a fully *included,* unrecognized, *special needs* student during the 50s and 60s. This situation was because there were no separate classrooms for those students who simply didn't learn to read or do the math, nor recognized as having a problem. I remember being harangued by a math teacher I liked for not studying hard enough when I had tried my hardest to learn the information. "What can we expect? You're just a girl." I have never forgotten those words from a good teacher whom I admired, and I stopped trying to improve my math skills, considering there was no reason. I was just a girl and not capable of doing higher math. To this day, math is beyond me, but I am not *dumb*, and I can still add faster than an adding machine.

After twenty years of teaching with eighteen of those teaching in high school, I taught Learning Handicapped at the high school level. I strongly believe that Full Inclusion, when done properly, is the way we should be teaching our students. Full Inclusion allows the learning disabled student to be in regular classes which build self-esteem and forces them to strive to achieve in a normal setting. As a nod to the naysayers, yes, there will be circumstances when it is necessary to have children segregated in special classes to meet their unique needs. However, these situations should be the exception instead of the rule. This exception becomes particularly important in high school where the stigma of being "special" can be exceptionally painful for our students.

The major problem for schools trying to go to a Full Inclusion model is not the students but the staff, including special education teachers and administrators. Many regular and special education teachers can be hard to sell on the idea. This problem is because they have had little to no experience dealing with the handicapped population. It frightens regular education teachers to seriously think they will be responsible for grading and accommodating the "sped"—special education students, who have a reputation for being very difficult to manage, nor do they want to dummy down their classes to accommodate these students. Special education teachers are leery for a number of reasons. They fear they will lose their jobs; they will be blamed if the students do not do well, and will be relegated to a position of being a teacher's aide instead of a teacher. These may seem to be petty concerns to most, but they are real and have to be dealt with before a quality program can be established in any school.

An example of a district that is doing it right is where I started my high school career. This district understands that you have to put in the hard work and money to make a great program greater. When they decided to go to the Full Inclusion model, the district spent the money on planning and implementing the program over a two-year period. They were willing to spend the money needed for training and preparing teachers and students for the changes. It had taken two years before they were ready to change to the new program, but by then, they had the regular and special education teachers supporting their model, as well as the students and parents.

All students have to go to their classes for math and English, but if they *don't get it*, they sign out of class and go to the resource classroom where they can get individual help. It doesn't matter if they are special education or regular students; anyone, who needs help, gets it. Since this system has been instituted, the majority of the students, including special education students, graduate with a diploma.

In this program, many of the special education students passed the California High School Exit Examination (CAHSEE) the first time they took it in the 10th grade. The school likes to tell what happened the second year of the program. All students are required to take the examination, even if they are not on the graduation track. No one was expecting much from the non graduation track students, but nine of them passed the CAHSEE. The school and staff scrambled to understand and study the program. They started looking for a method to help these students catch up, so they could graduate on time. To this day, students continue to surprise them each year. It is true that students will rise to the expectations demanded of them. Today, they graduate students in numbers well above the national average, and there is no reason that they shouldn't continue to do so for the foreseeable future.

This district is successful because they work as a team. The students are everyone's responsibility, and everyone is accountable for them. Regular education and special education teachers work together to provide the best training possible for all students. They are never satisfied and are continually looking for better ways of doing their jobs. Another essential element in their success is the willingness of the district to spend the money needed to maintain the level of training required. This district is no better off than any other district and doesn't have a secret stash of money to spend, but everyone feels the benefits of both regular and special education students. They must maintain the program.

Full Inclusion, in and of itself, is not the total answer to the problems faced by students and schools; anyone who thinks that is just foolish. However, it is a step in the right direction and goes a long way toward solving some very sticky problems. It makes special education students part of the fabric of the school and gives them the chance to develop a meaningful relationship with "normal" students, as well as to be able to develop a more rounded personality with self-esteem. It also helps the crippling effect of being stigmatized "special" because they are no more special than the regular education student. We need to show all students that even if they need help in some subjects, this doesn't mean they cannot function in normal society, study at the college level, or lead a normal life with a good job and family.

I've worked in a district that tried to go to the Full Inclusion model without any discussion or training. In fact, they held a meeting in the middle of the summer when most teachers were unavailable, and parents were ignored. They went so far as to initiate and design Individual Education Plans, known as Individualized Education Programs without the parents and placed all the Special Education students into regular classes. It was a disaster! Special Education students were even placed in Advanced Placement classes. They needed help!

I had twenty-eight special education students, some of whom were splendid students, and all of them failed every academic class in which they were enrolled. The regular education teachers were screaming for help. The situation was a nightmare. I wish I could say that things have improved at this school, but they haven't changed. Parents who could take their students out of the school, they did. This endeavor was an example of a good idea with good intentions, going haywire because of the lack of preparation.

It doesn't matter what system you use as long as it is well studied with the students' skill levels in mind and how the system will attend to the different levels. The first stated concern should be, "How will this model impact the students academically and emotionally? Will their needs be met and is the whole staff behind it?" It is my opinion that Full Inclusion is the best, but I am sure there are many who would like to argue with me. However, I've been on both sides of the battle.

To this day, I have an internal struggle when it comes to intellectual matters. I still have that little voice in my head telling me I am stupid and will never be able to do what I want, even though I know that I need to ignore it. Every class, every speech, every course is a secret battle, and I have never felt as if I did it well enough. I personally never want any of my students to feel that way.

I had a student who told me he wasn't worried that he couldn't read; he would learn in prison like his father and uncles learned. He believed you couldn't learn to read until you were at least thirty years old. Along with a system that had failed him and more like him, learned attitudes lead in a negative direction. He wasn't stupid nor was he a born criminal, but he had no expectations of being able to succeed and was prepared to pay the price. He wanted to read and write but knew he couldn't because he had been shown throughout his school career that he couldn't. I was told just to pass him and get rid of him. Personally, I blame the system for failing not only him but more like him. Some parents had the same learned attitudes.

Everywhere, we can find deplorable examples, as well as exceptional programs and teachers. I have also known students from the same system, who have succeeded despite everything, who were able to overcome low self-esteem, poor education, and were reared above and beyond what people expected of them. The majority of my students have found a niche in life and are happy.

I have taught school in Paraguay, California, Alaska, and Hawaii. I have learned that no matter where you are, the people are the same. They want the best for their children and worry about what will happen to them when they are adults if they don't get a good education.

Thank you, Kathy!

Given my experience, I know that *inclusion* has always been an attitude, as is *exclusion.* I was reared in Santa Rita, New Mexico in a mining camp for my elementary schooling. If you were a "big" company "boss" you lived Downtown. We lived on Booth Hill and in the Ballpark housing area. Daddy was a machinist. If you were a Mexican laborer—Mexicans were common laborers, you lived in Mexican-Town in a tin shack. And when we got to school we were somewhat divided according to social and cultural attitude, both on the playground and in the classroom. This division was segregation, but as children, we were only dimly aware of the rigidity of this social structure. I had a friend Ricardo. We played and talked with each other.

I lived on a ranch during high school. Again, there was a division of attitude. This time, the division was between the ranch-hand children and the rancher's children. My college was a desegregated school, while right across the line in Texas, there was no place for the black basketball player. My experience has been that school was a class system in society, without power to change dysfunctional attitudes about worth and ability. However, I can change attitudes within me. I never felt privileged over another. Blessed with this attitude.

An answer came a few years ago when I sat and visited with my friend Ricardo Munoz. As we shared tender times about our growing up, I asked for information about what happened to whom since we were together in that mining camp, I found the courage for a question, "Richard, how come you are not still in Mexican Town and playing ball with your compadres?" Incidentally, Ricardo was teaching at New Mexico A&M in Las Cruces, sitting with two degrees, and writing books. "Argie Ella, I didn't think I was different. My parents never told me that we were poor, uneducated, or disadvantaged. I had a good life. I had the hills behind me where I could run my dog. In my mind, it was you *white guys* who lived without opportunity. I also had a teacher who knew I was okay." And Ricardo's mother included her children with an attitude of *inclusion*. They received the rhetoric of being *included*. What they responded to was the belief that they were not less than; his mother's view was that they had opportunities and family; Ricardo's training from his mother was laced with *even though!* Always beans in the pot! My own unprejudiced mother would take me to the little Mexican store. I didn't know a difference existed, beyond poorness. Ricardo and I were friends!

Katrina De Hirsch says that the most important thing that we can give a child with problems is a *psychological* support system which makes a statement, "You are okay." Oh, how I wish the teacher who said, "Argie Ella, if you do not learn to read, you will not graduate from the 8th grade, let alone high school," had acted on the principle of inclusion rather than exclusion. Even in the 4th grade, I knew my teacher did not include me. It was my 5th grade teacher who wrote on an envelope to my mother, "This is delivered through the kindness of Argie Ella." I knew and felt what inclusion meant. Argie Ella felt supported, and she was motivated.

In college, I learned the teacher and consultant model of special education intervention. I knew that this model expressed a valid principle that held hope for the student. I was comfortable with it. It is a theory which would provide the psychological and teaching interventions which our *special needs* students need the most. This model is more than being a teacher of skills. It forwards the idea that a teacher gives students and parents understanding as to how skills are used on the journey for the survival of life. As individuals, we have the power to change our attitudes, to look through a lens that has hope. We can further our education so that Hope opens the windows. Finding answers can be a path to peace. Lessons learned!

Kathy, Brother Sam, Kathy C., and Argie during a party. All included in Aloha Days!

By artist Randy Reneer

Randy would say, "Have a Happy Heart!" With that comes the joy of including all in your circle of love. Inclusion!

Professional Consultant and CEO

36

Language Processing:
Deficit or Disability
Summary of Argie Ella's Challenges

Through the entire book, I have shared that having a difficult time learning to read has not been my only "hard to do" challenge. My overarching cognitive processing is complex and somewhat unknown with a far-reaching **Sequencing** deficit. This deficit, when packaged with **Developmental Dyslexia,** creates an overwhelming challenge to the tasks of daily living. Another deficit **Developmental Language Disorder** has been a communication nightmare. Yes! My life has been emotionally laden because the sequencing deficit has scattered confusion *everywhere with everything* that I have done or continue to do. Real!

A plan with logical and determined energy to understanding cognitive challenges is rewarding. Once again, research and observe to find answers. Some of what I have now included has been stated previously; however, this chapter brings salient points forward for continued consideration. I will attempt to explain.

Dyslexia

According to the **Mayo Clinic Staff**: *"Dyslexia is a learning disorder characterized by difficulty reading due to problems identifying speech sounds and learning how they relate to letters and words. Also, called a specific reading disability, Dyslexia is a common learning disability in children. Dyslexia occurs in children with normal vision and intelligence. Sometimes Dyslexia goes undiagnosed for years and isn't recognized until adulthood. There's no cure for Dyslexia. It's a lifelong* *condition caused by inherited traits that affect how your brain works. However, most children with Developmental Dyslexia can succeed in school with tutoring or a specialized education program. Emotional support also plays an important role."*

As a child, I had a difficult time learning to read, and as an adult, I continue to find that it is difficult to decode or say more complex words. Lifelong! On Sundays, I do not take my glasses to church so that I have an excuse not to read aloud if called on to read a verse of scripture. I graduated from Arizona State University where I earned Magna Cum Laude next to my name. It is the next-to-highest of three honors for grades above average. Nevertheless, scared to death of reading, I cannot sequence the sounds or remember more complex words! Embarrassing!

The developmental disorder of communication called dyslexia appears to me to be more than reading. I also know that without a doubt; it is a language deficit. I also know without a shadow of a doubt that whatever this language processing is called, it is familial. Genetic! It runs in the family; however, no two persons with dyslexia manifest it in the same way. The common thread, among all of the individuals who have a variety of different symptoms, is that they experience a deficit in reading, language, and communication more than the whole of the population. People with average or above average intelligence who have this developmental disorder, learn to compensate for what is an incredible response. The more understanding of the condition, the better.

According to the **International Dyslexia Association**: *"Dyslexia is a specific learning disability that is neurobiological in origin. It is characterized by difficulties with accurate and/or fluent word recognition and by poor spelling and decoding abilities. These difficulties typically result from a deficit in the phonological component of language that is often unexpected in relation to other cognitive abilities and the provision of effective classroom instruction. Secondary consequences may include problems in reading* *comprehension and reduced reading experience that can impede growth of vocabulary and background knowledge."*

Developmental Dyslexia

This book would not be complete if I did not openly share what has been my experience with what I have come to know as Developmental Dyslexia. As I have shared many times in this presentation, my Dyslexic condition appears to be an auditory deficit. That means to see a written word and transcribe it into a phonological representation is a very challenging task because of what I term as auditory memory. When I see a new word as a picture, I can learn the word. When I see the picture and hear the word in association with words that I have experienced with meaning, this is another help. I can say the name of the picture.

My question remains, would my problem be called a sensory deficit or an auditory memory challenge? Some would say that it is both. I believe I have a sensory deficit. The literature explains this to be a sensory memory problem that is the shortest term element of memory with the ability to retain impressions of sensory information after a given stimulus has ended. Some researchers have suggested that this memory problem only exists for language information. I agree!

I have an excellent visual memory. My auditory sensory memory has a deficit written across it with a stroke of a motor sequencing deficit. Not severe but enough to have confused me and made me feel *dumb*. This information may help you travel a road to find answers. Gene says my brain is a Duke's mixture of confusion that needs to be researched. Oh!

Do not let your deficits identify who you are or can be. None of us is perfect; we all have deficits. Only when the deficit interferes with our functioning does it become a disability. A deficit can become a disability depending on the severity of the deficit. Also, it can become an unrealistic disability by the person's attitude toward the deficit.

Now, I will say what I just stated in another way. Along with my difficulty with having auditory memory, to remember the vowel sounds and the order of sounds or sequence of the sounds, I had and still have what seems to be a *motor planning disorder*. I can hear the sounds or words in my head correctly but cannot sequentially and motorically produce the sounds as I hear them. The outcome feels hopeless when I am trying to communicate. I can't get the word from my brain and out through my mouth. Sometimes, I want to say, "Where is the road from my brain which hauls the sounds or the word to my mouth?" The mouth will not say what the brain is silently hearing. Frustrating! This processing is an irritation for me. I have to find another word that means the same; one that I can make my motor generate the right way. Words which are not multisyllabic may be generated correctly.

Some call this condition Apraxia, which means a disconnect between what the brain wants to say and what the brain can process with the lips, tongue, and jaw correctly. It is not due to paralysis but is a disorder of the nervous system. The language area of the brain could be affected. Apraxia of speech: a condition which has difficulty stringing syllables together in appropriate order or inability to do so. That's me!

Acquired Dyslexia

It is my understanding that there are differences between Developmental and Acquired Dyslexia. Developmental Dyslexia is where the reading skills have not matured properly. Acquired Dyslexia is where a brain insult causes trauma which damages learned reading, language, and communication skills.

It is common knowledge that Acquired Dyslexia is a reading disorder when brain damage occurs after the person has learned to read. This condition is known as Alexia. However, could an infant or a child who has not learned to read have had developmental dyslexia before the injury? Yes.

The condition called Alexia has a face identified as phonological dyslexia or in my opinion, phonological alexia. The person can read but has a notable challenge with grapheme-to-phoneme conversion. Letters are visual building blocks for words. A phoneme is *each* sound you hear that is associated with consonants and vowels, but it is only a sound. A grapheme is a letter or groups of letters that represent chunks of sounds; a graphene represents letters, numbers or symbols. Phonetics!

As I continue to visit with you about my cognitive challenges, I will not leave a substantial piece of the puzzle amiss or misunderstood. Here I go with another thread to be addressed.

Developmental Language Disorder

This disorder is when a person has trouble understanding what others are saying—**receptive language** or when a person has a difficult way of expressing thoughts and feelings—**expressive language**. It has a broad range of severity. Communication!

There are those who have suggested that this developmental language disorder is part of Asperger's. However, Dr. Paul Steinberg wrote for the New York Times that he questioned the increasing diagnoses of Asperger's, particularly among those who were diagnosed later in life. The basis of his argument; *"True Autism reflects major problems with receptive language (the ability to comprehend sounds and words) and with expressive language."*

Some things just do not fit. It is my opinion, based on observations that Asperger's Disorder does not belong with the autism syndrome.

Knowledge comes from the Autism Society, *"Adults with Asperger's Disorder frequently have good to excellent language skills; they simply use language in different ways. Children with Asperger's Disorder may not understand the subtleties of language, such as irony and humor, or they may not understand the give-and-take nature of a conversation."* And then more valuable information from the Autism Society, *"Another distinction between Asperger's Disorder and Autism concerns cognitive ability. While some individuals with Autism have intellectual disabilities, by definition, a person with Asperger's*

Disorder cannot have a 'clinically significant' cognitive delay, and most possess average to above-average intelligence." (Asperger's Syndrome-Autism Society)

Autism brings the *lack* of language skills, whereas Asperger's affects the *how.* Sounds like me with the *how!* We all have a bit of *this* or *that* to one degree or another.

Pulling this book together has given me some interesting insights about how differently we cognitively process information. I will now share an experience that I had with Gene, who is a retired professor. I felt that writing this book was for others and myself, but I have reluctantly found that the book has been for my husband and me. I shared how difficult it is for us to communicate because of our mixed challenge with receptive and expressive language. Gene made it through a doctoral program in a well-known university while reading about six to eight pages an hour. He read so he could assimilate information through his *receptive* language channel. The author was *expressing* words on the page. This slow reading, searching for comprehension, is a language processing deficit. That was not the end; he had to use his *expressive* language channel to show that he understood and could apply that which he had learned through the receptive channel. Again! His expressive language was used to express what he had learned from the receptive language. Excellent expressive language!

We can understand the challenge. Gene cognitively read at a slow rate because he needed to read that way to comprehend the information; however, hard as it was to wade through all this processing of information, when he did comprehend the material, he did not forget it! Had he been my student, I would have designed an intervention that would have addressed the rate of reading. I have successfully helped students develop the skill for comprehension by reading at a faster rate.

Gene recalled that in elementary school, he had the same challenges with his comprehension of receptive language. He sees, hears, and responds to the *details* of information rather than attending to the *whole* picture of the information. This processing is a deficit, not a disability.

An important step which I have taken to remediate my language processing has been to find my language as I write. The more I write, the more language I find. Language has come to me through writing this book: writing, reading, and writing again, and then reading again. Pushing myself to generate language for print extends my understanding of language, and this way of learning language has made its way to my brain more than learning by speaking. Seeing language in print has been a key. This seeing helps me use spoken language more efficiently and comfortably. I can first figure out the order or sequence of language as I have learned to write. After I have seen the order in print, I can hear my words in the proper order. I have taken my visual strengths to remediate my language sequencing challenge. What I am saying is that I need to see language before I understand language. This learning is a process. As a teacher, I had students *write to read* because I understand the process of visualizing language. Progress!

I will address my experience with those learning a foreign language. As a parent, grandparent, friend, and teacher, I have studied my observations which have caught my continued attention. I concur with those who say that different languages have different phonologies.

Those who have had a difficult time learning their native language or their mother tongue have also had a difficult time learning a foreign language. And why? This foreign language challenge is what I have observed. Those with a strong visual memory and who have a language processing deficit do not do well with foreign languages. Those with a strong auditory memory do well with foreign languages. However, I have seen those with the visual memory coupled with motor memory learn sign language in good order. I have shared what I have experienced, not what I have researched. I get excited when validated by observing this information again and again. I would have a difficult time learning a foreign language. Would you? Compensate with intelligence and curiosity!

I believe that the nature of one's Multiple Intelligences has a great deal to do with compensating for deficit weaknesses. Remember to use your strengths to remediate your weaknesses. If learning a foreign language is hard for you, use your cognitive strengths! You can do it!

This morning the question was posed, "I wonder how many teachers of foreign languages are aware of the wide differences in brain structure, functioning, and how they complicate one's ability to learn languages?" We tend to think that the individual differences in this ability lie on a simple continuum that runs from dumb to smart. In actuality, as I have studied, I understand that the issue is more complex than a simple dumb to smart approach. Read this book entitled *Please Don't Call Me Dumb!*

Last but not least, let us take a far-reaching look at the **sequencing** challenge which I could call a **Sequencing disorder;** however, rather than calling it a disorder, the literature smears the sequencing problem around and over all the *disorders*. Therefore, I am going to call it **Argie's sequencing disorder.** I have it, and I am still struggling.

Yes, I have the Argie's sequencing disorder while reading and writing. Which ideas come first, second, and does the phrase come before or after the noun or verb? I remember times when my book reports would have the end come first, then the first part of the book coming next and then the middle. I would study the report and finally get it right. Well, let us go even further back in time; I couldn't *remember* which sounds or syllables came first. The words seemed to sound correct no matter in what order the sounds or syllables occurred. And on and on with that reading thing.

Math wasn't any better. Time was a nightmare! I can't begin to tell you how I finally learned how to do that thing called *telling time*. No wonder we have digital clocks. Still, I ask how much time do we have before we must go. For me, time is without numbers in space.

The alphabet, days of the week, and months of the year have an order. When asked what comes before or after a letter, day, or month, I have to start at the beginning because I couldn't tell you what comes immediately before "w" before Tuesday, or before April without going through the whole order of things. Sequencing is everywhere you turn!

I know that stepping out of the elevator is a sequencing challenge. Which way do I turn, left or right, same with setting the table, I had to over-learn on which side of the plate to put the silverware? It seems in everything I do, *If at first, you don't succeed, try, try again.* I am not kidding.

One time, I got to the airport very early and one time very late. Sequencing problem! I could sit here and go on and on, but you have either determined that you have Argie's sequencing disorder or you are grateful that you skipped that one.

Over three months have passed since I fell. I know which side hit first, seeing how I look, but I would say that I landed on the opposite side. What is confusing is that sometimes the physical pain is felt on the opposite side and in my mind's eye that is the side that I visualize. Could this be a sequencing challenge or a crossed nerve signal? Damage!

I don't know if this has anything to do with anything, but is it another sequencing thing or a crossed nerve? Again, occasionally when I go to the dentist, he gives me a shot on one side of my mouth, and it is numb on the other side. Silly me! Which side is which side? Strange things happen to all of us. We shouldn't jump to quick conclusions. A studied approach to understand cognitive challenges should be planned with logical and determined energy. Find answers!

It has become essential for me to understand my brain with its sequencing challenge. This problem is not just in language processing, reading, spelling, and writing, but it is the overarching umbrella of what happens all day and every day. With language processing, it is difficult to recall the right words to develop an idea in a logical and organized fashion. The intellectual concepts are in the head but to get them to make sense for others is the challenge. Yes, it is a sequencing challenge from dawn to dusk. I will organize my life in an orderly fashion considering that I need to stop, look, and listen as to which step comes first. None of us is perfect, and all of us are unique. You are smart!

DO I HAVE DYSLEXIA or WHAT?
The *what* is a precious gift of seeing the world through lenses for which
there is no name.

As I step through life, I am honored to have you make a friend with my
book. Go and stop along the way to enjoy the flowers of spring and the
snow of winter, remembering that you are a unique and beautiful
creation. Share your gifts of hope with everyone and bring a happy heart
to the world with arms wrapped with the warmth of love.
You are a path.

You will be blessed to have the gifts of which I speak. Enjoy and
Celebrate!
How does Heaven see you? You are a gift.
I know that Heaven brings the Light of Truth and Truth is Hope. Every
living thing needs Light to live. Bring the Light of Hope?

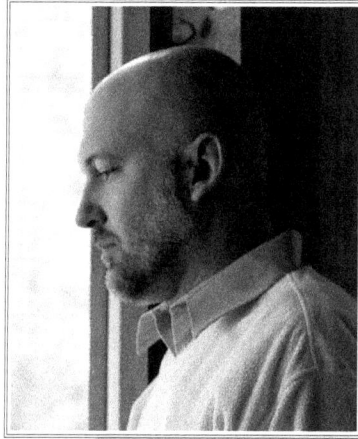

Program designer and musician, extraordinaire!
Thank you, Daniel. Designing the cover of my book is appreciated. I am grateful.

Long ago, scribed on a *now* precious piece of paper with the tender message "I love you," along with a rock, and a piece of wood—treasures touched my heart with gratitude for thoughtfulness, and my heart found tender tears of joy. To be found on the stairs, gifts left from the heart, my son wrapped the gifts in paper towels from the school's bathroom.

Enjoy your gifts!

May the Heavens bless you to bless others.

www.ingramcontent.com/pod-product-compliance
Lightning Source LLC
LaVergne TN
LVHW051621080426
835511LV00016B/2111